Praise for the work of Lynn Reardon

"In the horse racing industry, there is no work more important than that done by Lynn Reardon. Through her nonprofit organization, LOPE, Reardon has rescued, rehabilitated, and retrained hundreds of former racehorses and found them loving, lasting homes. Her comprehensive, innovative, and exhaustive efforts have saved the lives of innumerable horses and fostered new partnerships between horse lovers and former racehorses. She is truly a hero."
— LAURA HILLENBRAND, author of *Seabiscuit: An American Legend*

More praise for *Beyond the Homestretch*

"One of the most sensitive and humorous books that I have read in a long time."
— *Eclipse* magazine

"[Lynn Reardon's] prose is crisp, honest, authentic, full of self-deprecating humor and a passion for doing what is right."
— *Dressage Today*

"This has got to be one of my favorite books of all time — for a book addict like me that is really saying something. It reads like fiction, has a truthfulness about life that reminds me of Seinfeld skits and it is obviously written from the heart."
— *Thoughts on Dressage Blog*

"I have only known a few accountants in my life and none of them had a particularly good sense of humor. But Lynn Reardon's wit and self-deprecating humor make this a very readable book. Horse lovers and racing fans alike will enjoy these stories."
— ROBERT MILLER, DVM, horse behaviorist and coauthor of *The Revolution in Horsemanship*

"*Beyond the Homestretch* is a great read for any horse lover."
— JEFF WELLS, DVM, author of *All My Patients Have Tales*

"Lynn writes eloquently about her equine adventures, really bringing out the individual characters of her horses while also vividly depicting life on a Texas ranch."
— ALEX BROWN, creator of alexbrownracing.com

"It is the horses who provide the drama in the story, not the humans, and you will leave the story with a place in your heart for Thoroughbreds named Tulsa, Zuper and Nacho, as well as a certain 'disheveled rescue lady' in Texas."
— *Seattle Post-Intelligencer*

"This isn't a book that imparts specific techniques for rehoming and retraining retired racers, but instead a feel-good story that will inspire readers to pursue their dreams."
— Bloodhorse.com

"A superb read for those long evenings when sunset comes too early and outside is too cold! *Beyond the Homestretch* by Lynn Reardon is a marvelous journey not to be missed from start to finish."
— Tack n' Talk Blog

"Full of humor and insight and peopled with the unique characters that make up the world of racing, this is a can't-put-down book."
— Davenport Library, Iowa

"Lynn's passion and excitement for what she does comes shining through."
— *The Texas Horsemen's News*

"It's a terrific guide for anyone full of self-doubt about changing directions, who thinks they don't have the experience or the knowledge it takes to enter a new field."
— Serial Reinvention Blog

Beyond the
Homestretch

Beyond the Homestretch

What Saving Racehorses Taught Me
About Starting Over, Facing Fear &
Finding My Inner Cowgirl

Lynn Reardon

New World Library
Novato, California

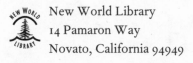

New World Library
14 Pamaron Way
Novato, California 94949

Text design by Tona Pearce Myers

Library of Congress Cataloging-in-Publication Data
Reardon, Lynn, date.
Beyond the homestretch : what saving racehorses taught me about starting over, facing fear, and finding my inner cowgirl / Lynn Reardon. — 1st trade pbk. ed.
    p.   cm.
ISBN 978-1-57731-956-6 (pbk. : alk. paper)
1. Race horses—Texas. 2. Animal rescue—Texas. I. Title.
SF338.R36 2011
636.1'2083209764—dc22   2010042712

First paperback printing, February 2011
ISBN 978-1-57731-956-6
Printed in Canada on 100% postconsumer-waste recycled paper

g New World Library is a proud member of the Green Press Initiative.

10 9 8 7 6 5 4 3 2 1

For Tom, whose philosophy and poetry set everything in motion

CONTENTS

INTRODUCTION

SEABISCUIT WAS A BAD-TEMPERED ROGUE, a willful loser at the track — until he found a trainer and jockey who understood him. From then on, he was unstoppable, a fierce competitor who consistently outran horses of much better physiques and pedigrees. He was the ultimate underdog. The crowds loved his cocky spirit and working-class ethos. Seabiscuit also loved Pumpkin, his kindly palomino pony horse, and he had a sweet habit of falling asleep on his cross-country train rides.

Secretariat was born on a lost coin toss, his birth representing a second-choice foal for his owner. He blasted the racing world like no other horse, with his tremendous height, deep stride, and overpowering Triple Crown win. Affectionately dubbed "Big Red," he was the Muhammad Ali of racehorses, brash, charismatic, and full of himself. His jockey, Ron Turcotte, rarely had to raise his crop or urge him on verbally — Big Red had a deep passion to win on his own. His autopsy revealed a heart three times the size of a normal horse's, a discovery that surprised no one who knew him or watched him win.

Seattle Slew, the 1977 Triple Crown winner, was born plain but athletic. One visitor commented that he had legs like telephone poles, straight, thick, and strong. A dynamic personality, Slew became so excited before each race that he would pirouette madly in the post-parade, a striking display of such strutting machismo that viewers christened it "the war dance." Tremendously intelligent, Slew was well-mannered off the track, showing special gentleness with children visitors. And for some odd reason, he loved snow and cold weather, seeming to happily anticipate each winter.

But what if Secretariat or Seattle Slew had been injured as two-year-olds? Or if Seabiscuit had never found Tom Smith and Red Pollard? We would never have known their incredible spirits and capacity for greatness, not to mention their entertaining quirks, such as loving snow or napping on freight cars. They still would have had all of that personality, that fire, that potential — just no racing career to bring it out, to give them purpose and challenge. What would have happened to Secretariat, Seattle Slew, and Seabiscuit then?

Every year, thousands of Thoroughbreds wash out of racing due to age, lack of speed, or injury. Often left to uncertain fates with auction houses, used-horse dealers, and inexperienced racehorse owners, they can even be at risk for the slaughter pens in Mexico or Canada. An equine athlete is a terrible thing to waste, especially one bred to give his all, to excel, to be the best.

I work with these athletes every day. Our organization — LOPE, or LoneStar Outreach to Place Ex-Racers — is a nonprofit devoted to finding Texas racehorses new jobs after their racing careers are over. We do this through our online services and adoption ranch. Over 145 horses have come to our ranch since 2004.

At the ranch, I have worked with every kind of racehorse — from the two-year-old youngster who is too slow to the game champion who still races at age nine to the twenty-year-old broodmare who ran in 114 races. I have seen all types of injuries and ailments: bowed tendons, bone chips, torn ligaments, slab fractures, paralyzed flappers, even tracheotomies.

To me, racehorses are winners even after their racing careers end. They have so much heart, athleticism, and intelligence — all they need is a chance to find that second career after the finish line. Of course, they could use a little help making that transition. Because it can be hard to change careers at first.

I can sympathize with that.

I used to have an accounting career, working in a Washington DC cubicle. Pale, stressed, and full of suburban angst, I was the least likely candidate to run a racehorse adoption ranch in Texas. Back then, horses were just my outlet, my weekend respite from spreadsheets. Only learning to ride as an adult, I took group horseback-riding lessons and strained to master the most basic equestrian skills.

But even then, I was drawn to racehorses — several resided at that stable, in training to become show jumpers and polo mounts. They charmed and inspired me, with their intelligent faces, beautiful conformation, and dark reputations as risky rides.

From childhood, I had secretly wanted to be a horse trainer. But I was a horse geek, a real goober around the barn. The instructors and trainers hid their smiles at my barn gaffes and painfully anxious riding style. Every trainer at the barn had grown up with horses, usually turning professional by their teens, a formidable résumé of equine mastery. I would never fit that mold — how could someone like me be a trainer? It seemed like an impossible, silly dream, plausible only in a Disney film.

I worked hard to improve my skills anyway: exercising polo ponies for free, trading barn work for lessons, teaching at a horse summer camp, anything to learn more on my modest budget. Slowly, my horse activities morphed into a vocation, a calling I could no longer ignore, however ridiculous it seemed to others — and often even to me.

Finally, I took the plunge, moved halfway across the country, and opened the racehorse adoption program.

At first I was an inept career counselor for the racehorses. My background in horse training was sketchy, and I had no experience managing a farm. So many racehorses came to our little farm so quickly, almost forty in the first year alone. I had to figure out how to work with them in spite of my poor skills, my fears, and my persistent sense of being an impostor.

Ashamed of my beginner status, I searched far and wide for horsemanship gurus, hoping to find training "Obi-Wans" who could turn me into a sophisticated professional. I longed to be more like the trainers I knew — brave, tough, full of expertise.

Meanwhile, more and more racehorses kept coming with their assorted ailments, sports injuries, and high-strung natures, all clamoring for help and intervention. They didn't have time to wait around for me to find the perfect tutor. So my on-the-job training program began immediately — run by the very best mentors of all.

PART I

The Starting Gate

Let me respectfully remind you —
Life and death are of supreme importance,
Time swiftly passes by and opportunity is lost,
Each of us should strive to awaken, awaken!
Take heed. Do not squander your life.

BUDDHIST PRAYER
taped to my accounting office desk

CHAPTER ONE

Spider's Bad Day

IT WAS 3 A.M., and I was trying to decide whether to shove pieces of rubber hose up a horse's nostrils. Spider, the horse in question, stared at me dully. His head was swollen to twice its normal size, and truly epic amounts of saliva, mucus, and something else I was afraid to identify were oozing from his mouth and nose.

My flashlight, long overdue for new batteries, flickered sporadically — it wasn't helping me make my decision. The dim light scared three-year-old Spider and he flinched, trying to huddle in the darkest corner of the pen. He was miserable and confused and the last thing he wanted was a light in his face.

I was scared, too. It was critical to keep Spider's adrenaline down. His breathing was already so impaired by the snakebite venom. If he began to panic, nothing, not even the last-ditch rubber hoses, could save his life. I'd never performed emergency procedures with rubber hoses before, not even for the sheer learning pleasure of it. Note to self — maybe it was time to correct this gap in my horse husbandry skills.

Several hours ago, as my husband, Tom, had been driving home from work, he had seen Spider violently shaking his head. I had been out riding one of the ex-racehorses at our ranch, trying to teach a young filly that there's a gait (actually, a couple of them) between walk and gallop. She was surprised — no one had pointed this out to her before.

By the time Tom got my attention and we ran to Spider's pasture, his nose was already starting to swell dramatically. We looked closely — two fang marks dotted his muzzle. He had been bitten right between the nostrils.

I speed-dialed our vet, Dr. Damon O'Gan, as I quickly led Spider toward the round pen near the field's gate. Spider had stopped shaking his head, but he was clearly in pain and kept balking at the lead rope. We made chaotic progress as Tom shooed Spider from behind, waving his arms and hat to keep him moving forward. Big John, Spider's pasture buddy, hovered around us anxiously, trying to help by crowding near Spider protectively. Normally, I would have been touched by John's devotion, but he was a huge horse with the proportions and gracefulness of a dinosaur — he nearly stepped on me twice. It was a distraction I didn't need.

Damon finally answered his cell phone. "Hello," he said in his Wyoming drawl. Even after several years in Austin, he never quite sounded like a Texan.

"Hi Damon, it's Lynn," I began.

"How are you?" Damon replied. He drew out this question with about three extra syllables and an odd offbeat iambic rhythm — as in, "Hoow arree you?" Damon never sounded flustered or rushed. I'm pretty sure I could call him in the middle of some huge task, like open-heart surgery on a horse in a field during a thunderstorm, and he would sound exactly the same ("Hello Lynn. Hoow arree you?").

"Fine, fine. Hey, I think Spider got bitten by a snake. He has fang marks right between the nostrils, and, God, his nose is swelling like an inch every ten seconds."

"Ah." Damon sounded relaxed and vaguely pleased. "That's very interesting. Lynn, can you tell me what the fang marks look like? How wide is the distance between them? Just an estimate is fine, no need to measure."

Great, no need to measure — because I don't usually carry a ruler in case of measuring emergencies. Another horse husbandry gap to fill. I squinted at the fang marks. How do you describe fang marks? It looked like Dracula had bit Spider: two pinprick dots, each with a drop of blood, were almost perfectly centered between the nostrils. I relayed this cinematic information to Damon, hoping he wouldn't ask to me clarify which Dracula (Bela Lugosi? Gary Oldman?).

"Lynn, you'll need to give him a 10 cc dose of Banamine in the vein. Check him every hour, especially the breathing rate. It's going to get ugly, and we might have to come out for a temporary tracheotomy procedure."

Damon then launched into a technical lecture on rattlesnake bites and how they can cause massive swelling in the head and upper respiratory systems. Horses can breathe only through their nose, so they can't use their mouth as a backup breathing system as we do. If the nostrils get blocked, horses can't breathe. At all. Which is not good for activities such as being alive.

Damon broke my morbid train of thought with an odd and ominous question — "Lynn, do you have a rubber hose you can cut up?" I did, but why? He said, "Cut two pieces, each about eight inches long, and be ready to shove those up Spider's nostrils if he looks like he is about to stop breathing. If things turn the wrong way, there's no way I can get there in time. It will be up to you."

I pondered the unpleasant images that came to mind. Damon said, "Call me every hour or so and update me. I'm on call tonight, so I can come out anytime. And good luck."

AS I WATCHED SPIDER AT 3 A.M., that conversation replayed in my head. Spider looked worse than I ever imagined a horse could look. His head was one huge oval, with no sign of contour from his cheekbones, jaw, or other facial bones.

His nostrils were caked with creeping cascades of yellow foam, and their normally large openings were down to the size of a man's finger. When I touched his nose, it was no longer velvety and soft — instead it felt like concrete. The hardness disturbed me the most: How could he breathe with such unyielding membranes in his nose? Worst of all, it hurt him. He tensed at my light touch, clearly in pain.

I never saw the rattler and was sobered by the damage one snake could inflict on a 900-pound horse. If Spider was in genuine peril from its bite, what would it do to a human? It was scary.

It seems strange that our pretty little twenty-six-acre ranch, just thirty minutes from Austin, would be home to such dangerous creatures. But Texas can be a wild and rugged place. It didn't seem untamed, as I looked around at the sturdy pipe fencing and large shade trees and listened to the occasional truck zoom by even at that late hour on Highway 21. But it can be, and I made a mental note to pay more attention to where I walked.

I snapped off the flashlight and sensed Spider relaxing a little in the dark. I walked slowly up to him, gently petted his neck, and put my ear close so I could listen to his watery breathing and count off the rate. I hoped for a good number, so the rubber hoses could stay in my jeans pocket. If the rate was too high, it would be time for emergency hose action.

In spite of his incredibly bad day, Spider put his head down and leaned against me looking for a pat. He was then only three years old and had never been ridden. He had been donated to our racehorse adoption program a few weeks before by a breeder getting out of the business. She loved Spider, her last homebred Texas Thoroughbred, and she had entrusted us with finding him a new home. Spider was a truly sweet colt, a 900-pound puppy with a happy-go-lucky disposition and a love of bananas that bordered on fetish.

As I counted his labored breaths, a finger of panic poked rudely at my mind. Pushing it away, I made an effort to think positive thoughts. I remembered the day I first met Spider. The breeder had donated nine of her horses to us. They had all arrived together in a huge semi-load-sized trailer.

The drivers opened the side gate first, and the mares tumbled out together down the ramp. The mares were all pretty and smart with lively eyes, and they immediately cantered off to the round bale of hay in a corner of the field. They weren't interested in me yet; they had their priorities straight.

Alice, the matriarch of the mares at fifteen years old, took charge of the field and bossed the younger, less-favored mares away from the round bale. In spite of her long trip, she looked pleased that we had the good sense to serve dinner early. She gave me a detached appreciative look, the type that a suburban matron might give to a waitress who was prompt with the drink order. She was dark bay, with deep intelligent eyes and the impressive belly of a many-times mother.

Then the drivers opened the second gate on the trailer, and all the geldings, plus Spider the colt, came leaping down the ramp. The boys weren't quite as smart about the trailer exit as the girls — it took them a while to figure out where the hay was in their pasture. They milled around, jostling each other, like guys heading for the draft beer line in a sports bar. There was tall Solomon, a big affable horse with tremendously oversized ears for a Thoroughbred. Then came JJ, another dark bay who resembled Alice (his mother) but with a macho swagger. JJ and Solomon began nipping at each other and bucking in unison, not sure what to make of this new place.

Eclipse came next, the intellectual of the group, looking embarrassed by the frat-boy antics of his brothers. He lingered near me, wanting to introduce himself properly. He was a beautiful red horse with a striking crescent mark on his forehead and calm, gentle eyes.

Spider was the last one out, following his siblings' big act like a rookie comic in a variety show. As he clumsily scrambled down the ramp, one of the drivers turned to me and said, "That horse is a stallion. Better watch out for him. He might be dangerous."

I looked at Spider and laughed. Spider was the most Bambi-like stallion I'd ever seen. He was a chestnut horse with a cute little star and snip of white on his face. His legs were long and gangly, and he clearly didn't quite know how his body worked yet. His head was a tad big for his body, and he had a sweet face. I couldn't help but like him on sight. He's just a kid, I thought to myself.

In the next few weeks, Spider established himself as the clown of the farm. He liked to turn over troughs and splash the water out. If he saw you in the pasture, he would run across the field to greet you, gangly legs flying, with a delighted "you-must-be-coming-to-see-me" look on his face. It was impossible to be in a bad mood around Spider's enthusiasm. Spider innately assumed that the universe was a benevolent, wonderful place where everyone was there to pet him.

I was looking forward to teaching Spider about ground work, saddles, and bridles. We had gelded Spider last week, and I was planning to start working with him in a few days. Poor Spider! In the past seven days he had been gelded, then bitten by a rattler. Not such a benevolent universe this month.

I felt so responsible for him. And I realized that right then, at the farm, in the middle of the night, I was the most qualified person to take care of him and to make the right decision. Damon was a solid drive away, Tom was not a horse person, and all of our immediate neighbors had less veterinary care experience than I did.

It wasn't an empowering feeling.

I concentrated on counting breaths, trying not to speculate about what exactly was dripping on my hair from Spider's face. The count was good. His breathing rate had stabilized from when I had last checked him an hour ago. The rubber hoses could stay in my pocket for now. I was too tired to walk back to the house, so I kept petting Spider. It wasn't much, but it was all I could think of to do. He wheezed and snuffled and kept leaning against me, not at all put off by my wet, stained shirt. My dirty jeans, grimy from riding, completed my ranch haute couture.

This was not the way I had planned to spend my forty-fourth birthday. Aren't people this age supposed to be confident and settled and at the very least not covered in horse mucus? Haven't they mastered their careers, gently settling into that "I'm watching the 401(k) plan grow" phase of life?

I pondered my previous life as an accountant. Had it really been so awful? I didn't remember any rattlesnakes or crushing sense of responsibility in that career. The offices were so clean and cool in August, not like this round pen in Texas, which still radiated heat at 3:15 A.M. The glamour of it all, I thought to myself. Spider nicely punctuated this thought by trying to rub his swollen head on me.

I spotted something white in the pen and bent down to pick it up. It was a napkin from dinner about six hours ago. It cheered me up to see it and be reminded of Tom. My internal whining faded, along with my fragmented panic, both overwhelmed by the distracting chatter in my mind.

Once we had given Spider his shot, all we could do was wait and watch the venom's progress. But I had been too worried to leave Spider, so Tom cooked a huge spaghetti dinner and brought it out to me in the field. We sat in his truck bed and had an oddly romantic al fresco dinner, quietly talking and watching Spider together. Spider's head was less swollen then. I could notice the night sky, always so big in Texas, and enjoy Tom's improvised truck-bed restaurant.

All of this business about changing careers was really Tom's fault. He was the one who started giving me those books on philosophy, the ones that make you think for yourself and indulge in other dangerous activities. *The Fountainhead. Man's Search for Meaning. How to Find the Work You Love.*

And music, too — Tom was always bringing me eclectic music. One of his first gifts to me was a Sur Sudha CD full of Nepali sitar music. I played it over and over again, as I planned my first trip to Nepal — just hearing the music made me feel bold and cool enough to attempt the trip. No wonder I had married him — how could I resist a man who courted me with philosophy and alternative music? And who catered me Italian dinners in the middle of dusty fields late at night?

Perhaps picking up on my soothing thoughts, Spider was now dozing lightly. He seemed to be in a relatively calm stupor. I tiptoed out of the pen, hoping to catch an hour of sleep before my next check on Spider. As I walked along the quarter-mile driveway to the house, thinking of Tom's philosophy books, I remembered why I had chosen this life.

I quickly glanced at the other horses to make sure all was well. That rattlesnake was still out there somewhere. Irish, the filly whom I had just taught the joy of trotting, was curled up like a sleeping cat. Zuper, our handsome, permanently retired gelding, stood guard over her.

I looked down at my work boots to make sure nothing was slithering under them. My bootlaces caught the moonlight as I strode quickly and steadily down the driveway. Compared to my office days, my shoes were rugged, my jeans loose, and my physique muscular and fit. In my twenties, I was an out-of-shape, pale chain-smoker whose job never required anything more physical than hefting big blue payroll binders.

In that moment, I decided that very few women celebrate their forty-fourth birthday this way, and that it would make an excellent story to tell my nephews. They already thought I was a rock star just because I rode horses every day. This story would knock them dead.

It was guaranteed that the rest of the day would be better — with such a dubious start, my birthday was bound to improve.

Back at the house, I fell asleep quickly and had scattered, surreal dreams about my past life as an accountant mixed up with horse images — of racehorses wandering in file rooms, saddles stacked next to industrial-sized calculators, and Spider splashing in the office water cooler, his head normal and his universe benevolent once again.

HOURS LATER, MY BIRTHDAY MORNING BEGAN with an early call from Damon. I was excited to report that Spider had stabilized — his breathing was steady and his swelling had leveled off. With his huge oval head and puppy eyes, he resembled a sweet-faced raptor.

We agreed on a plan — Damon and his new partner, Dr. Matt Evans, would examine Spider at 7:30 A.M. They were due back here midafternoon for a standing surgery on another racehorse, and they would recheck Spider then.

I was thoroughly disheveled, sleepless, and punchy from the middle-of-the-night nursing sessions. But I was cheerful — Spider was doing better, and the prospect of a birthday nap between vet visits hovered happily before me.

I had just an hour to shower and feed the other horses before Damon and Matt arrived. The shower was a must, for the sake of my relationship with the vets. They already sponsored our adoption farm, giving us huge discounts and lots of their nonexistent spare time. The least I could do was soap off the remnants of Spider's nasal debris.

Refreshed, I flung myself into clothes and grabbed the feed buckets. Storm and Ivy, the two horses in the pasture by the house, circled the porch listening for the tell-tale clanking. They were both slowed down by healing leg injuries, but they persistently lurched around the driveway with hopeful faces, their pace slow but relentless, with a *Night of the Living Dead* flair.

As I scooped the feed, I could hear hoofbeats lurching faster, beating a chant of "feed-feed-feed." I plopped two buckets in front of the zombie porch horses and hustled to the truck, lugging two buckets overflowing with feed. We don't have a barn, so I feed all the horses in their individual pastures — the feed commutes to them daily. I call this the "home gym"; my biceps are strong from carrying full buckets twice a day, every day.

At each pasture, I scoop feed into pails tied to the fence. The horses are always thrilled to see me. Well, to see the buckets — but at least I am holding the buckets. As the horses come to the fence, I reflexively stop and glance at each horse, checking for injuries. Any swelling? Limping? Blood? Any pawing or signs of stomach discomfort? Most importantly, do all the horses come to the feed? I have learned the hard way that a horse that stands aloof and doesn't want to eat is invariably sick or injured.

I barely finished my rounds in time — the vets pulled up as I was scooping feed into the last bucket for Big John, Spider's pasture friend. John spent the entire night dozing next to Spider's pen, keeping an eye on him and being a good equine nanny.

Dr. Matt Evans was out of the truck first, cell phone in hand, jogging to the fence as Spider looked up at him. Matt is a cheerful, happy guy with an open face that inspires trust immediately. He is a terrific vet and patient teacher and has the air of a 1950s television dad — slightly old-fashioned and tremendously likable. Matt also tells the corniest jokes imaginable — Dixie cup opuses that create waves of wincing at the punch lines.

Both Spider and I were curious: Why was Matt bounding up to the pen with his cell phone held out Olympic-torch style? "Wow, that is the *worst* snakebite I've ever seen," he exclaimed happily. "I'm sending it to my buddy at A&M right now." I gently touched Spider's head, telling Matt how much worse it looked four hours ago.

"Cool! Tell me what it looked like then," Matt said, eager to hear more.

"I've seen worse," Damon scoffed, as he good-naturedly began debating with Matt about who had seen the worst snakebite, and what exactly qualified as "worst."

A word about vets: They aren't like normal people — the weirder an ailment, the worse a case, the more interested and engaged they become. Vets are scientists at their core. They aren't squeamish like me — blood and gore are engineering terms to them, components of a system needing tune-up and repair.

Remembering that a civilian was present, Matt and Damon broke off their debate. During their conversation, they both were deftly prepping medications, already beginning their examination of Spider. A second debate, as friendly as the first, started over whether to inject Spider with steroids as an extra precaution. Matt quoted the latest vet journal findings; Damon pointed out his most recent field experiences.

"So, we'll be back around two," Damon called over his shoulder as he packed up the vet kit. "To do Storm's hoof procedure." Matt grinned, clearly looking forward to a standing surgery in our driveway — the highlight of the day for him. Freaks, I thought to myself, all vets are freaks.

I wasn't looking forward to Storm's hoof procedure — Storm had a persistent infection on his coffin bone from months of recurring abscesses. Our intrepid vets would be surgically taking out the infection — a process I couldn't quite envision, nor did I want to.

A few hours later, however, I was watching the surgery under one of our shade trees. Bleary-eyed from lack of sleep, I squinted at the sight of Damon cradling Storm's hoof as he meticulously removed the infection — by scraping it off the bone, deep inside the hoof, with a sharp-edged surgical tool.

Not able to see inside the hoof, Damon did this "by ear," listening to hear whether the bone sounded crisp or spongy as his tool rubbed against it.

"So, do you guys hear the difference?" Damon asked, scraping louder for our listening pleasure. Blood dripped and pooled on the sterile sheet under Storm's hoof, as our cat, Mama, watched with avid interest like a vampire kitty. Sweat dripped down my neck. Damon scraped steadily. Mama licked her chops and edged closer.

Finally, the surgery was over. As Damon cleaned up his instruments, Mama darted to the still-fresh blood drops, doing her best to sneak a quick taste. I decided I had earned a birthday beer. Meanwhile, Matt was checking Spider again, counting off his respiratory rate, examining his nostrils.

The hot August sun showed no sign of wavering. I drank down the cold beer and opened a second bottle, a rare event for me; I figured the snakebite and the hoof surgery merited a doubleheader of a birthday toast.

Matt had a surprise verdict on Spider. He wanted to perform a temporary tracheotomy — just to be safe, in case anything else put stress on Spider's fragile airway. Matt smiled as he prepped his instruments and pulled out a tracheotomy tube — so far, this had been a dream job day for him. I was less enthused. Time for me to head back to the house. I was nauseous from veterinary overload over the past twenty hours. But I had one more birthday surprise in store.

"Lynn, can you assist?" Damon sounded odd. He had been fighting the flu all week. After a full day of equine vetting in the heat, it was finally hitting him hard. I knew exactly how he felt. Tracheotomy assisting can be strenuous, requiring strong shoulders, good balance, and steady nerves. Uh oh.

As I stepped into position, cradling Spider's head on my collarbone, I sighed at the truly sad thought that this wasn't my first equine tracheotomy. At least this time, I knew to keep my eyes closed and my ears tilted away from the incision site. Matt deftly cut into Spider's neck, exposing his trachea and inserting a tube to keep it open to the air. Spider, groggy from sedation, rested his heavy jaw on me and drooled, his day even weirder than mine.

LATER, SITTING ON THE PORCH, I marveled at a birthday that started with a near-fatal snakebite, crested with an under-the-tree hoof surgery, and ended with a surprise tracheotomy. My best birthday gift would turn out to be belated — Spider recovered fully within a few days, a medical comeback that wowed even Matt and Damon.

My head spun from the beer. I drifted along in my thoughts, wondering when I would finally be a "real" horse professional, confident, competent, and unfazed by any vet emergency. Even the racehorses still wonder about me sometimes, their heads cocked quizzically at my abrupt movements, awkward lead rope techniques, and constant stream of chatter. Occasionally Tulsa and Zuper, two of the permanent horses, will exchange looks as I walk by, as if to say, "She's an odd one, but she's all we've got."

As I cradled my empty beer bottle, memories of my former riding teacher, Tory, surfaced. "Ride or die!" was her favorite motto; it was quite an experience being her working student. Her other credo was "That horse will kill you, Lynn." Tory was what a horse trainer should be: tough, athletic, and fearless, not to mention a master of horse vet care. I fell far short of that ideal.

I didn't learn to ride until I was an adult, taking weekly group lessons at a big stable. My childhood fantasy of effortlessly riding the Black Stallion in the Kentucky Derby quailed before the reality of my adult muscles ineptly gripping the saddle, my face contorted with anxiety and embarrassment.

By my thirties, I stopped riding regularly — it was too hard on my budget and ego. But then one day, I saw an ad for polo lessons. I decided to call and ended up trading barn duties for discount lessons. I saddled the lesson horses Saturday mornings and cleaned the tired school tack, slathering it with a dubious concoction called Horseman's One Step.

By day, I worked as a nonprofit finance manager — I'd keep an eye on the clock, just waiting for quitting time to dash out to the stables. Although I was competent in the office, my confidence vanished at the barn door. I was so determined to improve my riding, to prove myself, that inevitably I would tense up, start tripping over hay bales, dropping halters, and generally making all the horses nervous.

My clumsiness was often funny, and even I had to laugh at my desperate horse passion. Secretly, I harbored an ambition to be a horse trainer, a dream I was careful to hide. The horse pros would smile at my "adult beginner" riding style and my obvious desire to emulate them. All the trainers I knew had been riding since preschool, racking up decades of horse experience by their late twenties. Not exactly my résumé.

Soon, I discovered that the polo players needed help exercising their extra horses. You didn't have to play polo well; you just had to be able to ride a horse while leading another one or two, tugging them along like dogs on a leash. This was called "riding a set."

The players I rode for were careful to assign me only gentle horses to exercise. I was happy to ride anything for free at first — but soon I longed to ride the spirited horses, especially the ex-racehorses, the young ones fresh from the track and still in training for their new job. They had powerful physiques, intelligent eyes, and dangerous reputations — the epitome of the kind of horse I should avoid.

Naturally, I was desperate to ride them.

Clearly, I needed a mentor, a horse trainer to take me on as an apprentice, to teach me how to ride the "real" horses, the best horses, the racehorses. A few months later, I heard about Tory, a local horse trainer. The other riders at the polo barn said she could ride any horse, no matter how unruly. She would take young horses from the racetrack, retrain them, and then sell them. Rumor had it that she could be abrasive and difficult, but she was the best horsewoman in town.

One rainy Saturday, I was riding a polo pony in the indoor arena. Fred was a kind horse who liked to amble along slowly. He was the worst polo mount ever, due to his utter lack of speed or ambition. But he was beginner-safe for riding, and his owner traveled frequently. I was exercising him so he could stay fit for his power walks on the polo fields.

A trailer pulled up with a rumbling flourish. A tall, young woman with massive, curly auburn hair jumped out of the truck. Within minutes, she had unloaded three horses, saddled one, and ridden into the ring leading the other two. "Hi," I said quietly from the other side of the arena, fully expecting to be ignored.

Which I was. Intent on her horses, she rode around the ring rapidly, frequently lapping Fred and me. Furtively, I studied her, marveling at her deft handling of the horses. Her hair was pushed back with a colorful fleece headband, and she wore black leather chaps with bright pink fringe and a big initial T. She slouched slightly in the saddle, on a sleek hot rod of a bay horse, holding the lead ropes of the other two.

Her horses were clearly young and green, probably just off the racetrack. They seemed well behaved enough. But I could see the telltale signs of spirit in their mischievous eyes and sassy movements — they seemed unpredictable, like the bad kids in school who smoke and loiter in the hallways, looking for trouble. One of them, a gray mare, began to buck on the end of the lead rope. She leaped high in a terrifying, satanic gymnast maneuver. Tory — for it had to be her — didn't even bother to look; she just said, in a bored tone, "Quit." She then flicked the lead rope lightly in the mare's direction. The gray immediately settled back to normal, looking sheepish. I was impressed.

As I led Fred back to the barn, he shied away from a hay bale that he'd passed every day that week. Trying to imitate Tory's oh-so-bored tone, I straightened my shoulders, flicked the lead rope at Fred, and said, "Quit."

Ever graceful, I managed to hit myself in the eye with the rope. Fred looked offended and spooked again. Just on principle, I thought.

As it turned out, Tory was looking for a working student. Screwing up my courage, I managed to get an interview — a trail ride with Tory and her barn friends. I was scared, but excited; Tory could be the key to my dream of riding spirited racehorses.

The following Sunday, I showed up for the interview with Tory. Her barn was lit up in the gray afternoon with overhead lights flickering, women laughing, and bright colors flaring in unexpected places. Tory's riding buddies consisted of several dashing horsewomen — all carefree, pretty, and confident.

Insults, jokes, and insider anecdotes rocked the barn aisle as I stood there awkwardly, my earth-toned riding garb marking me an outsider. The barn glamour posse mostly ignored me, occasionally shouting something incomprehensible at me, like, "How *cute* is Wicky being?" or "Toss me the Swedish meatball bit, would you?"

Every "first day at school" memory merged in my mind — I looked down at my hands, fully expecting to see them clutching a dorky metal lunch box.

Tory had the tallest figure, the longest hair, and the fastest walk of the barn posse. Her clear, slightly husky voice carried over all the others as she barked orders, mocked the girls, and occasionally cussed at a too-slow-to-move horse, chicken, or barn cat — all of which flitted in and out of the barn aisle like a livestock game of Red Rover.

She assigned me a horse, a brooding beige-colored mare with the clever name of Brown. As I fumbled with the saddle and bridle, Brown pinned her ears in annoyance. The other women were already mounted and trotting off. I vaulted awkwardly on Brown, struggling to catch up as we headed out to the bridle paths behind the farm.

The day was a blur of equestrian failure. I was miserable on Brown, who hated me. The posse politely averted their faces, careful not to stare as I flailed at every obstacle, like crossing a creek, cantering up a hill, or simply trying to keep up with them. Brown alternately balked, refused to slow down, or sulked, ears glued to her neck in outrage. I slipped and slid in the saddle, trying to hide my dismay. This was nothing like the sedate group riding lessons or my leisurely walks on Fred.

No one slowed down for me. The posse continued its spew of giggles and chatter, their horses behaving beautifully, their fringed chaps and pastel fleece headbands dancing colorfully, their long hair whipping princess-like over their backs. In comparison, my budget breeches, rubber boots, and sensibly short hair seemed woefully geeky — not to mention my flailing riding style.

My inner teenager rose up, defiance winning over fear — I was going to finish this ride, no matter what, and then I'd slink back to my suburban apartment in despair. After what seemed like hours of riding across meadows full of holes, hopping up deer-infested embankments, and jumping over fallen logs, the ride finally ended.

Tory took pity on me, inviting me back for another "lesson." "Next time, try *not* to floss the couch," she ordered. Baffled, I nodded, afraid to ask how exactly I had applied dental hygiene to furniture. Maybe it had something to do with the "Swedish meatball" bit.

"Around here, you need to ride — or die." A cascade of posse laughter followed Tory's pronouncement — clearly this was a favorite barn punch line.

I drove home that day in a chastened frame of mind — wondering if I had just met Obi-Wan or Darth Vader.

A SNUFFLING SOUND INTERRUPTED my beer-inspired Tory memories. Startled, I looked up to see Tulsa Mambo grazing by the porch, his black coat blending into the night air. Just his white hind ankles were visible, eerie bobby sox floating in the dark.

Tulsa Mambo is my favorite horse — not for his perfect build (he has bumpy ankles), sleek beauty (he likes to roll in mud), or impeccable training (he can be opinionated under saddle). It's his mischievous sense of humor and cynical, Frenchman-like gallantry that make him so special to me.

And because he was one of the first Texas racehorses I ever met, an ambassador to the local racing scene here, a key player in the story of how our adoption program grew from a website to a full-fledged ranch in just a few months.

CHAPTER TWO

Tulsa Mambo

TWO YEARS EARLIER, one summer afternoon in 2003, Tom and I were on the backside of Retama racetrack in Selma, Texas. As we walked between the endlessly long barns (called "shedrows"), the usual equine rush hour swirled around us as horses commuted to the track for their morning workout.

Beautifully turned out, the racehorses were meticulously groomed, shining in the dawn. Their exercise riders also took pride in their appearance — wearing jaunty fringed chaps, bright helmets, and gaudy shirts emblazoned with their barn racing colors. Female exercise riders, called "gallop girls" no matter what their age, stood out in the sea of jockey machismo, their riding style more refined and elegant than that of their male counterparts.

The actual race trainers rarely ride; instead they pace along the track rail, like football coaches on the sidelines, muttering to themselves as they watch their horses gallop. Most trainers could easily fit into a Dick Francis novel, with their disheveled attire, wind-creased faces, and sharp-eyed worldview.

The racehorses danced on their toes with anticipation as they approached the track, their pony horse babysitters jogging beside them. As the jockeys steered their mounts up on the track, the horses immediately showed their age and experience. The young two-year-olds galloped sideways, crablike, heads bobbing at every new sight. Seasoned veterans broke into smooth runs, every stride an efficient pump of equine power. The champions of the moment, the ones winning today or about to win tomorrow, strutted arrogantly, throwing challenging glances over their arched necks, fighting the bit playfully.

It was easy to see which horses needed new careers — they moved with stiffness from old injuries or radiated a tension too nervous for competitive racing. My favorites were the couch potatoes, the still-maiden racehorses that ambled around the track, gazing placidly at the other horses dashing by, never once feeling a twinge of competitive fire or a faint urge to keep up with (let alone overtake) the sprinters in the passing lane.

Behind the scenes at a racetrack is always a disorienting jumble of rumbling diesel trucks, tautly alert young horses trotting on the dirt pathways between shedrows, gallop girls shouting to each other over the wind between their hurtling horses, random sprinklings of barn cats, feral kittens, and goats (the favorite stall companions of racehorses) wandering boldly in the barn aisles, and horses "playing" (a race term that really means "bucking like a mad bronc") on the starfish-shaped automatic walkers.

As a pedestrian, it's up to you to watch for horses suddenly trotting up from behind, their riders glaring if you don't leap out of the way quickly enough. In Texas, most trainers spit regularly, either chewing tobacco or dusty saliva, creating another hazard. The cats will rub up against your legs, the more enterprising goats will casually head butt your torso, and the kittens will flee from you on principle. Horse heads will snake out from the open stall windows, usually just looking for a peppermint treat, but sometimes aiming for a quick mouthful of your shirt, jeans, or arm.

Lack of savvy isn't tolerated here. Neither is slowness, in horses or people — nearly everyone walks fast and talks even faster, a carny cadence faintly discernible. There is a touch of greatness in all the people — and a touch of the con artist, the film noir character with a sentimental side. Racetrack people will surprise you — almost always pleasantly.

The horses all have a touch of greatness, too. Whether fast or slow, young or old, they reflect their ancestors in their sleek bodies, their well-shaped heads, their alert eyes, and their purity of purpose — to run, to race, to win.

I love the racetrack and all its colorful characters, both equine and human. In 2001, after my tumultuous tenure as Tory's working student ended, I discovered a nonprofit racehorse placement program called CANTER near Washington DC. On Saturdays, I found myself walking with Allie, the bubbly program director of CANTER's mid-Atlantic chapter, around a West Virginia racetrack. "Okay, go pet the racehorse . . . awww, he's *so* cute! Lynn, get in the frame with him. Helllooo, racehorse, *smile* for the camera!" Allie giggled and snapped photo after photo. Her upbeat, optimistic view of track horses was refreshing — she shared and encouraged my fascination with the dashing Thoroughbred racehorses, teaching me much about their racing lifestyle.

Her nonprofit program helped racehorses find new careers after racing. Allie put up free racehorse classified ads on a website, creating a bridge for race trainers to find nonracing homes for their horses. Allie said, "These race guys, they are so great. I love them! But they have *no* clue about the web, about how to find people looking for riding horses. Most of them don't even have email, let alone a digital camera!" The racehorse listing service was a big success. Allie's colorful ad descriptions and pretty photos attracted many people, mostly cheerful horsewomen like herself, all eager to give the racehorses new homes.

A few months later, in early 2002, Tom and I moved to Texas — we wanted new careers and a quieter lifestyle. We liked Texas, its open spaces and its straightforward, friendly people. The plan was to get "normal" jobs, save money, then gradually transition to our dream careers: for me, horses; for Tom, filmmaking or design.

Within a year, inspired by Allie, I started a nonprofit racehorse service

named LOPE — short for LoneStar Outreach to Place Ex-Racers — a
Texas version of her program. Allie had made it all seem so easy and fun.
I figured LOPE would just require a website and a couple of track visits
each month — no need for large amounts of my time or outside funding.
Texas Horsemen's Partnership, the state race trainers' association, quickly
partnered with LOPE — a stamp of approval that gave us instant credibility at the tracks. The three largest Texas racetracks also endorsed our
listing service, allowing us access to their backside shedrows.

As Tom and I walked through the Retama racetrack chaos in 2003, we
tried to talk with trainers about listing their less-than-stellar racehorses on
LOPE's nonprofit website. A man mucking out a stall looked at us curiously. I stepped in with my well-rehearsed spiel: "Hi, are you a trainer
here?"

This question, if delivered cheerfully, usually yielded me a curt nod.
At that nod, I broke into my description of LOPE's program, explaining
the nonprofit website classifieds, stressing the no-cost (no-risk) price tag,
and outlining the process to list a horse with our service.

Keith was a classic racetrack surprise. A tall, broad-shouldered man in
his midfifties, he looked like he was born on a track. His white hair peeking from under a battered cap, Keith cut a very barn-seasoned figure in his
faded jeans and worn cotton shirt, handling his horses and grooms with
gruff kindness. Quiet at first, he slowly warmed up to our conversation,
words finally flowing more easily, accompanied by a soft drawl.

Keith had been a paratrooper, then an engineer, before becoming a
race trainer. Growing up on a ranch, he returned to horses after years of
designing skyscrapers. "I did all right, liked building things. Till they promoted me, wanted me to schmooze clients, socialize and stuff. I wasn't any
good at that, knew it was time to get back with the horses."

Keith led a dashing black gelding named Tulsa Mambo from the stall.
I had seen more impressive, taller horses that day, flashier ones with big
blazes and white stockings. But Tulsa caught my attention immediately —
his eyes were wise, and he carried himself with a certain bemused air, as if
he found everything entertaining and interesting.

"I just want him to find a good home," Keith said. He petted Tulsa on the forehead gently. "We got him last year, and he's worked hard for us. Won money, too. But he's seven now and I don't want him to break down." Tulsa spotted Tom and the camera, and he swiveled his head curiously toward the shiny clicking box. "He's in great shape," Keith said, "but he has those ankles, so he won't pass the vet."

Tulsa had osselets on his front ankles. They looked almost identical, as if Tulsa had decided to wear matching bumpy bracelets. At the time, I didn't know the technical term "osselets" — everyone just called them "racing ankles" or "racing jewelry."

Osselets start as a stress injury to the joint capsule — usually caused by the repeated concussion of racing hard. The joint capsule tears, then "sets" with extra bone deposits that eventually calcify into "jewelry" form. Some osselets are so severe that the horse's ankle will barely flex, stiff from the bone deposits and premature arthritis. Others are mild, faint traces of a once-strenuous athletic career, rarely causing problems. Tulsa's were somewhere in between — not too bad, but Olympic jumping probably wasn't in his future.

"Now, he knows how to win a race — he did that seven times. And he's a good horse, wouldn't ever buck or anything like that. But he has been known to run away with an exercise rider now and then," Keith added.

Tulsa yawned in the sun, with a "What, me?" look of faux innocence. I could see him mischievously lulling his rider into a relaxed ride, then suddenly bolting off for fun down the track. Smiling, I played with Tulsa's mane — he snuffled around my hand, looking for a peppermint.

Keith was worried about Tulsa and asked several questions about how long it might take him to find a home. The race meet was about to end at Retama, and Tulsa needed to leave before Keith moved on to the next meet in Houston. That was a good five weeks away, though — it seemed like a shoo-in that Tulsa would be snapped up before then, with his good looks and charm.

Keith still looked anxious. "I don't want to sell him to the wrong type.

But he needs a new place real soon." Sometimes when a race trainer needs to move a horse quickly, horse dealers will move in, offering to buy the horse cheaply. The dealers usually then flip the horse at an auction for a fast profit. Auctions are the roulette of horse sale venues. Nice people attend these sales looking for reasonably priced horses — and so do less-pleasant individuals, such as rougher cowboys and meat dealers. Racehorses, full of nervous energy and high spirits, rarely show well in crowded auction arenas, often scaring off the kinder, less-hardened bidders.

As we talked, I could see Keith needed reassurance — flippantly, I said, "Hey, don't worry. He's going to find a great home before the Houston racing starts. And if for some freak reason, he doesn't — well, I'll buy him then. I could use a nice riding horse."

Keith cheered up immediately and tried to hide his relief by bustling around Tulsa, shooing him into a new pose for the next website ad photo.

Tom was petting Tulsa, too, by the time we left — fortunately he hadn't heard my casual comment about buying Tulsa. But I wasn't worried. The horse was dark and handsome and had a sense of humor to boot. Irresistible combination.

A MONTH PASSED and I forgot about my conversation with Keith. The listing service had become busier and busier, taking more of my time than expected. More time than I really had, with my part-time teaching gig and full-time employment search.

My original plan had been to find a "normal" job and gradually transition to horse work, but this had hit a snag, as the job market in Austin was at an all-time low. With his economics background, Tom had strung together a series of consulting projects and temporary jobs, but I had more difficulty lining up employment. Then I saw a job listing for a part-time horseback-riding instructor; excited, I applied immediately.

Like a good DC professional, I showed up early for my interview/ lesson. Bobbie, the barn owner, looked more like a school nurse than a horsewoman. It was hard to tell her age. She was short and stocky, with brown hair carefully done like my mom's and glasses. Bobbie peered doubtfully at me, clearly skeptical of my qualifications to teach lessons. Her other instructors were half my age and had twice my experience.

Two regular students were there for their usual lesson with Bobbie — pleasant soccer mom types, both named Judy. Bobbie had assigned me a huge palomino horse named Flash. "Oh, Flash is such a good boy," one Judy said cheerfully. "Very safe."

That must mean he won't break out of walk, I thought. "Would you like to borrow my crop?" the other Judy asked, confirming my hunch. I declined, sensing that the crop would be a sign of weak riding, a black mark in an interview I needed to pass with flying colors.

The outdoor arena was good sized, with small jumps, several barrels, and two large shade trees. Bobbie stood under the trees, directing us while sipping on a Big Gulp and answering her cell phone. I was the lone English rider, with my polo saddle strapped to Flash's massive body. As we walked our horses across the ring, I could feel Flash beginning to balk, his hooves barely moving with heavy dinosaur steps. The Judys shot me sympathetic looks.

My legs were already burning from pushing and squeezing against his sides. Flash began to wiggle at the walk, head bobbing, ears flattening. Well, at least something was happening — I wasn't making it easy for him. I became locked in a world that narrowed to my legs, Flash's back, and his ears.

Bobbie was watching me, her eyes cool even from a distance. As she ordered us to trot, Flash's cement sides softened imperceptibly (just as my legs were beginning to twitch). He glared at me over his shoulder, his baleful expression reminiscent of Brown. "Same to you, Flash," I thought, squeezing intensely with my calf muscles again, and then, with a grunt from Flash, we were actually trotting.

Flash had a lovely, comfortable trot — his ears registered astonishment, but also resignation, at his own speed. As the Judys gasped, I pushed even harder, making Flash step out and lengthen his stride — we began to lap the Judys.

Bobbie was laughing. I was out of breath (as was Flash), sweating heavily in my helmet, lurching in the saddle with my now unsteady legs. But I had passed the interview — I was officially the new rookie riding instructor at Bobbie's stables.

TEACHING RIDING LESSONS PART-TIME WAS FUN, but it created an erratic schedule that sometimes clashed with the racetrack photo sessions. On the weekend before the meet change to Houston, I was back at the Retama racetrack taking pictures. As I was finishing up that day, I kept an eye on the clock, ready to dash back to teach a lesson at Bobbie's barn. Keith found me walking quickly between the shedrows. "Hey, a lady is coming to see Tulsa now. If she doesn't take him, he's yours," Keith said, obviously delighted at the prospect. Like most race trainers, Keith just assumed I was an expert rider — even though all I did at the track was take horse photos, then post them on a website.

I smiled weakly, wondering what the hell I had gotten myself into. He said, "Come watch if you want. She sounds like a nice lady, but I don't know if she has experience with track horses."

Damn. She better have experience, I thought, as I headed toward Keith's barn.

Katie showed up a few minutes later. She was about thirty-five, with a perky pageboy haircut. She chattered on about how much she loved horses — she was looking for a trail horse to ride on the family ranch.

Katie's elderly father accompanied her, and he positioned himself in a dangerously fragile-looking chair parked in front of the feed room, watching the proceedings avidly. His daughter giggled, lobbing questions at Keith, reminding me of a girl on a mall shopping spree — with her dad along to pull out the plastic at the key moment.

As Keith got Tulsa ready, with Katie looking on, her father caught my eye. "My Katie, she's a real horse lover. And she is good with them, too — she'll probably want to jump right on him now."

"She must be a good rider," I said hopefully. Her father nodded emphatically, launching into a description of Katie's prowess as a child show rider.

Meanwhile, Keith was explaining to Katie that Tulsa hadn't been worked in several weeks. Ever since he had decided to retire Tulsa, Keith had kept him from racing as a kindness, to make sure Tulsa didn't accidentally injure himself right before retirement. Like a beat cop pulling desk duty before his pension kicked in, Tulsa was being kept away from any chance of danger.

But if he was being confined in a stall most of the time, that meant he wasn't getting much exercise. Tracks don't have open pastures — the racehorses stay in their shedrow stalls except when being raced, worked out on the track by their exercise riders, or cooled out on the automatic walkers.

Tulsa walked demurely beside Keith, looking docile and kind. Katie smiled, saying she understood Tulsa might be a little "up" and full of himself — and that was not a problem. Could she see him trot?

I held my breath. Sure enough, as Tulsa started jogging next to Keith, a sudden gust of air appeared beneath his bay legs. Tulsa began bucking playfully on the end of the lead rope. He still managed to trot; he just added a graceful levitation in between steps. "Hey, stop that," Keith barked. But he knew it was futile.

Tulsa actually was being polite, if you understood racehorse manners. He kept a respectful distance from Keith while he "played"; he never once tried to pull on the rope or kick out in Keith's direction. But none of this made an impression on Katie, who understandably looked nervous, her brave comments about "up" racehorses fading at the sight of Tulsa cheerfully cartwheeling beside Keith. She and her father left, happily horseless, to look for a less gymnastic trail horse somewhere else.

Keith seemed pleased as he handed me Tulsa's lead rope. "Looks like you got yourself a nice horse." Tulsa looked at me innocently and yawned again, suddenly the world's mellowest racehorse. A conspiracy theory darted across my brain, as I looked from Keith to Tulsa — they both appeared to be grinning.

It seemed surreal — how could I possibly own a bolting, perpetually amused racehorse named Tulsa Mambo? But I did.

At that moment, I was nervous about riding any horse. The first year in Austin, I enjoyed teaching children's lessons, but the pay was tiny, averaging $7 an hour, which put quite a crimp in my rent budget. Then I hit upon a brilliant strategy to bridge my revenue gap: I would boost income by emulating Tory, by taking more serious training cases, and maybe even investing in equine resale prospects.

Not a good idea.

MY HEAD SNAPPED BACK SHARPLY as the paint horse threw his head between his legs. "Just like TV rodeo," I thought as I left the saddle. I landed hard on my back, spewing a string of curse words.

Jenny and Steven, the paint's owners, were watching from the barn. I quickly shut my mouth, hoping to confine any lingering sailor language to my throat.

"Guess I better get back on him." I smiled, trying to look unruffled. My jeans were caked with manure, thanks to Rusty's aim. My back stiffened painfully as I lurched over to him.

Rusty was my training client, acquired soon after I launched my services as a pro horse trainer. Armed weakly with homemade business cards and Word flyers, I somehow managed to attract Steven and Jenny with my marketing plan.

They had purchased Rusty at an auction. "I've always wanted a paint horse," Steven had said during our first meeting, waving his beer can in Rusty's direction. "And there he was. I bought him for hardly anything, bargained with his owner in the parking lot."

A short, three-year-old gelding, Rusty was mostly white with splashes of reddish brown here and there. He had looked up at me, his eyes big, brown, and not terribly analytical. Steven had patted him, prompting a nuzzle from Rusty. "I love this little guy. Even named him after my grandson. Rusty's a good horse, but he's young. He needs some more rides on him — can you do that?"

Looking at Rusty's small stature and calflike expression, I had asserted that yes, I could definitely do that. But now I wasn't so sure. Rusty had been well behaved for our previous rides, but he seemed possessed today.

I strode over to Rusty, ignoring my clenched stomach and his worried expression. With a cowboy tough move, I remounted, pulling the reins up hard like I'd seen polo trainers do. I'd show Rusty who was in charge — and ride out his bad behavior.

Rusty bucked harder this time, flinging me sideways. Against all odds, I landed in the same manure pile again. I lay on my back for a moment, looking up at the hot Texas sky. Jenny tittered. Rusty started to graze. Embarrassment kept me on the ground, my cheeks flushing even under my sunburn.

Of all things, accounting motivated me upright again. Bobbie's lesson pay wasn't enough to cover my share of the household bills — I needed this training gig. "Guess I'm not approaching this right," I mumbled to my clients. "Let me try to figure out why Rusty's so upset."

It turned out to be his girth, which was too tightly buckled and pinching his skin, an amateurish blunder on my part. Steven and Jenny took the scene in stride, my buck-off not unexpected for a "gal" trainer in their world. "He wouldn't have bucked me off, I guarantee you that," asserted Steven, arms folded across his stocky chest. "I weigh a lot more than you."

Inexplicably, I wasn't fired, my ineptitude mistaken for equestrian refinement. "We want a lady rider to work Rusty. None of that cowboy rough stuff."

RUSTY PROVED TO BE THE FIRST leg of a bumpy road. Within a few months, I had been thrown off several times — every horse seemed to buck, rear, or both. One of the rearing horses even fell over on me. My budding confidence was seriously bruised, not to mention my back and shoulders. By the time Keith handed me Tulsa, I was backing off the horse work and even scanning the want ads for accounting jobs.

My courage weakened by my horse rearing-and-flipping carnival ride,

I promised myself I'd find another home for Tulsa. Back at our rented pastures, I hastily improvised a small pen between two large fields so that Tulsa could slowly get used to the idea of suddenly being outside all the time. When he arrived, full of muscle and energy, he'd run playfully at the pen walls, skidding to a stop inches from the fence.

A true prankster, Tulsa especially liked to pull this stunt when I was nearby, seeming to enjoy my gasps of horror. Eventually, I refused to watch this "chicken" game, resolutely averting my eyes when I walked by, afraid I'd see Tulsa sliding to a heap, tangled in cable fencing and pipe posts. Without an audience, Tulsa soon grew bored with the game, contenting himself with dozing in the sun and nibbling on hay.

After a month, I finally let him loose in the big pasture. Watching anxiously, I opened the gate — wondering if Tulsa would race around the open space like a fiend, perhaps whacking into trees in an adrenaline-crazed rush.

Tory had always been careful to slowly familiarize her ex-racers to larger spaces. Other riders at the barn whispered about wild, crazy racehorses, fresh from the track, pumped full of drugs and aggression — everyone seemed to have a story involving track horses, wire fencing, and a shotgun. I wasn't sure what to expect from Tulsa, a horse who already had demonstrated a flair for playing recreational chicken with pipe fencing.

Tulsa walked slowly through the gate, looking mildly interested. He then sauntered around the entire pasture perimeter, sniffing the ground occasionally, until he was back at the gate. Then with a sudden, fluid movement, he started trotting gracefully around the field again, seeming to retrace his steps, sidestepping the rocks and larger mud puddles, a look of concentration in his eyes.

As he rounded back to the gate again, he paused, and then accelerated, this time into a full gallop, an equine projectile, hooves cutting deeply into the rain-softened earth, powerful strides of tremendous velocity flinging from his body, an impressive and slightly scary sight.

He tore up his improvised track around the pasture, his steps hitting the same spots as before, a confidence whipping out from his tail, a cocky pleasure apparent as he looked around for an opponent to beat. He never misstepped, never hit a mud puddle or rock — he knew where he was going, since he'd already done a preflight check twice, at the walk and trot. For all his exuberant speed, he was in control, a professional athlete understanding how to use his body and push his muscles for best performance.

His victory lap over, Tulsa slowed to a stop, dropping his nose to the tall grass, relaxed after his refreshing sprint. Keith's comments about Tulsa bolting with his exercise riders echoed in my mind — it was hard to believe this placid, grazing horse had been running full tilt just seconds ago.

After watching Tulsa's playful pasture races, it took me months to work up the nerve to ride him. To boost my morale, I researched Tulsa's history, trying to learn more about his background and handling. At the track, there were many different stories about Tulsa — some said he had injured his shoulder badly years ago in a race. Another trainer disagreed, claiming Tulsa had weak stifles, not shoulder damage. Two different riders told me that he reared, he bit, and he was known for being mean and erratic.

A third rider, a superb problem-horse trainer, brushed aside these reports, insisting that Tulsa was a good horse who had been treated roughly by the other riders. He told me, "That Mambo horse, he's a smart one. Only run off or reared on jerks who were hard on him, who tried to bully him. I never had any trouble with him. He was my favorite ride of the day."

In the professional racing arena, Tulsa was a typical working-class racehorse. He won over $53,000, earning it the hard way, in purses spread out over sixty races and five years. By contrast, Smarty Jones, winner of the 2004 Kentucky Derby, won over $2.6 million (plus a $5 million bonus) in nine races and retired at age three to a stud career. As I soon discovered, most racehorses are like Tulsa, hardworking midlevel runners, minor league players who steadily accumulate respectable winnings but never hit the big time.

Though Smarty Jones and Tulsa had widely disparate careers, they had some famous relatives in common — such as Mr. Prospector, Native Dancer, and Bold Ruler. But shared lineage is normal for racehorses. All Thoroughbreds can be traced to three Arabian stallions imported from the Middle East into England near the turn of the seventeenth century. These studs were then bred to quality native mares to produce horses with both speed and endurance. Bred selectively for speed over centuries, the modern Thoroughbred is the fastest of all horses. They have been clocked at speeds close to 40 mph over mile-long tracks and also are known for their competitive spirit (or heart) in races.

Tulsa raced all over the country, from Minnesota to Indiana to Texas, changing hands frequently. Keith picked him out of a farm sale, in spite of his age and ankles, sensing Tulsa had some wins left in him, seeing something in his eyes that made Tulsa stand out — even in a dusty field full of other horses.

Keith owned Tulsa for only about nine months, but quickly became fond of him. "Right after breakfast every morning, there he'd be, putting his head out the stall, wanting to know what's going on," Keith told me. "Most horses would just as soon take all day to eat their breakfast, but Tulsa, he likes to do things. He likes to work, gets bored if nothing is going on."

A clear portrait was emerging of Tulsa: smart, bores easily, and likes to occasionally toy with people. Clearly, it wasn't a good idea to leave him inactive in the pasture for much longer — he wasn't the type of horse that idles well.

A few months had passed since my most dramatic equestrian accident. I had been riding a young mare regularly, a sweet gray with kind manners. My rather naive plan was to give her some riding miles and then sell her, maybe as a polo prospect. Lilly's short stature and kind temperament made her a good candidate for that career — plus she was fun to ride, a truly gentle horse.

One morning, while I was mounting Lilly, she abruptly reared, her neck smacking into my face, catching me off guard. Stunned, I clung limply to her mane, watching helplessly as she lurched sideways, on her hind legs, swaying toward the now very terrifying pipe-and-cable fencing.

I should have ended up underneath her, with many broken bones. Or been flung into the cable fencing with multiple lacerations. Instead, as Lilly fell backward, I managed to slide sideways, my body reflexively choosing to fall into the cable fence rather than beneath the 900-pound horse. By pure luck, I hit the cable right where it happened to be weak; it popped out from its rusty moorings on the pipe post, releasing me to the ground, tangled in stiff, wiry fencing. I was frightened and bruised, but not seriously injured.

As it turned out, Lilly wasn't misbehaving; she had been hit with a sudden onset of a neurological condition, a true freak accident, nothing I could have prevented or known about. A sad-faced vet came to the farm, shaking his head as he examined Lilly's reflexes. "Looks like maybe EPM," he said, explaining how this disorder can erupt suddenly, caused by protozoa attacking the nervous system. "Or maybe a brain tumor," he sighed. "Hard to say if she'll recover — probably not, but you never know. I wouldn't ride her again, just to be safe." Stunned, I managed to find Lilly a home as a companion horse, where she could be a pasture pet without ever being ridden again.

Still traumatized, I fought a subconscious assumption that all horses were going to rear or have some kind of unpredictable physical ailment. To say the least, my riding style regressed rapidly. Ashamed, I was ready to retreat back to weekend riding and group lessons.

And here was Tulsa, my unexpected acquisition, ready to be ridden. With his reputation, I knew there would be little chance of finding him a new home — unless he had some riding time that didn't involve high-speed galloping. But my budget was tiny; there were no funds to pay an outside trainer. And somewhere in my psyche, an impostor feeling rankled. How could I run a racehorse placement service and be afraid to ride one?

Slowly I inched my way from lounging to saddling to mounting him, working in a small corral more suitable for riding Shetland ponies than racehorses. Tulsa seemed to shake his head in pity at me, often dozing in boredom at my snail's pace. He even appeared to roll his eyes one particularly sad day when I mounted him, then jumped off within thirty seconds, my heart thumping fearfully. When I finally rode him, he was kind and willing, almost with a touch of gallantry, occasionally touching his nose to my stirrup, as if trying to reassure me, to calm my anxious breathing.

Tulsa's old injuries showed during the rides. He was stiff on one side and had bumpy gaits, his racing ankles now weak shock absorbers. Even more, his personality showed — he was opinionated about where we should go, exuded a jaunty cheerfulness during trotting, and liked to make faces at the neighbor's horses over the fence. Tulsa reminded me eerily of Charles, a chatty European polo pro from my exercise rider days, a slim man who liked to smoke, make cynical witticisms, and curse in French while riding his herd of moody polo ponies.

Tulsa was often spirited during the premounting phase — due more to his mischievous sense of humor than to true misbehavior. You had to be able to take a joke, a pretended spook as you stepped into the stirrup, in order to ride Tulsa. Once you were in the saddle, he was a perfect gentleman — content to walk and trot sedately in the fields.

Still, I remained alert, his amused eyes and reputation as a runaway always in my mind. I didn't fully trust him, even after many rides together. And maybe I didn't trust myself either. My horsemanship was now teetering back to my original "clutch the mane and forget to breathe" riding style. What if I started "flossing couches" again, as I did so often at Tory's barn? Maybe Tory's assessment of my skills was correct — I belonged in safer equestrian waters with the other adult amateurs.

Tory's stable was an exciting, disorienting chaos of polo ponies, hunter show horses, and off-track prospects. I learned many useful things there, such as the properties of the infamous Swedish meatball bit (a double-looped contraption, it created humane, but firm, leverage on a horse with brake problems); the definition of a couch (a placid, beginner-safe horse such as Brown); and the proper way to avoid flossing said couch (don't treat the reins like a rappelling rope, hanging heavily on the horse's mouth for balance).

Under Tory's tutelage, I worked hard to improve my skills. I rode her quieter horses, traded stable chores for private lessons, learned to play polo ineptly, and eventually even acquired horses of my own — but when I left, I was still light-years away from being a professional trainer. My riding did get better, although not good enough to safely ride Wicky (short for "Wicked Witch"), Tory's moody, massive mare, or the racehorses in her pastures. Tory frequently reminded me that ex-racehorses were green, prone to bolting when riders like me even breathed the wrong way — just way out of my league. "That horse will kill you, Lynn," was a steady refrain, tossed my way whenever I looked wistfully at her best prospect, a pretty black filly straight off the track.

Soon my premonitions about Tulsa proved correct. After weeks of uneventful riding, Tulsa and I were having a bad day. "Quit!" Tulsa side-stepped violently, catching me off guard as I tightened his saddle girth. The reins tangled in my fingers as I clumsily hopped out of his way, try-ing not to buckle my own hand into the saddle billets. "Hey, knock it off!" I tried to sound confident, my high-pitched voice betraying me.

Snorting, head high, Tulsa prepared for another spook, ears twitching in his intended direction. I yanked the reins, turning his head toward me (and away from wherever he was headed without me), wondering how I was possibly going to mount him.

The October wind was collaborating with Tulsa, blowing in popping gusts that sent leaves and random debris all around us. Ever mischievous, Tulsa seemed to be taking full advantage of the wind's excuse to misbe-have, with his usual pretend feistiness tipping over into an Academy Award–winning performance. True to Keith's word, Tulsa had never bucked once I mounted up; his antics were always confined to before the ride. But my hands shook as I grimly tangoed with Tulsa, looking for a moment when he would stand quietly — so I could get in the saddle and stop his fun.

The wind smacked at my face and hands, its speed and tempo increasing, forcing eerie noises from the tree branches scraping our roof. At least it wasn't cold — a Texas autumn is balmy compared to Virginia and DC. Finally, after several attempts, I climbed awkwardly into the saddle. "Let's go, Tulsa. Walk on." I tapped my stirrup gently against his flank, normally the only incentive Tulsa needed to launch into a rapid trot down the path.

Tulsa tensed, flinging his head up, blowing hard through his nose — PSSHHT! PSSHHHT! — dancing nervously from side to side and doing all kinds of things except walking. My fear masquerading as assertiveness, I kicked harder, much harder than is wise on an ex-racehorse. "*Let's go*," I shouted over the wind, while Tulsa flicked me an aggrieved look over his shoulder. I aimed his head toward my favorite path, along the creek bank with its pretty trees and brush piles, and kicked again.

Tulsa managed to move both reluctantly and rapidly — a spurting lurch that would have been funny if I wasn't on his back, which felt tight and dangerously coiled beneath me, much like Lilly's had right before she reared. The wind whacked my face harder, a pounding hammer effect that matched my breathing — I was scared and confused. Tulsa felt erratic, unpredictable, and dangerous under the saddle.

The path was right in front of us, just a few paces past a brush pile. Staring at the trail fixedly, determined to get there (ride or die), I smacked Tulsa's rump with my hand, kicked again, anything to get him moving forward, to keep him from rearing or bucking or thinking of something even worse. Tulsa hopped forward another half step, then stopped sharply, his hindquarters nearly dropping to a sitting position. Tensely, I prepared for another massive kick, berating myself for getting on such a crazy horse, for putting myself at risk again, for ever wanting to ride fiery racehorses.

Tulsa whipped his head around his shoulder, his nose nearly touching my boot, his right eye staring at me intently. Before I could react, he whipped his head back, flipping it up and down, pointing his forehead toward the brush pile. Then again his head came to my knee; he looked at me, and gave another emphatic flip of his nose. As a crazy image of someone playing charades floated across my brain, Tulsa turned away, bobbing his head violently toward the brush pile, its dead tree limbs and leaves rustling in the wind.

Perplexed, I followed the direction of his nose with my eyes, simultaneously realizing that the brush rustling sound was odd, a little too loud. The wind dropped helpfully, as my gaze settled on a funny-looking upright branch in the pile, the rustling sound now more distinct, an angry sound, a staccato sound, a reptile sound — a rattlesnake.

I had never seen a rattlesnake before, except at a zoo — and the zoo snakes weren't upright and undulating, enraged and ready to strike from ten feet away.

Tulsa looked over his shoulder one more time, as if to say, "Do you get it now?" He was scared, his tense body no longer a dangerous mystery.

I loosened the reins and sat back, giving Tulsa his head and decision-making power. Deftly, he sidestepped and reversed, executing a series of maneuvers that quickly removed us from snake-striking range, but without any abrupt, rattler-tempting moves.

Mama, the small gray cat that ruled the porch, emerged suddenly — she had spotted the still-angry snake. With typical feline arrogance, she marched toward the brush pile, her six-pound frame radiating an "I'm going to kick your butt" attitude.

Aghast, I jumped off Tulsa, leaving the reins looped on his neck. "Stay," I said absurdly. Who orders a racehorse to stay? Tulsa looked quizzically at me as I bolted for Mama, scooping her up before the snake could.

Mama squirmed in disappointment, annoyed at my interference, ready to rumble with the rattler. As I plopped her in the house, then jogged back to the driveway, I speculated on what mischief Tulsa had started during my cat-saving absence — no doubt galloping halfway across the ranch, taking extra care to roll in the mud with the saddle, step on the reins, and break them. Or maybe he had trotted between the trees, catching the dangling stirrups in the branches, ripping their expensive leather straps. Lost in thoughts of tack destruction, I turned the corner of the porch rapidly, then stopped in shock.

Tulsa was standing right where I left him, looking bored, like an old cow pony taught to ground tie. He walked over to me, nuzzling my arm, ready for his ride, his eyes as wise as ever.

Tulsa has many imperfections — he is mischievous, with weak ankles and a twisted sense of humor — but he has taught me a new horsemanship principle, one that even Tory never knew.

Racehorses, the most unlikely of equine Lassies, can be couches, too.

I decided to keep Tulsa, glad for the lease on his hastily rented pastures — a seemingly simple contract that soon changed everything for Tulsa, LOPE, and me.

CHAPTER THREE

Zuper

A STIFF MARCH BREEZE WAS BLOWING used stall bedding around the Sam Houston Race Park shedrows. In 2004, the Houston track was fairly new and well kept — but windstrewn manure can bring down the look of the best facility.

Tom was filming a video about our racehorse placement program and our newly purchased adoption ranch. The morning gallops had been peppier than usual, thanks to the gusting cool air — several racehorses were extra exuberant, hopping and careening around the track.

Tom's camera captured an outrider, settled comfortably on his big horse, chatting on the cell phone, his head rocking gently with the saddle motion. The outriders patrol the rail, their Western saddles and stout horses setting them apart. The cops of the track, they make sure the racehorses stay on course. If a horse suddenly bucks or bolts, putting his jockey in peril, an outrider will calmly maneuver his mount nearby, ready to intervene if needed.

"Hey, lady." An outrider reined his horse near me. He was lean and hard faced, with a grim scowl lining his features. "Lady!" Startled, I looked up, nodding, feeling like a naughty cocker spaniel. The outrider trotted his charger-sized horse next to me as I walked along the rail. "Barn J —

there's a trainer gal there. Her horse got injured last night — go see her. He needs a home." I nodded again, wondering why he was taking the time to tell me about this horse. He didn't seem like a going-out-of-his-way kind of guy.

"Barn J," he barked again, as he spurred his horse past me. Tom followed, laden with camera equipment. As we passed the first row of barns, Jay, a race trainer with Will Smith good looks, popped his head out of a stall. "Hey, lady!"

That's me.

Jay was a fast-talking, cheerful huckster type — according to him, he had the best horses, with Olympic jumping talent, ready to be purchased for mere pittances. Those pittances were always on the high side, and the Olympic horses always had "minor" injuries like bowed tendons or calcified ankles. But Jay was a bundle of pleasant contradictions. His horses were well handled and groomed to perfection. And his prices had a way of dropping suddenly if the buyer seemed like an especially good home.

I quickly introduced him to Tom. Jay had a tendency to flirt with all women under age sixty. Nothing personal — it was an odd form of chivalry with him. Jay got to the point. "You been at Barn J yet? Ask for Robin — she has an injured horse there. Nice horse — he got hurt real bad last night, needs to find a place."

Hmm. This wasn't like Jay — he hadn't tried to list a horse or sell Tom a TV from out of his truck. Surprised, I seized the chance to cut the conversation short — skies were getting heavy with clouds, we better scoot on over to Barn J before it rained. "Tell Robin I sent you," Jay shouted as he disappeared back into the stall, unwrapping a polo bandage for a small bay mare.

I wasn't sure where to find Barn J — the Houston shedrows were laid out at odd angles to each other, in asymmetrical rows. Since each barn had about fifty stalls, guessing wrong meant many retraced steps. As I walked toward my best guess, Kelly appeared around the corner. Another master of rapid-fire banter, he immediately regaled me with his latest saga of "almost" winning on the track. Proudly, he bragged about his best horse, how she was going to win big this month, just watch and see.

Tall, muscular, and bald, Kelly looked like he rarely got mocked for his girlish name. He was fond of his horses, all rogues like him, and he whispered baby talk to them when no one was looking. His favorite phrase was "dog gentle" — nearly always shouted — as in, "This horse is *dog* gentle, follow you anywhere. Bites sometimes but just to play. *Dog gentle!*"

Kelly had a horse to list — but the gelding had rolled in mud and needed a makeover before we took a photo. As I flipped open my notebook to jot down the horse's name, yet another trainer wandered by, a blonde woman with surprisingly clean jeans for the shedrow lifestyle.

"Kelly, I got a horse that needs a home," she said, worry in her eyes. Kelly introduced me ("This is Lynn, that horse lady"), and her face lit with relief. "I heard about you from the racing office" she said. "My horse got injured last night, and I've been just sick about him." It was Robin. Eager to meet her horse, I followed her to Barn J.

Zuper was gorgeous. A husky bay with an endearing splash of white on his nose, he exuded wisdom and Buddha good cheer. Zuper was nine years old, ancient for a working racehorse. His right front ankle was grotesquely swollen — the injury had created a triple-sized ankle, like a cartoon character hit by an anvil.

Robin was another racetrack surprise. Her shy smile, print shirt, and maternal anxiety gave her the look of a soccer mom instead of a race trainer. She fussed over Zuper, adjusting his halter, brushing his forelock out of his eyes, as she described Zuper's mellow personality.

"I don't ride so much anymore, but he always takes care of me. I just hop on him bareback with a halter and lead rope, and go for a ride around the shedrows. He's always laid-back and quiet." Zuper was also the barn's Christmas tree — each December, Robin would drape ornaments and tinsel on Zuper, topped by a Santa hat, for her Christmas card photo.

Haltingly, Robin described how he had hit a bad piece of ground in his last race and stumbled, twisting his ankle violently, the torque of his large body combining terribly with his high speed. Near tears, she berated herself for putting him in the race.

"Before the race, when we came to get him ready, he just threw a fit. Wouldn't stand, acted all crazy, didn't want to be saddled. And I thought what is *up* with you, boy? Nothing ever bothers this horse. But I put him in the race, and he got hurt — he must have known something wasn't right in his leg. And he was trying to tell me, and I didn't pay attention."

As Robin talked, she kept petting Zuper. He dipped his head closer, clearly fond of her. Zuper's injury was serious, a fresh tear of a previously damaged suspensory ligament. Robin explained that he needed months of pasture rest, that the swelling would subside but the ankle would never be the same. Zuper looked calmly at me, with confidence and poise, an expectation of good times in his eyes.

"I don't want to sell him," she said emphatically. "Just want to give him to a loving home." Zuper arrived at our adoption ranch soon after, one of the first arrivals.

EVER SINCE I HAD BEGUN the listing service in spring 2003, race trainers had tried to give me injured or slow horses. As I soon learned, stall space is limited at the racetracks and most trainers don't own farms. There is no room to give an injured horse time to rest and heal. Most trainers do their best to find homes for their horses — but the options can be limited. And the threat of auction (and "used-horse" dealers) is never far away.

I hated saying no. The trainers were so earnest, so hopeful that I could take in their horses. Like Keith, they all thought I was a professional horsewoman, most likely with a ranch somewhere near the track. In their industry, a professional is paid to train and "finish" horses in a particular discipline. The top trainers would focus on young or troubled horses, the most dangerous types of equine clientele.

That was not me. The reality was, Tom and I lived in a small apartment near the University of Texas in Austin. Our fellow neighbors were mostly college students, all slightly disheveled and financially strapped like us. They assumed we were either elderly grad students or unemployed professors, nodding to us deferentially in the laundry room and avoiding our balcony overhang for post-keg-party antics.

I was still teaching riding lessons at Bobbie's stable. She had a second ranch, about forty minutes away, where she retired her old school horses. As part of my expanding work duties, I fed Bobbie's ancient horses there on weekdays. The property had a big house, two barns, and lush pastures dotted with a lumbering herd of elderly equines. The tenants were Randy, his wife, and their two daughters. Randy had a giddy personality and deep voice pitched through much-neglected teeth. He also carried a rifle in his truck and liked to show it to new visitors.

My feeding chores kept me busy, requiring frequent visits to Bobbie's retirement ranch. Usually, Randy was my only company — I learned to be careful what I said to him, as his reactions were unpredictable.

Randy had a weak memory, rarely recognizing Tom despite his many visits to the farm. Spotting Tom on the property, Randy would come zooming up in his truck (rifle on the front seat), squinting suspiciously through his tinted windows. Once he realized it was Tom, someone he was supposed to know, Randy would pause, his brain desperately flipping through memory cells, then bellow in greeting, "Hey... hey guy!"

A potential lesson client once made the mistake of chatting too long with me. As the man sat in his rumbling truck parked between the main barn and Randy's house, Randy popped out, door slamming, hissing in wild-eyed fury, "Not in my backyard!" Was the truck too noisy? Were we talking too long? No explanation was forthcoming, just more enraged muttering through clenched teeth. Although his rifle was nowhere in sight, the incident was sobering, a reminder of the fine line between "colorful" and "soon to be incarcerated" in Texas.

There was another ranch next door, with a cottage-style house tucked at the end of a long driveway flanked by knee-high grass. Wistfully, I asked Bobbie about the place. She said, "Oh, those people are kind of strange, keep to themselves. Unfriendly. House isn't worth much either."

With tenants like Randy, Bobbie's idea of "strange" must be spectacular — clearly I should avoid the neighbors. Still, the little ranch seemed so peaceful, with its big trees and hobbitlike house. I often looked at it longingly during my feeding duties, daydreaming about owning a farm, no longer tiptoeing around erratic tenants and financial woes.

One day, while filling up the water troughs for Bobbie's retirees, I saw a man with glasses wheeling a trash can down the driveway next door. As I debated whether to approach him, Randy wandered by. "Hey, girl," he shouted, usually the preamble to a long conversation about catfish or lotto.

That was all the incentive I needed. Throwing down the hose, I sprinted over to the neighbor, leaving Randy behind, swaying on his porch, Bud Lite in hand.

The neighbor turned out to be Al, a tax attorney with a dry sense of humor and not a single firearm to his name. His wife, Mae, worked for a large bank in Austin — the traffic-laden commute was wearing on them. They were just beginning to think about selling the ranch, maybe putting it on the market in a year or so.

Mae and Al liked the idea of helping horses. After a couple of meetings, we struck a bargain — we would rent the fields for $20 per month. We drew up a simple lease that included a purchase option. And just in time — Tulsa was soon on his way from Keith's shedrow.

TOM WAS ALSO TAKEN WITH THE RANCH, his Colorado childhood cementing a deep appreciation of the outdoors in him. He took several photographs of the property, including an especially artistic shot of the cottage framed by trees and pasture growth. Lit by late-afternoon sun, the ranch house was a tranquil beacon amid the lush, almost raucous nature swirling around it.

Ever the philosopher, Tom immediately made a flyer of the photo with the title "Goal: To secure the purchase of the 26-acre ranch" centered boldly above it. He posted the flyer in our bedroom, to inspire us with income ideas despite the tight job market. Taped to the wall across from the bed, the ranch image floated before our eyes, usually the last thing we saw before falling asleep at night.

As if sensing our new lease, more racetrack trainers approached me, offering to donate horses. Soon came a filly named Peanut with a hairline fracture. "Got a horse for you," her trainer said. "She's a nice one, just needs some time to rest her knee." Boomer, a mooselike gelding with zero speed, quickly followed Peanut into our rented fields.

Then, a month after Boomer's arrival, Mae emailed me unexpectedly. "We've decided to put the ranch on the market now. If you'd like to make an offer, please let me know by next Thursday." This gave us ten days to decide.

By now, we had fallen in love with the property, its scenic pastures and trees creating instant (and much-needed) serenity in our lives. But Tom and I had about $1,000 to our names — probably not the offer Mae and Al had in mind. The ranch's price was about $185,000, a bargain compared to the $600,000-plus cost for similar farms back in DC. So we leaped into action, frantically contacting mortgage lenders, family members, temp agencies, and racing organizations. Tom rustled up a short-term but well-paid consulting gig. I pitched racing industry and animal welfare philanthropists, writing and calling any foundation I could research on Google.

On the ninth day of the deadline, a donor stepped forward, funding our horse care budget and a tiny stipend for me, a near-exact match to my pay at Bobbie's lesson barn. "There's just one catch. I want to be an anonymous donor. Otherwise, all kinds of groups will hit me up for more money." The native Texan grinned, his eyes disappearing in well-earned laugh lines. "I'm guessing you won't have a problem with that, though — just so long as you get the check."

With hours to spare, Tom and I made an offer on the ranch, an offer that Mae and Al accepted.

IN THE BUSTLE OF ACQUISITION, the enormity of the purchase didn't sink in until move-in day. We officially took possession of the ranch on a cold February weekend in 2004. The first night was eerie, the country quiet ominous to our city ears. Finally, we fell asleep, fatigued from moving day, our new dog (hastily adopted from a local rescue center) curled up at the foot of the bed.

Coyotes woke us up within hours, screeching and yipping like deranged women in peril, just outside our window. Shaken, we tried to laugh it off, but sleep eluded us for most of the night. The dog, Sophie, had no such problems — she slept deeply even through the coyote serenade, seriously undermining our confidence in her watchdog abilities.

The coyote population wasn't our only challenge. Running the ranch was full of strenuous chores, like putting up fencing, repairing broken gates, and mowing long-overgrown pastures. The grass was crazy tall, with thick, tangled layers of thorny ivy — as I picked my way across the fields in search of long-buried water faucets, it felt spookily alive and springy under my feet.

Near the house, the weeds had completely taken over, erupting into five-foot-high stalks, complete with bark and grasping roots. Snakes were everywhere, along with rabbits, armadillos, lizards, and large rodents I called "field mice" — even though it was obvious they were really rats. Strange piles of dirt poked up from the ground; they were fire ant mounds, home to thousands of the meanest insects I'd ever encountered. Fire ants are tiny, yet sting with the ferocity of hornets, leaving behind blistering welts that burn and itch for days.

In addition to liberating water spigots from jungle growth, basic horse-care tasks seemed daunting — especially now that I was solely responsible for them. Figuring out how to get hay to the ranch, then store it out of the elements, was alone a tremendous puzzle. Local hay farmers don't advertise on the internet or in the phone book. Instead, most dealers rely on word of mouth. Others prefer "drive-by" advertising — in the form of hand-lettered signs posted on rural roads, often cryptically worded ("Hay $7 Call 265-1235").

When I asked neighbors to recommend a hay supplier, I got answers like, "Well, I've been using Lorenzo's son up there near Temple but only for rounds. That fellow, what's his name, the guy with the red sign up by the Exxon — I use him for squares. His number's on the sign but he doesn't check his messages too much."

My DC networking skills were useless here.

I found a big general store nearby — Callahan's — where I could buy horse feed, buckets, and fencing materials. They also sold cowboy boots, hardware, seeds, books on agricultural subjects (my favorite title: *Raising Meat Goats for Pleasure and Profit*), grain for every type of livestock, and women's clothing.

The bespectacled store manager, Mike, was lean and taciturn, always running to find a customer some obscure pig-breeding product in the warehouse. Embarrassed to ask basic questions about animal husbandry, I instead fed him information about our nonprofit ranch operation, hoping to wheedle a discount. "Nope, not today," Mike would say, dropping his eyes and turning away, heading for the latest crisis at the live baby chick aisle. "But keep asking me."

UNTIL MARCH 2004, the initial herd of racehorses was small, just Peanut, Tulsa, and Boomer. Although they were good-natured and easy to handle, it took all of my fledgling skills to keep their food rations flowing steadily, to tend to their injuries, and (most importantly) to monitor their personality quirks.

For example, Boomer was kindly but dim. He followed Tulsa's lead — never a good idea. Tulsa liked to nip him playfully, each love bite shaving off some Boomer skin. He goaded Boomer into ill-advised activities, like galloping through slippery mud and rolling in manure. Predictably, Tulsa seemed intent on playing practical jokes instead of providing good leadership.

One afternoon, I separated Boomer, putting him in the next pasture, to keep his coat away from Tulsa's teeth. All seemed quiet enough — until I heard hoofbeats. Tulsa was running up his pasture, near the pipe fence separating him from Boomer. Boomer decided to play, too. He began running on his side of the fence, on our paved driveway with its traction-unfriendly asphalt surface.

Tulsa edged closer to the fence; Boomer galloped up the driveway, hooves already slipping, perversely avoiding the safe grass next to the pavement. The horses were having a blast, their tails flagging cheerfully, their heads up with excitement. They kept looking over at each other, just like racehorses do to challenge their opponents, an equine version of trash talking.

Boomer was squealing happily, his head turned completely to the right as he galloped next to his buddy, trying to catch Tulsa's eye. There was just one problem. Boomer wasn't looking where he was going — which was straight for our large white gate at the end of the driveway. Tom and I both began yelling at Boomer and Tulsa to stop now, whoa, *whoa!*

With a vaguely baffled air, Boomer finally looked our way. As he spotted the gate, now all of twenty yards away, a cartoon look of dismay suddenly filled his eyes.

With Wile E. Coyote acrobatics, Boomer valiantly tried to stop, slamming down his chunky rump, a sickening sound of hooves screeching on blacktop. He was a big horse — stopping on a dime just wasn't an option.

He slid into the gate, his head and forelegs wedging in its long slats, his hindquarters spinning out to push him deeper still, his head now on the other side. Terrified, I ran to the gate, certain I was going to see jagged lacerations and lots of blood. When horses feel trapped, they often struggle and thrash to escape, inevitably creating worse injuries.

Boomer was nestled — almost peacefully — in the gate. Slowly he sniffed the grass on the other side, so tantalizingly close to his nose. Then he nonchalantly pushed backward and shook, slipping the gate off like a giant, metallic horse blanket, and began grazing placidly, his mind too dense to entertain panic.

The consequences were minor. Two small scratches for Boomer. Three broken slats and a bent hinge for the gate. A good laugh for Tulsa. And one near–nervous breakdown for me.

The ranch needed some better leadership — in a hurry.

I BEGAN A HIGH-SPEED QUEST for local horsemanship mentors. Kelly, the race trainer at Sam Houston Race Park, referred me to AJ, a Morman cowboy whose motto was "We eat broncs for breakfast." A former race trainer, AJ understood off-track horses well. "He makes them *dog gentle*," asserted Kelly. I took several lessons from AJ, learning the "cowboy cool" way to tie rope halters and cinch Western saddles.

Bobbie recommended Woody, her tobacco-spewing farrier/hay farmer/colt breaker. Woody could gossip for hours, spitting between juicy revelations, all while rapidly shoeing horses. His anecdotes were entertaining, his strong Texas drawl lending color to the simplest story. With Woody on the job, I no longer needed to search the roadside for hay or blacksmith advertisements.

Then I met Lisa, a hunter/jumper show competitor who could ride the worst-behaved horse in the hottest weather and still look immaculate. She shopped the LOPE website regularly, looking for jumping prospects. We soon struck up an email correspondence. Articulate and witty, Lisa was a welcome change from cowboys — and she was a neighbor, her hilly farm only fifteen minutes away. She became my "go to" consultant on more complex horsekeeping questions, her sensible advice always couched in proper grammar (and without any excess saliva).

ROBIN INSISTED ON DELIVERING ZUPER herself. A few weeks after our meeting at Sam Houston, her sturdy truck arrived at our ranch, pulling a horse trailer. Zuper filled it completely, his round rump peeking out from the back doors.

Zuper looked even more handsome than I remembered. Robin had groomed him for his new home, his rich mahogany coat soft and shining, his black mane freshly trimmed. His ankle looked less swollen as he carefully backed out of the trailer.

Tom and I had prepared a small pen, adding deep pine shavings and fresh hay. Tulsa grazed in the adjoining field, his presence hopefully providing reassuring companionship for Zuper.

Robin walked Zuper from the trailer. To keep him relaxed and reduce strain on his injury, she had sedated him before the trip — but from the look in Zuper's eyes, the tranquilizer was wearing off.

He looked around, confused and worried — this wasn't the racetrack. Where was he? What was happening? Tulsa and Boomer came trotting up to the fence, adding to the excitement. "Hey, new guy!" their bright eyes said, "Come over here and run with us." Zuper snorted and pawed at the shavings, popping his head up to neigh at Tulsa.

A warm hug, an averted face with tears already starting, and Robin was gone. Zuper trotted and bucked when he saw the trailer leaving. He stomped around the pen, head held high, his body radiating power and speed in spite of the cramped quarters.

I could see why he had been such a successful racehorse. Even injured and sedated, he looked like a formidable athlete, the kind you never rule out, like a seasoned older quarterback who can suddenly uncork a huge pass in the last seconds of the game.

But as Zuper limped around his pen, I felt sorry for him — he was handsome and intelligent but clearly too limited by his injury for any consistent riding. The type of horse Tory and the polo pros would shun, with his permanently injured ankle.

AS I HAD LEARNED AT THE POLO SCHOOL, the DC polo world was much more enamored of young, sound horses. One day a group of us lingered at the barn after our lesson, watching the boarders turn their horses out into the pasture. As a woman named Barb led her new horse away, a polo student whispered, "Useless!" The bay mare pirouetted, her dainty strides and sculpted head showing her Arabian bloodlines. She was pretty, with a diva personality — Barb hovered around her, delighted to be an entourage of one.

Barb, a polo player in her fifties, had rescued the mare, whisking her from a home ignorant of horse care. The seven-year-old mare had never been trained or ridden — she didn't know how to carry a rider, let alone play polo or jump a course.

As soon as Barb was out of earshot, an instructor let loose. "What was Barb *thinking*? That horse will never do anything. It's too late to train it, plus it looks like it has an old tendon injury. Look at how it moves — awful!"

The other students nodded assent, casting looks of disdain at Barb's mare, eager to agree with the pro. Disapproving murmurs rose.

"That mare definitely isn't going to help Barb's polo game."

"Barb's getting all PETA on us."

"Somebody sell her a real horse. That thing's a disaster."

I nodded knowingly with the other students, not sure why Barb's mare created so much controversy. But I made note — clearly rescue horses were uncool and worthless to this crowd. And the ladies who saved them didn't get much respect either.

ZUPER EPITOMIZED the polo barn's definition of useless. As I examined his swollen leg, I noticed signs of older injuries. Zuper was a living roadmap of a racehorse's athletic life — he had bowed both his front tendons and torn the suspensory ligament on his left front at least twice, and he had a misshapen front hoof. An X-ray later revealed a healed fracture in that ankle, too.

But Zuper carried himself like a Kentucky Derby winner. His walk was arrogant and long strided — he sauntered across the pasture like it was an Olympic arena, on his way to pick up the gold, his limp a minor detail.

Zuper's sire was Zuppardo's Prince, the leading stallion in Louisiana for a record ten years. Zuppardo's Prince's stud career spanned an impressive twenty-one years. He sired 579 foals with lifetime earnings well over

$16 million. Zuper inherited his father's elegant head, blazing speed, and eye for the ladies.

At the start of his race career, Zuper was known for courting mares during track workouts, nickering suggestively as he galloped beside them. Once gelded, he concentrated on racing instead of flirting — earning nearly $180,000. Even as a gelding, Zuper still preferred mares and female riders, his Southern gentleman ways making him a favorite with both.

His appetite for winning was obvious — Zuper loved to run and went proudly to the winner's circle ten times. In a sport dominated by adolescent three-year-olds, Zuper was a rare sight at age nine, a senior citizen in active racehorse circles.

But now, on our ranch, I was worried about Zuper — I didn't want Tulsa bullying him, maybe pushing him away from the feed buckets. Tulsa had already established that he didn't handle power well. He wasn't above taking advantage of Zuper's sore leg.

During their first joint feeding, I tied the buckets far apart on the fence, hoping the distance would discourage Tulsa from stealing Zuper's food. After I scooped the grain, I hovered protectively between the buckets, scowling at Tulsa. As Zuper ate his dinner, Tulsa made a move and darted toward Zuper's bucket. "No! Tulsa, go back!" I said, my eyes fixed on his mischievous eyes.

Tulsa's face changed expression and he backpedaled rapidly, his hooves scuffing up clouds of dirt. Zuper had seen Tulsa coming, too. Out of the corner of my eye, I saw a white nose, a pinned ear, and a dark bulk swinging.

And then I was in the air.

I landed heavily on my left hip, several feet away, marveling at how rapidly the ground met me. Zuper had swung his hindquarters at Tulsa, a sudden move designed to cow Tulsa, to warn him away from Zuper's feed bucket. He accidentally bumped me instead, his minor rebuke to Tulsa launching me skyward.

Brushing myself off, I stood and looked at Zuper. He was walking over to Tulsa's feed, the new sheriff in town, ready to eat out of whatever bucket he felt like. Impressed, Tulsa and I both acknowledged the shift in leadership — Tulsa giving up his bucket, me heading back to the house, letting Zuper protect himself from now on.

I didn't feel sorry for Zuper after that.

A FEW WEEKS LATER, Zuper's rehab hit a snag. Zuper began lurching painfully, barely putting weight on his left foreleg. He had been sore for days, and I couldn't figure out why. His bad leg was healing steadily — though it was still swollen, he rarely limped on it anymore. Now it was his good foreleg that was the problem, which didn't make sense.

I ran my hands up both front legs, eyes closed, trying to feel heat or swelling. Zuper's old injuries made his legs feel strange; the tendons were thick from scar tissue, creating diagnostic difficulties for my unsophisticated technique. There was no heat or swelling — good. And no sign of puncture wounds or blood — good. But Zuper was painfully lame — bad.

The vet who had diagnosed Lilly's neurological condition no longer made ranch calls except in dire emergencies. If we took Zuper to his vet clinic, he would be fully under the care of "Dr. Death," our nickname for the pessimistic DVM. Dr. Death seemed certain that any vet case would end badly — an attitude that far outweighed his skills, as his clinic patients often took turns for the worse.

I thought maybe Zuper had developed a hoof abscess — a blister inside the foot. Because hooves are extremely sensitive (like human fingernails) and bear the full body weight of the horse, an abscess is very painful. Until it drains (a polite term for "the pus oozes out") from the bottom of the sole, the horse is miserably sore, sometimes holding the afflicted hoof off the ground. The sole is tender and hot to the touch until the abscess resolves (another polite term for "oozes pus").

While Zuper showed the classic pain symptoms of an abscess, his hoof sole wasn't warm or sensitive. I could tap all over the bottom of his foot with a hoof pick — not one flinch. Stumped, I decided to consult my Texas Obi-Wans.

AJ counseled apple cider vinegar and a cotton wrap — to pull out whatever inflammation was lurking in Zuper's leg. "Cider vinegar's a drawing agent," he declared. After several applications of AJ's remedy, Zuper and I smelled liked a strange Thanksgiving salad, but Zuper improved only slightly.

I floated my abscess theory to Woody. Flexing Zuper's leg between his muscled hands, Woody shook his head. "This tendon's sore. It's the tendon, not the hoof — see?" He pinched Zuper's lower leg tightly, provoking an annoyed look from the horse. "He don't like that, must be the tendon. It's not tight like it should be."

Doubtful, I looked at Zuper's tendon — the last time it had been tight was probably in 1997, before his race career started. As his injuries multiplied over the years, his tendons had steadily thickened with scar tissue. I couldn't detect any sign of tautness, not even on his pain-free leg.

I turned to Lisa next, and Zuper's strange case sparked a flurry of emails between us. Careful to phrase my questions nonchalantly (hoping I didn't sound as desperate as I felt), I waited eagerly for her email replies, feeling like a veterinary stalker. With Spock-like logic, she advised a "wait-and-see" approach: Zuper would get worse or improve, either way providing more information.

Zuper himself finally solved the mystery: one morning, he was walking normally, a cluster of flies buzzing around the top of his hoof, now wet at the hairline. Defying gravity, a deep, large abscess had managed to drain up there, instead of down through the sole. I was never so happy to see pus and flies.

Zuper's abscess was a sobering reminder of how little I knew about horse care. My ranch management skills were even weaker. Maybe the ranch was a mistake, a well-intentioned (and heavily mortgaged) house of cards, ready to fall at any moment. In a flush of optimism, I had quit Bobbie's lesson barn, certain that more donors would follow our anonymous Texan contributor. As the reality of our sputtering cash flow set in, I eyed employment classifieds again, looking for part-time bookkeeping work.

Then support appeared from unexpected sources. After months of my leaving LOPE flyers on Mike's desk, Callahan's decided to sponsor the adoption ranch. "I told you to keep asking," Mike smiled, enigmatic as ever. Half-price gates and fencing materials flowed our way, along with much-needed advice on repair techniques.

One day, I went to a local farm to take photos of a racehorse. Jorge, the Thoroughbred's owner, was a dignified Latino man in his sixties. Full of rugged vigor, he still broke his own colts and did all of the ranch work. After the photo session, Jorge thrust some homegrown gifts at me — a jar of fresh honey and a fifty-pound bag of pecans. "For helping the horses, please — take this from me," he said.

Race trainers, especially Keith and Robin, spread the word about our start-up adoption farm. Used halters, horse blankets, liniments, oats, and cedar shavings regularly followed me home from the track, usually thrust into my hands with a gruff, "Here, I don't need this. You can have it."

One trainer, a Runyonesque character complete with cigar and battered fedora, pulled me aside. "Heard you're that lady, you help the horses. I want to do something for you." Drawing closer, he unfolded a Daily Racing Form. "Bet on the number 5 horse in the third ráce. He's a long shot, but it's a done deal. Know what I mean? Bet big on him, you'll be able to buy hay for a year."

I passed on that one.

ALTHOUGH OUR RANCH SEEMED PEACEFUL, it teemed with vivid creatures, especially at night. Assorted wildlife and semi-domesticated animals streamed across the fields. After dark, possums, raccoons, giant palmetto bugs, and the occasional armadillo laid siege to our porch. The nightly coyote concert was accompanied by owl calls and the cries of their prey. Nocturnal toads screeched with howler monkey cadence, loudly reminiscent of Stephen King scenarios. Sophie, our dog, was obsessed with the amphibian population, trying to swallow whole any toad or frog she encountered, a sight that only reinforced the horror novel ambiance.

During one evening feeding, I spotted Zuper staring fixedly at the adjacent field. Following his gaze, I glimpsed a ghostly group of white cattle, a good thirty head, their massive bodies moving with eerie quietness. A neighbor's prize livestock, they had wandered across the deep gully separating our properties. Zuper kept guard diligently, returning to his feed bucket only after the herd meandered off our pasture, heading back to their home.

Stray dogs sometimes crossed the ranch, usually too frightened to pause. When an especially motley pack appeared, randomly darting around the trees, looking for trouble (and maybe Mama cat), Zuper stepped in. He charged at full gallop, head down, teeth bared — chasing the canine gang out of his pasture and off the ranch.

Sophie slept through that incident, though she did rouse herself later to bark at the porch possums.

ALTHOUGH THE DONATIONS from Callahan's and the race trainers were helpful, I still needed to raise more funds for ongoing horse costs. Free publicity soon appeared from regional horse publications who were interested in covering our adoption ranch. Zuper turned out to be a talented equine supermodel, posing shamelessly whenever a camera crew appeared. Casual visits from local reporters became feature stories in the *Dallas Morning News* and the *New York Times*, thanks to Zuper's heavy-lidded profile and uncanny ability to charm photographers.

Soon after Zuper's arrival, Alex, a world-weary newspaper photographer, followed me through the fields, clearly expecting a dull shoot. Zuper walked up to him, stopping a convenient ten feet away for lens focusing. As Alex lifted his camera, Zuper raised his head and stared nobly into the distance, looking every inch the regal champion. Then he stretched his neck, ears pricked forward, and directed his large, soulful eyes directly at Alex. He held that pose perfectly, for several minutes, while the delighted photographer snapped shot after shot. Alex was no longer bored or cyni-cal. "He's a good-looking devil," he gushed. "Will he let me pet him?"

Not surprisingly, Zuper attracted a formidable fan base. Tom dubbed him the "Sean Connery" of horses, commenting, "He looks like he should be smoking a pipe, with a Bond girl nearby." After his photo was posted on our website, over a dozen people emailed, eager to adopt him. One by one, Zuper's previous racing owners and trainers contacted me, asking about him and telling me stories about his best races.

Richard, his first race owner, offered to retire him. "He can come here anytime and live in our back pasture. Won't ever wear a saddle again, I guarantee it. He was always special, just a great old class horse." Robin called regularly to check on him, and she slipped me $20 bills ("for Zuper's carrots") whenever our paths crossed at the track.

Even a racetrack gambler emailed, asking me to thank Zuper for all the times he won. Calling Zuper his "Old Money Making Buddy," Dick wrote: "It was absolutely wonderful to see my second-favorite horse's pic-ture in the *Dallas Morning News* today. That boy won me alot of exacta, trifecta, and superfecta money here at Lone Star Park. I am glad that he is being well taken care of in his 'Retirement Years.'"

Clearly, this "useless" horse had a tremendous impact on many peo-ple, some of them quite hardened. And I already relied on him for many key duties. Seeing Zuper in our pastures gave me confidence — at least someone here was competent on the job. He was too valuable to be adopted out.

Instead, I promoted Zuper to assistant ranch manager — a wise move, as a trailer full of racehorses was on the way, and I needed all the help I could get.

PART II

The Stallions

Throw your heart over a fence and your horse will follow.

UNKNOWN

CHAPTER FOUR

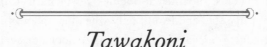

Tawakoni

A TRAILER LOAD OF FOUR HORSES, including Tawakoni the stallion, arrived at the ranch shortly after Zuper's promotion in April 2004. As I talked to the driver, our new neighbor, Jesse, walked over. Randy had departed recently, taking his family and rifle with him.

Jesse sidled up to my husband, Tom. "That stud horse, be careful. Don't let your wife near him when she's at her time of the month. He'll kill her." Tom stared at him, appalled. Jesse adjusted the duct tape on his boots and adopted a wise air. He sauntered away, trailing a wake of flapping tape and eau de Pabst.

Shielded from this exchange, I watched Tawakoni take charge of the pen. He strutted, looking every bit the stallion. A powerfully muscled, black bay with a massive neck, he was thoroughly masculine. Tawakoni was excited — he gave a couple of horse shout-outs, which sound like snorting sneezes with a bit of whoop mixed in.

Naturally, I didn't have much experience with stud horses. My mind flipped through the catalog of unpleasant descriptions I had heard about stallions: They maim other horses, attack people, and must be handled like serial killers with chain restraints. Their caretakers should never show fear or they'd face dire hoof-slashing, teeth-ripping consequences. And of course stallions are extremely erratic — a calm one can turn vicious for no apparent reason. Only highly skilled, professional horse trainers, preferably men, could work safely with stallions.

A stallion had been boarded at Bobbie's lesson barn — he had a sad existence, kept in a stall and let out only when his stall was cleaned. He would run around the arena, frantic and frenzied, looking pent up and dangerous.

Tawakoni definitely commanded respect. He didn't seem like a gelding — there was something more intimidating in his eyes and bearing. I could tell Tawakoni wouldn't tolerate bullying or manhandling. The new place and long trailer ride had brought out his "You talking to *me?*" look.

Fascinated, I hung my arms over the fence and watched as Tawakoni restlessly walked the pen perimeter. He didn't acknowledge my presence but finally chose to stand next to me. Cautiously, I extended my palm toward his neck. Tawakoni ignored me, then suddenly swiveled his big head toward my hand. I froze, looking for Jeffrey Dahmer in his expression. I felt a soft exhale of warmth as he breathed on my fingers and then briefly touched his nose to my wrist. His head swiveled away again, as one of his buddies neighed across the pasture, and he nickered in return, a deep, rumbling sound. So much for the killer stallion myth.

Pete, the trailer driver, was a chatty, affable fellow. Bib overalls, red shirt, red face, red bandana. He was impressed by Tawakoni and his three gelding buddies and kept talking excitedly. "That old boy, he's built like a roping horse, for sure. Bet he'd fly out of the box. The big one, reckon he'll be a jumper." The other horses with Tawakoni were Texas Monarch, a tremendously stocky horse; Victory Dawn, a tall, elegant six-year-old; and Wise Indulgence, the darkest bay of the four.

Pete kept up a running commentary for the next hour — on everything from our pecan trees ("You gonna harvest the pecans? Lemme tell you the best way. First, you get a shaker machine . . .") to his favorite horse ("Yep, old Blaze, he was a quiet one.") — as we tried to usher him back to his truck.

Jesse loomed over the driveway horizon a couple hours later, watching as I fed hay to Tawakoni. "You need to talk to your husband," he muttered, shaking his head and spitting for emphasis, a damp form of punctuation. Jesse was a horse trainer, usually working with young horses. A few weeks after he moved in, I watched from our porch as Jesse worked with a spooky Appaloosa.

As I squinted across the ten acres of pasture separating us, I could see Jesse doing various things to the horse. He chased the Appaloosa around the corral, saddled him, and slapped the stirrups around, then inexplicably tied the horse's head to his tail and left the corral. The horse waited patiently. Jesse finally reappeared, beer in hand, and untied his tail from the bridle. The horse stood, plotting, until Jesse put the beer down and put his foot in the big Western stirrup. The Appaloosa promptly bucked Jesse off before he had a chance to mount.

The horse had worked out a good strategy — Jesse couldn't progress past putting his taped boot in the stirrup without being flung off like a flea. Back to the Pabst. Jesse climbed up on the fence and stared at the horse.

I was fascinated by the cowboy mime show — what would Jesse do next? Tie the horse's tail to something else? Finish the beer? Duct tape the horse's hooves?

Jesse disappeared behind the barn, and emerged with what looked like an empty burlap bag. He puttered around, stuffing random items like cans and paper trash into the bag. The sack was now bulging — the horse took one look and leaped away. Jesse was quicker and grabbed the horse's lead rope. After much pawing and spooking, the horse stood still long enough for Jesse to strap the feed bag to his saddle. Then Jesse left. The horse hopped around a little but decided to claim the field sans Jesse as a victory — he began grazing, ignoring the burlap and leather confection on his back. The next day, the horse was in the same pasture, still wearing the saddle and burlap bag, now bored by both.

I never saw Jesse ride him.

Jesse wasn't cruel at heart, just a throwback to a rougher frontier era often glamorized on television. Jesse probably was younger than me but looked like he could be my father (or a pretty tired uncle). His face was battered from more than sun and wind damage. Hard drinking, possibly drugs, maybe prison, all showed in his wary eyes, his deeply lined cheekbones, and the hard set of his jaw.

But Jesse was intelligent, and I could see he was kind, even if he hid that in self-defense. His son liked to cavort around the property in a cape, playing *Lord of the Rings* — it was a real sign of evolution at work that Jesse tolerated this without comment. And Jesse liked our adoption ranch, offering a bargain rental rate for stalls and the occasional use of his ancient tractor.

WITH JESSE BACK AT HIS HOUSE and Tawakoni quietly munching hay, I headed back to the house. A big dinner, a rented DVD, and by midnight Tom and I were in a deep, unworried sleep set to the soundtrack of a soft rain.

Till the screaming began around 2 A.M.

I staggered out of bed — what was *that*? A wild, high-pitched shrieking was coming from Tawakoni's pasture, carrying across the quarter-mile driveway like it was outside our window.

He must be hurt, I thought. Something horrible must have happened. Tom thrashed blindly across the bedroom, trying to simultaneously pull on his jeans and find the flashlight. I fumbled for our emergency vet supplies (first-aid cream, cotton gauze, felt leg wraps) and the car keys.

The rain was still falling, only now there was a sharp, howling wind; the tree branches swayed erratically, making snapping sounds. Our driveway lights were out — it was pitch dark, with a screaming horse, loud wind, and rain competing for my ears. We headed for the car, but then I spotted the fallen fence posts. Tulsa, Zuper, and Boomer must have pushed aside a section of weak fencing, then trotted up the alley separating their pasture and Tawakoni's pen. Texas Monarch's pen also bordered that path.

Newly arrived horses, fresh from the track, need time apart from the rest of the herd here. Often edgy, a horse in an unfamiliar pasture might kick out at abruptly introduced pasture mates. And all the horses from Tawakoni's trailer still wore racing horseshoes with sharp cleats — one kick could mean serious lacerations and muscle damage.

Slipping, I ran unsteadily across the wet, muddy field. The wind threw debris in my eyes, and I ducked around trees and fire ant hills. Sure enough, there were Tulsa, Boomer, and Zuper, all taunting Texas Monarch and Tawakoni. The shrieks from Tawakoni were tremendously loud at close range. One fence stood between him and Tulsa's marauding gang; it seemed woefully inadequate to the task. Tawakoni was enraged, offended, and ready to attack. He bucked, he reared, he kicked out at the fence. And he screamed — over and over again — a pterodactyl sound of prehistoric fury.

Tulsa, ever the wiseguy, immediately ran when he saw me — this was the best prank ever, breaking the fence, teasing the new horses, and making me chase him. The normally ponderous Boomer was emboldened by the wind, and he ran, too (though very slowly). Only Zuper had mercy on me, pausing to let me halter him.

Thunder rumbled ominously. I was soaked, with slippery hands clutching Zuper's lead rope. Tulsa and Boomer raced in the dark, coming closer to me with each pass. Zuper danced in place but held steady. Somehow I had to round up Tulsa and Boomer, then get all three horses in a secure pasture — all before the storm hit, with lightning, hail, and big, Texas-style rain.

Tom's flashlight bobbed on the other side of the driveway, giving me a bearing. I headed for the light, with Zuper in tow, hoping Tulsa and Boomer would follow him. Zuper nickered impatiently, and soon the other two were walking behind us, looking chastened. Tulsa had a moment of rebellion at the gate, but Zuper's well-timed nip foiled his escape attempt.

Shaken, I wondered how I was going to find a home for Tawakoni. The challenge now seemed daunting, either to find someone who wanted a stud horse or to geld him (and risk disappointing his previous owners).

All those killer stallion myths didn't seem silly now. Right out of the gate, I had a huge adoption challenge on my hands. What was I thinking, agreeing to take a stallion?

LAST WEEK, IT HAD ALL SEEMED SO REASONABLE. First, I got a voice mail message: "Lynn, I have two nice horses to donate to your program. Please call me, it's Judy Cascio."

That name sounded familiar. I quickly looked her up — she and her husband, Bubba, ran Cascio Racing Stables. Bubba was a legend in Texas horse racing. He had trained Dash For Cash, the most famous Quarter Horse racehorse in history. Winner of over $500,000, Dash For Cash showed even more talent as a stallion, siring over eight hundred winners with earnings topping $39 million.

Most Quarter Horse race trainers don't cross over to Thoroughbred racing — the breed and the length of their races require much different training techniques. But Bubba switched to Thoroughbred racing easily. Within a few years, he was one of the most successful trainers on the Southwest circuit. Judy was the ranch manager, supervising the training of the young horses as well as the family breeding business. By 2004, their farm stood several of the best race stallions in Texas.

I called Judy back on a rainy afternoon, crouched on the floor near our front door, which was the only spot inside the ranch house with decent cell phone coverage. Through the sound of rain on our metal roof and the moody cell service, I strained to hear Judy's quiet voice.

"Lynn, *shshsh* is a nice gelding, you'll love him. Nothing wrong with him except *shshsh*. And Tawakoni is a real gentle *shshsh*. Bubba said *shshsh* the other day. *shshshshshsh* dark bay and tall. *shshsh* they need to move fast. Can they come to your place by *shshsh* weekend?"

"Yes, that sounds good," I blared, hoping Judy could hear me over the storm and static.

Then the rain eased off, and I heard Judy clearly: "Great, so we'll send the four horses then. And don't worry about Tawakoni — he knows these geldings, so he'll get along with them. He's not like most stallions. I hope you can place him as a stud — we'd like to send a mare or two to him someday. Bubba thought about standing him here, but we've got so many other stallions, all with such good bloodlines."

Uh oh, I thought. Four horses? Stallion?

I couldn't say no now — Bubba and Judy were important people. If anyone knew an excellent stallion prospect, it was Bubba Cascio. According to Bubba, Dash For Cash was originally scheduled for gelding, his gangly physique not showing much studlike promise. Most male racehorses are gelded, unless their pedigree and conformation are outstanding. Stallions can be more challenging to train, often prone to either flirting or fighting during workouts. But right before the vet appointment, the young colt gashed his shoulder, a minor injury requiring stitches.

In a 2002 *American Quarter Horse Racing Journal* article, Bubba talked about the incident: "We got ready to cut [geld] the other colts and Dash's shoulder still wasn't quite healed up — still had stitches — so we didn't want to throw him down [to geld him]." Instead, Bubba decided to start training Dash under saddle. "The first time I tacked him up, Dash still had those ol' dried-up stitches. I just cut them out and we went on with him, still planning on cutting him when we had time." Not long afterward, Dash and his rider went out for an initial gallop. When they returned, the jockey's face "looked like it had been sandblasted and he couldn't get his breath," said Bubba. "I knew right then we had a runner." Bubba called Dash's owner immediately, advising, "I don't think you want to cut this one."

It was a huge honor that the Cascios would donate horses to our start-up adoption ranch, especially a stud. Listening to Judy's description of Tawakoni's temperament, I was reassured. She and Bubba had trained Tawakoni attentively, giving him a good foundation in manners. How much trouble could one of their stallions be?

A lot, actually, if I couldn't find anyone to adopt him. I was still new at adoptions. As opposed to a regular horse sale, an adoption from our

ranch requires references, an approval application, and a limited bill of sale
— just like adopting a dog from the pound. Developing adoption policies
and procedures was then still a work in progress, requiring several consultations with Allie, the racehorse placement lady back in the DC area.

Peanut, the filly with a slab fracture in her knee, was our first adoption.
She was injured in her last race, a hairline crack etching across her knee,
the pressure twisting the joint. Peanut had a ton of heart and refused to
yield to the pain — instead she drove for the finish line, finishing in second place in spite of the fracture.

Small and feminine, with a soft red coat, Peanut didn't look like a horse
with a broken knee. She moved normally at the walk, with just a faint hitch
in her stride at the trot. Slab fractures are usually slender fissures, hori-
zontal rather than vertical, that heal well with pasture rest. But if the knee
isn't rested, if the horse is still ridden, a much worse injury is likely to
occur, like multiple bone chips or a severe fracture requiring euthanasia.

Peanut, an uncomplicated filly, enjoyed grazing and slow saunters
around her paddock. Not sure what to expect, I listed Peanut for adoption
on our website. To my amazement, she had a new home within weeks.
Lydia and Tony had excellent references and a tree-lined farmette near
Austin. They were happy to nurse Peanut's sore knee, letting her rest for
several months in their pasture. Carefully following our instructions, they
didn't ride her until her injury was completely healed — and Peanut paid
them back by becoming a gentle trail horse, the family's favorite mount.

TAWAKONI REQUIRED a much more specialized home. I decided to consult Ruby, a local racehorse breeder and trainer.

I had met Ruby a few months earlier, when she called to list a horse on
our website. After a couple of shouted cell phone conversations, I went to
her farm to take photos of the horse for the website, curious to see a Thoroughbred breeding operation.

As I drove through the farm gate, not sure if I was in the right place,
I saw horses on walkers and several barns. Large bird pens bordered the

driveway. A tomboyish figure strode around the corner, in boots, jeans, and cap, two long gray pigtails bouncing on her back, shouting at someone over her shoulder. I recognized the voice (and decibel level) from our phone calls.

Ruby bellowed hello and ushered me through the guinea hens, peacocks, and kittens littering the driveway. "Joe's an ugly horse," she proclaimed. "But he's a nice fellow. Head like a hammer, though. Ugly!"

As I fumbled with my camera, trying to keep up without stepping on the poultry and felines scattering in Ruby's wake, she stopped and grabbed my elbow. "How OLD are you, anyway?" she asked abruptly. Startled, I dropped my camera case on one of the slower birds. "What?"

"How old are you?" she asked impatiently. I told her, and she beamed. "I knew it! I have a daughter just about your age, Helen. You should come ride with her next week here. She's a WONDERFUL rider, you know. You could take lessons with her and her trainer." Ruby waited for my answer, foot tapping.

Fortunately, we had arrived at Joe's paddock, and I could defer my answer for the moment. "There he is — poor Joe. He is homely, you know." Joe did indeed have a rather large head, but he also had gentle eyes and an athletic look to him.

"He's BROWN," barked Ruby. "Not even a bay. Just plain old BROWN. Ugly horse."

I felt like I should defend Joe. He was sweet and mellow, standing peacefully for his photos, nuzzling Ruby as she insulted him repeatedly. While I took pictures, Ruby kept up a steady conversation. As she told me about her horses, her new stallion, and her farm, I could see how proud she was of all of them. What I couldn't do was get a word in edgewise — Ruby was a river of information, with a powerful current and lots of rushing noise.

"So, you will be here next Monday. To ride with Helen. Some other girls will be there, too. Bring your saddle." These were declarations, not questions.

I threw a soft fly line into the river. "Thank you, but I don't have a trailer or horse to bring."

Ruby snorted. "You'll ride one of our horses here, of course. Ten o'clock." She peered up into my eyes. Her face was kind, if her tone was commanding. And she really wanted me to come on Monday. I smiled, recognizing the warmth under the bullying words. Joe turned and pricked his ears for the camera, smiling back at me.

Ruby became a supportive, if overbearing, friend, offering ranch advice, hosting riding lesson "playdates," and explaining Thoroughbred bloodlines. I called her about Tawakoni, but her response was skeptical. "What's his race record? I don't care about his breeding, just tell me what he did on the track! Hmmph. I'll check it out and get back to you. But you probably should geld him — just make a riding horse out of him, too many mediocre studs out there."

A few days later, Ruby left me a curt voice message. "Lynn, this is Ruby. Cut them off."

Ouch. I later found out that Ruby was predisposed toward gelding in general. Ruby's big personality was legendary in Texas racing — there were many stories about her rather direct approach to problem solving. One friend told how Ruby used to have an intact male dog on her property. In Texas, many ranch owners don't neuter their male dogs, especially their herding and hunting dogs — either to use them for breeding or to keep their protective instincts as sharp as possible.

Ruby's dog kept getting into trouble — he'd run off her ranch, aggravate the neighbor's livestock, and chew up fencing. One day, her neighbor called; the dog was on his place again. Ruby retrieved the dog and marched him back into her house, heading straight to the kitchen. Picking up a sharp knife, she hoisted the dog on the table and deftly neutered him on the spot, her fifty years of ranching experience making this just another livestock chore. Problem solved.

I decided to seek other opinions on Tawakoni. Another Thoroughbred breeder, Pam, had recently crossed my path. Pam was a diminutive Southern belle, a race trainer as well as breeder. Her original lilting Georgia accent now blended extravagantly with a Texas drawl, and her rushing soprano banter took on epic dimensions.

Pam had heard about our racehorse listing service at Retama track. She still owned several of her retired racehorses and hoped to find them homes. My first visit to her ranch prompted much excitement, drawing a crowd of dogs and lots of noise.

"*Lynn!* How are you? Come see my newest filly, she's just gorgeous! Henry, you get down now, you're acting like a heathen of a sheepdog. These dogs — Bob! Come get the dogs... BOB!"

Pam's cell phone bleated. "Billy? *No!* She needs that other medication." Dogs barking. "Hush! No, not you, Billy. It's Henry, he's crazed, won't stop barking. *BOB!* Get the dogs!"

Brief silence, then Pam turned to me. "Anyway, how *are* you, Lynn? Did Ruby call you, I told her to, I said, Ruby! You must call Lynn about ... BOB! Damn it, get Henry and the other dogs!"

Bob, Pam's husband, wisely chose not to hear the commotion, driving off in his tractor to the other side of the farm. Pam ushered me to a stall housing a dapper chestnut gelding. "Rally should be a show horse. Isn't he *gorgeous?* I told Bob, I said *Bob*, Rally would clean up at the A circuit." Pam would know, too — she had decades of horse-show experience and was once a top competitor in the show ring, boldly riding over jumps nearly as high as herself.

Remembering my day at Pam's farm, I had a hopeful thought. Maybe Tawakoni could sire jumpers instead of racehorses? Excited, I called Pam to ask her opinion. Her response was muted. "Well, I don't know. Maybe. Is he tall?" Her lack of enthusiasm seemed to put her on Ruby's side of the question — only much more politely.

My neighbor Jesse was too scared of Tawakoni to comment rationally on the topic. Plus I didn't want to hear any more about his theories correlating stallion attacks with my hormonal cycle.

At least Pete, the chatty transport driver who'd dropped him off, was pro-Tawakoni: "You oughta find some big ol' cow outfit around here and get that son-of-a-gum breeding ranch horses!" While I appreciated his optimism, I wasn't sure how to find cattle ranches in the market for a "son-of-a-gum" to sire baby cowhorses. Neither was Pete.

AS I SOUGHT ADVICE, I also researched Tawakoni's bloodlines and discovered his father was Grindstone, winner of the 1996 Kentucky Derby. Tawakoni was descended from Thoroughbred royalty, from great racehorses like Swaps, Mr. Prospector, and Native Dancer. But Tawakoni's racing career was undistinguished — as a three-year-old, he had developed chips in both knees, requiring surgery to remove them. Knee chips are a common injury in racehorses. A small fracture, usually due to impact stress from pounding speeds of 40 mph, will produce a bone flake or chip. If left alone, the chip can wedge in the joint groove, causing pain and arthritis.

Tawakoni's sire, Grindstone, also had knee problems. As a two-year-old, after only two races, he came up sore during training. Radiographs revealed a chip in his left knee; surgery was immediately scheduled to remove it. Just nine months later, Grindstone ran in the Kentucky Derby. He wasn't expected to win. The official video of the Derby shows him in fifteenth place on the backstretch, hardly a good striking position. As the front runners turned down the homestretch, all eyes were on a horse named Cavonnier, ridden by Chris McCarron.

Cavonnier was darting up a hole on the inside rail and was going to take the race from Unbridled Song, the odds favorite and the steady leader in the race till then. The commentators were breathless, shouting, "Here comes Cavonnier up the inside." The crowd was cheering, and everyone knew it was going to be an exciting finish. They had no idea.

As Cavonnier surged ahead, just a few lengths from victory, a startled announcer yelled, "It's *Grindstone* coming up the outside. He's closing *stoutly*!" A dark blur sprinted past the fading Unbridled Song and drew even with Cavonnier's tail, then hindquarters, then head.

Grindstone won by a nose — in a photo finish.

But within days, Grindstone was retired. Another chip fracture had erupted in his knee. He was put out to stud, siring many successful race-horses, including Birdstone, the 36-1 long-shot winner of the 2004 Bel-mont Stakes. And Tawakoni.

After watching Grindstone's gutsy win on video, I had qualms about following Ruby's advice. In addition to his stellar pedigree, Tawakoni had excellent conformation with a well-proportioned physique and athletic movement. His night of screaming aside, Tawakoni had settled into the ranch routine nicely — he had a good temperament under all the testos-terone.

One morning, he nickered affectionately at me as I brought his break-fast, his eyes soft. I started talking to him with every feeding, asking him how his day was going, complimenting his manners, and explaining the fascinating blend of carbs and protein in his grain. Tawakoni seemed to enjoy the timbre of my high-pitched voice, pricking his ears as soon as I began speaking. He'd bob his head and stretch his neck out for petting whenever I praised him.

Finally, I decided it was time for Tawakoni to leave his pen, to enjoy the larger pasture with his friend Texas Monarch. Nervously, I haltered him and began leading him through the pen gate. Tawakoni respectfully kept his distance, never crowding me or pulling on the lead rope, his head tilted toward me, listening for my voice.

In spite of his Schwarzenegger physique and inherent machismo, Tawakoni was full of gracious chivalry — I sensed no threat from him. Irrational as it would seem to Jesse, Tawakoni knew that I was female and therefore to be treated with courtesy.

However, Texas Monarch was a gelding, a male buddy, and therefore subject to different standards. Tawakoni liked to "play" with Texas Monarch, grabbing him by the neck with his mouth and dragging him a few steps here and there. Tex put up with the roughhousing without com-plaint, careful not to annoy Tawakoni by protesting too much. Big and round, Tex was also quite the macho type — he and Tawakoni made a good team, the classic hero and sidekick.

They were both such "guys" with their poor table manners and sloppy habits. Tex liked to splash in the trough — especially after he had just stepped in manure, fouling the water with his excrement-encrusted hooves. Tawakoni rolled in the dirt regularly and enjoyed throwing his hay all over the pasture. Feeding time was a frenzy of bucket flipping and grain spilling, as they gobbled down their food before their next game of "How far can Tex be dragged by the neck?"

Tawakoni and Tex usually had hay or twigs in their manes, no matter how often I groomed them. They both disliked mane-comb-out sessions, making faces and fidgeting like teenage boys enduring a haircut from Mom. If I was overzealous, maybe putting conditioner or detangler in their manes, Tawakoni and Tex would head for the muddiest corner of the pasture and roll, determined to remove all evidence of my salon work.

THEIR MASCULINE PERSONALITIES reminded me of a horse at Bobbie's lesson barn — and his worst Halloween ever. At Bobbie's barn, Halloween was a big occasion. My students lobbied relentlessly for a special holiday class, an evening Halloween costume show instead of the usual group lesson. Expecting an entertaining class, with kids dressed in costumes and maybe some braided manes on the horses, I arrived early to decorate the arena.

I draped Wal-Mart cobwebs on the fence, hung an inflatable spider in the corner, and made small bags full of candy and plastic Halloween jewelry for the students. Dressed in my usual worn black turtleneck, I donned a black skirt and a plastic witch hat. Pleased with my budget creativity, I waited for the students.

The students came early, giggling, half-costumed, and dragging bags of mysterious "things" for the horses to wear. The girls refused to tell me what the costumes would be — they wanted to surprise me.

Courtney, a good student with thick red braids, had a flair for the dramatic. She wore a Las Vegas showgirl costume, complete with shimmering, grasslike skirt, big jewelry, and bright turban with cascades of plastic fruit. Her mother had carefully applied her glamorous makeup, deep blue eye shadow, pink blusher, and glossy red lipstick.

Courtney's assigned horse was Trooper, a bulky gelding with a placid nature. Long ago, Trooper had been Bobbie's stallion, fathering several of the younger school horses. Though gelded years ago, he still retained the muscular neck and dignity of his stallion days. Trooper was tall but gentle, with a lazy streak — an ideal lesson mount.

Like Tawakoni and Tex, Trooper also was a real "guy"— with the personality of a long-retired college football player, now out of shape but still fond of flexing in front of the mirror. He was the alpha leader among Bobbie's horses and often bossed them around in lessons, never allowing them to crowd his space during group trotting sessions.

As I watched Courtney braid his thick tail, I tried to guess what decorations she had in mind for him. Maybe hanging fruit on his saddle? Or she could make him into a bouncer — though that was a subtle costume concept for a girl in fourth grade. Or would he be something else Vegas related, like a slot machine?

Courtney pulled out an extra big, brightly colored cloth. It looked like a garish tent with an immense elastic band stitched into it. She and her mother descended on Trooper, with other students pitching in. Peals of laughter floated over Trooper's back; with his height, he towered over the girls, hiding their machinations from me.

"Miss Lynn, *look* at Trooper," Courtney said proudly. Trooper threw me a look of despair — Courtney had turned him into an equine showgirl. He had a turban on his head, secured with pink ribbons. Plastic fruit balanced uneasily on the turban and also were tied in his mane. His reins were festooned with bows. Glitter decorated his muscular neck and shoulders.

The pièce de résistance was the blue-and-yellow "tent": Courtney had fashioned a giant skirt that fit ingeniously into the Western saddle, the fabric falling gracefully over Trooper's massive rump. Big as it was, the skirt still could cover only about half of Trooper's thick hindquarters and long legs. He looked like a big, hairy Copacabana dancer — in a miniskirt.

Trooper was horrified. He kept trying to make himself small, to scuttle into the shadowed corners of the arena, before the other horses saw him. Whenever Courtney turned away, he'd furtively tug at his skirt, trying to pull off the embarrassing costume.

Trooper scowled fiercely at the other horses, but for once they had the advantage and could trot near him with impunity — because he was dressed like a showgirl. And there are very few guys, equine or human, who can pull that off without losing macho leader-of-the-pack status.

Maybe Tawakoni could. But I wasn't about to try putting a skirt on him to find out.

JUST WHEN I WAS READY TO GIVE UP and follow Ruby's advice, Julia called me. A local horsewoman with a show-horse breeding farm, she had recently lost her senior citizen stallion. Julia had grown up in Houston, competing in barrel racing, dressage, and equitation before settling into hunter/jumper events.

A neighbor of Pam's, she had a gorgeous ranch in the Texas Hill Country. Her elderly stallion, Wilbur, had died at age thirty-two — in midseduction of his favorite mare. Julia gave him a hero's burial, in honor of his devotion to his work.

"I'm not sure I'm ready to replace Wilbur." Julia's voice was sad. "He was such an exceptional stallion, so gentle with the mares. I only pasture breed, and few studs handle that well."

I was impressed. Most stud farms operate under the premise that the stallion will hurt the mares if left alone with them. Instead, a handler holds the stallion (usually with a chain lead inserted in the stallion's mouth). A mare, also restrained, is then brought to the stallion. Some farms put the mares in "stocks," small pipe cages that prevent mares from kicking the stallion during breeding.

Pasture breeding is much simpler and potentially more dangerous.

Mares are turned out in a field with the stallion and breeding takes place without human interference. Julia let her mares stay with Wilbur until the final stages of their pregnancies. She was certain that the mares felt more secure in his presence, thus keeping their hormone levels at ideal, non-stressed levels until the foals were born.

I immediately formed a mental picture of Julia — she must be statuesque, formidable, and athletic, like Ruby or Tory, to own a breeding ranch. Plus, she had been a barrel racer in her youth — that sport attracted brash girls with big personalities and a fondness for glitter. She probably wore brightly colored cowboy boots and gaudy T-shirts with slogans like "Don't Mess With Texas."

A few days later, Julia came to meet Tawakoni in person. Of course, she was petite, soft-spoken, and rhinestone free, attired in classic horse-woman garb: well-cut trousers, pastel shirt with hay clinging to the sleeves, and sensible, nonbright boots. Her elegant bearing spoke of the show ring rather than the rodeo arena.

As we chatted, Tawakoni came up to the fence — Julia had a feminine voice, much more musical than mine. He responded to her immediately, holding his head out for pats and treats, confident that she had horse cookies somewhere in her pockets. Julia was thrilled with his personality and good looks. She haltered him and led him as if he were a pony, trusting his good judgment and obvious intelligence. Tawakoni walked calmly behind her, looking over at her trailer expectantly.

Contrary to all the stud experts' advice, Julia turned out to be the most effective stallion handler ever, joyfully adopting Tawakoni within fifteen minutes of meeting him. Tawakoni soon took up residence at her farm, siring beautiful jumper foals and managing a harem of doting mares.

The first time I saw Tawakoni there, holding court in a gorgeous pasture with two mares, his appearance stunned me. He was massively muscled, his neck thick with sinewy definition. The hormonal requirements of stud life had transformed him — his testosterone-fueled physique was now the ultimate in equine machismo.

Tawakoni galloped toward us, snorting. His thundering strides were intimidating, powerful — and showed no signs of slowing. "Here he comes," said Julia. "Be careful not to get between him and his mares." She stepped aside, smiling. I bunny-hopped to the fence, a much less cheerful expression on my face.

"Tawak, how *are* you? Look who's here to visit you, just because you are so special. And handsome, too." Julia's voice took on tones usually reserved for lap dogs.

Tawakoni stopped and walked over to Julia. Her head barely reached his shoulder, yet Tawakoni melted into a docile calm at her voice. His head swiveled toward me, just as at our first meeting long ago. Tawakoni's cheeks and jaws seemed twice as large now, his face sculpted with masculine confidence.

"Hello, Tawakoni," I said.

Tawakoni extended his head. I reached out and patted him, marveling at how small my hand looked on his nose. He exhaled, breathing on me, his eyes warm with recognition.

"Tawakoni remembers you!" exclaimed Julia. "I can tell by his face. He has this certain wide-eyed look for people he knows and likes. Now, he has this slit-eyed expression for people he doesn't like..."

As she talked on, Tawakoni's face softened further. He stood beside her, halterless and tame, a living contradiction of killer stallion stories. Within a few months, his first foals had hit the ground, all tall, handsome, and kind — just like their father.

Julia is now the only expert I consult about stallion behavior.

CHAPTER FIVE

Captain Boo

B Y AUGUST 2004, the word was out at the racetracks about our adoption ranch — twenty horses had arrived in five months, more than double what I had expected for the whole year. The horses came in all shapes and sizes, from dainty fillies to husky middle-aged geldings. Their Jockey Club registered names were exotic and entertaining (often with deliberate misspellings) — like Big Boy Slew, Shaman Chocolate, Ease to the Edge, Fille Du Lac, and Avenging Tree.

Doing a pasture roll call each feeding, greeting the horses by name as they trotted to their buckets, always boosted my mood. Compared to my accounting days, my world was now poetic, full of musical words and metaphoric names. And lots of horse manure.

Fortunately, most of the horses were easy to handle (no more stallions), with uncomplicated athletic injuries — the equivalent of pulled ligaments — needing only pasture rest. Zuper's den mother presence settled the new horses quickly, making the herd relaxed and peaceful and less likely to get into trouble.

Our latest horse, Captain Boo, lived up to his Halloween name. He was a black gelding, full of muscle, with a strangely scarred eye. When he was a weanling, a horseshoe had been thrown into his face. His eye had

taken the brunt of the blow, and a fibrous pink scar protruded from it —
giving him a distinctly spooky air.

He was the first horse to be sent here by Laura, a diminutive yet sturdy
gallop girl. All of five feet tall, she moved with the confidence of an Ama-
zon. Her normal workday started at 4 A.M., galloping fiercely competitive
horses like Boo on the track. On racing nights, it ended as late as midnight,
after she ponied her last racehorse to the starting gate.

She left me a message about Boo, her voice strained with urgency.
"Hey, I got a horse here, he needs a home right away. He got hurt in his
last race. It's his ankle. Trainer will send him off to the sale in Seguin if he
don't get a place." I could hear hoofbeats clattering, horses snorting, and
stirrup irons clinking in the background — Laura had called right from
the barn, possibly even from horseback.

The Seguin sale is a general livestock auction. In this type of auction,
usually the animals are rounded up and sent through the big sale arena,
grouped by type of livestock (cattle, goats, horses). As the animals cluster
together, with numbered signs fixed on their rumps, the auctioneer calls
out a specific number. Buyers shout their bids, trying to size up the cow or
horse as it trots around with the others. Meat dealers from slaughterhouses
often frequent this type of sale.

By contrast, a horse-only auction is designed to show off each horse's
sales value. Before the sale begins, prospective bidders can ride and handle the horses. Horses are then auctioned off one at a time, giving them a
better chance for a good home. Sometimes the individual sellers will present their horses in the ring, taking the microphone and describing their
talents and training.

But horse auctions can be risky, too. Back in my DC days, I once went
to a sale in Maryland, tagging along with a trainer from the polo barn. Tina
was looking for an older horse for one of her clients, a heavyset man with
limited riding skills.

The auction house was like a giant barn, with a series of stalls and pens
behind the sales arena. A big horse caught Tina's eye — he looked like a

knight's steed, with large-boned substance and a broad back. "How old is this one?" Tina called over the stalls, trying to find his seller.

The big horse was crowded in a pen with several other horses. He huddled next to an even bigger horse, a reddish-brown paint mare. Her coat was muddy and unkempt. She turned to nuzzle her nervous charger buddy — her face was incredibly sweet with large, dark eyes full of warmth and trusting cheerfulness. I halted, arrested by the humanity of her gaze.

"He's just *three*!" A shrill voice carried from the other side of the horses. It came from a wiry, disheveled woman in her fifties. "He's a real lover, just like his mama there. That's her, next to him — she'll still let him nurse sometimes. That old girl, she'll be a nice babysitter mare for someone. She's twenty-four and got those bad ankles, but she throws the nice big babies, don't she? I'd keep her and the young one, but I got twenty horses on three acres — some of them just got to *go*."

Pausing for a breath, flicking cigarette ash down her torn pastel parka, she then started into a long story about all the money her horses would bring. The mare took a couple steps closer to us, looking for attention, her gait clumsy. I looked at her ankles and a chill tightened my throat. Even my novice eyes could see the arthritis and large bony spurs around each joint. She could barely walk — a death sentence.

Tina pulled me away, muttering. "Crazy lady, probably a rescue nut, one of those hoarder types. That mare's only heading one place and not for a lot of money. She's earned a better end than that." I glanced at the mare again — her Da Vinci expression still haunts me today. A meat dealer bought her, a squat, sunburned man with eyes like concrete.

That was the last auction I ever attended.

THE MARYLAND AUCTION regularly had racehorses come through its arena. And many Texas auctions are held near tracks — racehorses are a common sight at those. Often fresh from the track, racehorses enter the ring wild-eyed and snorting, kicking out in excitement, their taut physiques full of nervous tension. Heads thrown high, prancing wildly in place, the racehorses aren't popular with bidders. People shake their heads and keep their hands down, leaving the bidding to the more risk-tolerant professional trainers or the meat dealers.

When LOPE first started, horse slaughter was still legal in Illinois and Texas. An average of 67,000 horses were slaughtered each year from 1997 to 2006. In 2007, the practice was banned in those states, and the remaining US plants were shut down immediately. Statistics on the number of racehorses sent to slaughter can be difficult to pin down. Ten percent of total horses slaughtered has become the generally accepted estimate, given that racehorses usually represent 10 percent of all U.S. horses in a given year.

Although horse slaughter is now no longer practiced in the United States, some states have unsuccessfully introduced legislation to open new plants. Animal welfare groups are lobbying for a federal ban on horse slaughter to block such efforts in the future. American horses are still purchased by meat dealers, then shipped to plants in Mexico or Canada. Sadly, Mexico is especially known for its barbaric, outdated methods of slaughter. With its proximity to Texas, Mexico looms as a dangerous destination for local auction horses.

So, Boo wasn't a good candidate for the horse auction, especially with an old fracture splintering again. Boo had reinjured his ankle in his last race — a race he tried to win, pushing gallantly against the burning pain. Boo was Laura's favorite horse to ride — she couldn't stand the idea of him ending up in a slaughter pen, with his pride, beauty, and winning ways counting for nothing, his worth reduced to the mere weight of his meat.

On the phone, Laura said, "He's one of those proud horses, know what I mean? I'd gallop him in the morning and he'd carry himself so fine, so full of himself. But he's a good boy, never pull on me or nothing bad like that. Boo's a nice horse."

I agreed to take him immediately, arranging a trailer ride with a local transport service ("You call, I haul," the business card stated proudly).

At the track, Laura led Boo out of his stall, personally loading him on the trailer. Slender but strong, Laura exuded gymnastic toughness, brusquely pushing aside a groom's offer to help. She impatiently flipped her dark hair from her eyes, looking me over, wanting to be sure I was a good home for Boo.

Boo was gregarious and strangely handsome — his scarred eye was rakish rather than creepy, lending George Romero panache to his wide forehead and sculpted face. "Wow, what a good-looking horse," I said, immediately wanting to pet him. Laura's face softened. "He *is*, isn't he? Watch his leg there, though, it's sore."

As Laura guided him to the trailer, it was clear she loved Boo and that he returned the feeling. The wind picked up, blowing her unruly hair back in her face. But this time, she didn't push it away, dropping her head and letting it cover her eyes. Laura's voice was quiet. "Take good care of him. And he's on the stuff, so give him some time."

The stuff? Feigning a knowledge I didn't have, I nodded wisely. I wanted Laura to feel good about sending Boo to us — I could tell she was doubtful about me, glancing at my suburban Gap jeans and battered Saturn, not exactly the badges of a Texas horse expert.

At the ranch, Boo settled into the "new horse" pen in our first pasture. The field was empty, but he could see the other horses in the adjoining field. Just like Tulsa, Tawakoni, and Zuper, Boo needed some alone time in a reduced space as part of his transition from the racetrack.

Typically, a new horse needed to be alone only a week or two before meeting Zuper, then the rest of the herd. The transitions were smooth and easy, thanks to Zuper's watchful supervision. Tory's barn had been full of melodramatic stories about wild racehorses tearing up fences and other horses. I now chalked these up to exaggerated gossip or perhaps overzealous marketing.

WHEN I FIRST MET HER, Tory had several racehorses spread across her paddocks, all straight off the track. She purchased them with an eye for either polo or jumping prospects. The wanna-be polo horses were short and round with pretty heads; the jumping prospects were tall and willowy, with powerful necks.

Local equestrians soon heard of Tory's off-track horses. Patty, an amateur polo player, promptly bought a little brown gelding. Sarah, a neighbor, snapped up a leggy, beautiful bay to be her next show jumper. Every few days, another racehorse would be spoken for — but they still remained at Tory's farm.

"Don't even *look* at him, Patty," Tory ordered. "Your horse needs to stay here for at least another two months, letting down from the track. That's all included in the price. Trust me, he's not ready until the spring. Needs more time in the oven." Patty looked baffled but stayed away obediently.

At the time, I shared Patty's confusion — why couldn't she pick up her new horse? Or ride him? The brown gelding looked calm and quiet — and he had already been at Tory's farm for weeks. Tory was mysterious, evoking the cooking metaphor again and throwing in a couple of "Those horses will kill you, Lynn," for good measure.

It seemed ridiculous, a bizarre rule designed to raise the price of the horses, to tack on "oven" pasture fees. Unless there was a health reason — could it be that racehorses need some quarantine time? Or maybe Tory hoped to frighten the buyers about their new horses, then offer training services for more money? Her lack of explanation was frustrating — and reinforced my less-respectful theories.

IN THE NEW HORSE PEN, Boo walked gingerly on his sore ankle. Other than his hesitant gait, there wasn't much outward sign of the injury. His pastern felt a little warm with an almost indiscernible swelling. Laura had told me that Boo had an old condylar fracture, now stressed again. I had never heard of a condylar fracture. An image of Afghanistan and Kandahar came to mind — Boo's injury sounded exotic and dangerous.

"He needs some rest," said Laura. "No riding for a while, just pasture turnout and time to be a horse."

During the first dizzying months of racehorse arrivals, I relied on the medical instructions of their race trainers. Their prescriptions were usually the same, even if the ailments varied.

Big Boy Slew had a minor tendon strain needing pasture rest. Avenging Tree had a chip in his knee. "Just turn him out for a couple of months," said Eddie, Tree's trainer. "The vet said he ought to heal up well enough for riding — but he can't race anymore." Like Tulsa's, Shaman Chocolate's ankles were festooned with racing "jewelry" — but of a larger and more ornate variety. The treatment? Some vacation time in the fields.

But I was worried about the stressed, possibly splintering old fracture in Boo's ankle; he needed to see a vet, just to be safe. Fortunately, I no longer had to worry about Dr. Death's pessimistic bedside manner. A couple months before Boo arrived, a new vet in Austin emailed me about his practice, Austin Equine Associates.

"My name is Dr. Damon O'Gan, and I want to introduce myself to your organization. I am opening an exclusively equine veterinary practice that will service the Austin area. Our main areas of interest are diagnostic ultrasound and sports medicine related injuries. I would love to become involved with your organization in any way."

During our first meeting at an Austin Starbucks, Damon outlined his notion of "involvement." As I showed him our mission statement, ranch photos, and newspaper clippings full of Zuper's image, Damon nodded thoughtfully.

"Part of my philosophy as a vet is to give back to the equine community. We'd like to sponsor you for vet care. We can offer a 70 percent discount. Now, we don't have a clinic yet, but we are a fully equipped mobile service. I hope that'll work for your organization?" Damon's face was serious, his precision haircut, pressed shirt, and crisp khakis making almost a military impression (an assessment that would turn out to be hilariously incorrect — I later discovered that Damon was a former ska musician).

"Uh, yes, that definitely would work for us." I tried to sound professional, nearly spilling coffee on Damon as we shook hands on the sponsorship. Damon brushed aside my stammered, effusive thanks. "It's our pleasure. We're glad to help," Damon said with extra calm, probably taken aback by my caffeine- and excitement-fueled chatter. "Call us any time you need vet help — we'll be there."

NOT ALL OUR DONATIONS came so easily. Initially, LOPE's annual budget was small, with expenses under $60,000. Even so, fundraising was a challenge. Our anonymous donor's support constituted almost half of that — but was limited to two years only. In theory, the remainder would come from foundations, individuals, and horse adoption fees. Although I had worked for nonprofits for many years in DC, I had no fundraising experience. My role had been in finance and office management — I tracked the funds once they arrived but had little idea how to acquire them.

Fortunately, Julia and Pam soon teamed up on one of their neighbors, a dignified physician-turned-racehorse-breeder. Faced with the irresistible force of two lady ranchers, Dr. Wilson agreed to give us nearly a hundred bales of oat hay. Oat hay is much more nutritious than grass hay, the equivalent of protein-rich granola for horses. A deep amber color, it is thick and weighty, a great fodder for any livestock — especially ex-racehorses needing a carb-rich diet, to add some pounds to their greyhound-fit physiques.

There was just one catch — we had to pick up the bales ourselves. Lisa, my hunter/jumper neighbor, gave us her flatbed trailer and lots of advice about how to stack hay for the two-hour drive home. On the way to Dr. Wilson's ranch, we picked up Pam and her husband, Bob, their hay-loading expertise completing our expedition's needs.

Hay was scattered all over Dr. Wilson's front yard. His ten acres were crowded with a baler (a giant contraption that sucked up loose hay, then spat out bales), three trucks, and several farm hands throwing the bales into tidy rows. Despite our team, the work was slow and exhausting. It took us all day to load the hay, drive home, and then unload it. In a neighborly gesture, Jesse offered to store our excess bales at his barn — to keep them off the ground and out of the elements.

A few weeks later, Jesse moved out to another farm about ten miles away. It was an abrupt departure, following a rent dispute and a marked increase in Jesse's Pabst consumption. As I looked at the now-unoccupied barns and paddocks next door, it hit me: our oat hay was gone.

After many promises to bring back our hay, swearing it was "accidentally" moved, Jesse stopped returning calls. Grimly, we tracked down his address, paying a surprise visit. Tom and I ended up having to load and unload the heavy bales yet again, liberating them from Jesse's new barn. We weren't about to let anyone rustle our donated oat hay — not as long as we had arm muscles and a borrowed flatbed trailer.

The oat hay took up residence on our porch. Filled with feed bags, riding tack, grooming tools, and three kittens abandoned by Jesse, the porch had become an improvised barn. The hay was a huge hit with the kittens, who played endlessly in the bales each night; Tom and I would watch them through the living room window, their feline antics better than anything on cable TV.

SOON THE AUSTIN EQUINE ASSOCIATES CREW came to X-ray Captain Boo. To no one's surprise, he did have an old condylar fracture, a stress injury almost exclusive to young racehorses in training. These hairline fissures occur at the bottom of the cannon bone, entering the fetlock joint and extending upward. Usually treated with surgery and screws, condylar fractures have a good prognosis for full recovery.

Boo's old fracture had indeed healed nicely. There was no sign of new joint damage. Instead, the radiograph showed inflammation around another old injury, a sesamoid fracture that Laura didn't know about. This fracture hadn't healed well at all.

The critical functions of the equine sesamoid bones don't really have an equivalent in human anatomy. To my layman's eye, the closest might be the back of our heel, where the Achilles tendon and other important things attach. The equine sesamoids are two small bones sitting on the back of the horse's fetlock joint. The suspensory ligament attaches to the sesamoids, and if the sesamoids are unstable, the ligament becomes strained and can tear.

Boo's sesamoid bone had shattered, then healed without surgery. Scar tissue walled off and surrounded each fragment, creating a lumpy foundation for his suspensory ligament. It was amazing he had ever run again, let alone raced competitively. A re-injury was inevitable, with the amount of pressure racing speed puts on equine ankles.

Surgery wasn't an option — his sesamoid was in too many pieces to pin — and if the fragments were removed, it would leave him without any anchor for his ligaments, a recipe for truly catastrophic injury. I listened to the diagnosis, terms like "lateral vertical from distal" and "medial branch" jumbling in my head. Boo could be ridden again, after more pasture rest, but would never be able to jump or barrel race or play polo. Any kind of high-impact sport was out of the question.

Still, Boo was lucky. Laura had stepped in and made sure he wasn't sent to the sale. Most racing people I knew were like Laura, Keith, and Robin — they cared about the racehorses and did their best to do right by them. They were happy to donate their horses to our ranch or list them on our website.

Some trainers took more convincing, such as Jim, a race trainer I met one day at the Houston track. I was at his barn, arranging the transport of a racehorse Jim trained (but didn't own). Some race trainers own the racehorses in their shedrows, but most operate as hired trainers for other owners. Often racehorse owners aren't true horse people — they might be lawyers or doctors or stockbrokers who own racehorses as part of a syndicate. Hiring an experienced race trainer to condition the horses is key to their racing operation.

"You here to pick up Sherman? He's been a good racehorse, just has that old bumpy ankle. Owner said you'd come for him. Me, I just send mine off to the killers if they can't do nothing no more," drawled Jim, his tired blue eyes daring me to wince, cry, or judge him. He waited, in the hot Houston sun, dead certain I'd show some stuck-up Yankee ways or PETA sensibilities. Drawing my best weapon, I smiled. "Well, then you'll really appreciate what I do. I run a service for just those kinds of horses."

"Hmmph," Jim snorted, not believing my tales of adoptions and good homes. But he listened without spitting (a courtesy I appreciated), and he even helped shoo Sherman (a notorious balker) into the waiting trailer. As the trailer pulled away, Jim looked me over again. "You got a card or something? I might call you if I got one like Sherman, one that can still be a riding horse. But I won't be sending you any cripples — like I said, I send those to the killers."

Sighing, I handed him a business card and brochure. A partial victory was better than none.

WITH HIS MULTIPLE RESTRESSED FRACTURES, Boo temporarily fit Jim's definition of crippled. But during his first weeks at the ranch, Boo was alert and excited. He would pace the fence line, sometimes neighing a challenge to Tulsa and Zuper two fields away. Zuper ignored him but Tulsa sometimes nickered back, agitating Boo even more. Remembering Tulsa's delight in teasing Tawakoni, I compulsively checked and rechecked the three fences between him and Boo — we didn't need another premature horse mixer, courtesy of Tulsa's escape artist skills.

However, Boo was gentle whenever I entered his pen. He never pushed past me or tried to snatch feed from my bucket, patiently waiting to be served. His eye scar always startled me — I would be on his "good" side, and then he'd turn, showing the damaged eye. The pink scar tissue was a symmetrical lump, looking like an angry eraser stuck in the middle of his pupil.

Boo's good eye had a kind expression, and I learned to discern that same friendliness even in his damaged eye. He was a husky, powerful horse, his sleek black coat giving a gunmetal sheen to the muscles beneath. And Laura was right — Boo was a proud horse, his fence pacing sessions conducted with a cocky strut and arched neck.

His pride was hereditary. Like Tawakoni's, Boo's pedigree contained Kentucky Derby history. His sire was Captain Bodgit, a formidable racehorse in his day. Captain Bodgit was stocky, with blinding speed and a reputation for tremendous heart. His signature move was a dazzling final kick, a talent for flying up the homestretch in the last few seconds of a race and stealing a win.

Once in his homestretch sprint, Captain Bodgit was completely committed — his racing videos show him all-out, no reluctance, giving 100 percent to beat that other horse. In the 1997 Kentucky Derby and Preakness, he came within a head of beating the winner, Silver Charm. His last-minute surges pushed the other horses in the field, too — his presence meant faster times for all the competitors.

Like Grindstone, Tawakoni's father, Captain Bodgit retired during an exciting Triple Crown series. The day after the 1997 Preakness, he came up sore. His tendon was strained — his racing career was over. Captain Bodgit had injured the same leg several months earlier; it had healed well but weakened the leg overall. The second injury created too much risk for Captain Bodgit to keep racing safely. He was put out to stud instead, siring multiple winners with total earnings over $7 million.

I was struck by the father-son similarities. Boo had a condylar fracture, then recovered to return to racing, only to become injured again. Like his sire, Boo had a fierce competitive desire; he loved to race and win with exciting final sprints near the finish line. And Boo took after his father in looks — dark, athletic, and well muscled with powerful hindquarters and a handsome face.

I WANTED TO HEED LAURA'S ADVICE about Boo and the "stuff" — whatever it was. Online research yielded some answers. The "stuff" turned out to be Equipoise, a legal anabolic steroid used in horse racing. Equipoise is a testosterone-based drug. Its positive effects include enhanced muscle mass, improved appetite, boosted immune functions, and superior athletic performance. While many racing barns use Equipoise or other steroids regularly, considering it a given to be competitive in the sport, other trainers shun it.

Keith, Tulsa's race trainer, didn't like steroids. "I don't like to run them on that junk. Makes them feel like champs all the time. They can't tell how they really feel — so I can't tell how they feel. What if a horse is hurting and don't know it? That horse might just break down during a race and get in a bad wreck. I'd rather run horses that can win on their own."

In addition to boosting performance, Equipose has an unsettling side effect — it can make geldings behave like stallions. A normally mild-mannered gelding will try to mount mares and fight other male horses while under the Equipoise influence. After Tawakoni, this wasn't news I wanted to hear. Equipoise is also sometimes what adds that overall "zest" to a racehorse's personality, a combination of ADD and competitive fire that gives some racehorses all the appeal of a frat boy on crack. Interesting to watch, but not something you want to take home to your family. Or buy at an auction.

Now I understood why racehorses show so poorly at auction — most of them have steroids in their system. Also, their racetrack life is highly structured, a strict regime of challenging exercise, high-powered feed, and dawn-to-dusk bustle. Being pulled abruptly from their usual routine, thrust into an environment full of strange horses and noises, must set their Equipoise-enhanced nerves into overdrive.

I had no idea that steroids were a factor in racehorse behavior. Like most people, I just assumed that racehorses were high-strung and hyperactive by nature. Eager to show off my newfound knowledge, I brought up Equipoise often during my racetrack conversations. Throwing the term around made me feel like an insider — and almost made up for my suburban wardrobe. The race trainers seemed impressed, staring at me intently whenever I raised the Equipoise topic.

I later found out I was mispronouncing "Equipoise." Instead of saying it phonetically ("Eq-wha-poiz"), I went for the less obvious sea mammal pronunciation ("Eq-wha-pus," as in "porpoise"). The Gap jeans were rapidly becoming the least of my credibility issues.

After that, I just said "the stuff" or "steroids" — even I could get those straight.

WEEKS PASSED AND BOO MELLOWED into a Halloween teddy bear, his winter coat giving him an appealing fuzzy air. He gained weight steadily on our oat hay and donated feed, his race physique softly filling out. I watched him closely, looking for signs of lingering steroid effect.

Boo's pacing sessions slowed to leisurely walks, then stopped entirely. He no longer neighed at the other horses, disappointing Tulsa, who still tried to get a rise out of Boo by nickering provocatively. Boo ignored Tulsa, preferring instead to graze or nap. He especially liked to sleep in the sun, stretched out in the grass narcoleptic-style.

One morning, I decided he must be off the stuff. Boo had been alone for nearly three weeks. However, Zuper was already on the job with a different horse, a nervous youngster in need of babysitting. Pondering the options, I instead put Boo with Cow Paddy, a huge, good-natured gelding recently arrived from Keith's shedrow.

Cow Paddy also had a sesamoid fracture, but with a single clean break instead of Boo's shattered fragments. Before his racing career, Cow Paddy had been raised on a ranch, even doing a little cattle roping. He had been tremendously relaxed in our fields, the open spaces maybe reminding him of his childhood days. Since Keith didn't use steroids, I knew Cow Paddy would socialize easily with a new horse. Boo and Cow Paddy seemed like a compatible pair, with their matching injuries and dark bay coats. I left them grazing together in the shadiest part of the field.

As I walked back to the house, my cell phone rang — it was a local TV news station, and they wanted to film here after lunch. Bustling to the porch, I grabbed the grooming kit and headed toward Zuper's pasture — he would need a quick beauty makeover for the TV crew.

Suddenly, an all-too-familiar, Tawakoni-like scream of equine machismo hit my ears — it was Boo, who was clearly still on the stuff. He was nearly unrecognizable from excitement, pumped up with bravado and misplaced affection. Full of lust at the prospect of companionship, he was actually mounting Cow Paddy, a horse nearly twice his size and not at all interested in alternative equine sexuality.

Cow Paddy was deeply, dangerously offended. So offended, in fact, that he bit Boo on the lip, leaving a bloody twist of tissue hanging — tipping Boo's face from rakish to gory in a matter of seconds.

Shrieking, I scrambled over the fence, trying to stop Cow Paddy from biting off more of Boo. Cow Paddy, his good nature strained to the breaking point, eyed me warily, and then he decided to leave, stalking off indignantly. Boo retreated to a small run-in shelter, his passion thoroughly extinguished, his mouth dripping blood.

Shocked at Boo's rapid transformation from gelding rapist to chastened slasher-film victim, I pawed at my cell phone, dialing Austin Equine Associates and worrying about the camera crew on the way. I moved Boo back to the new horse pasture, demoting him to solitary confinement, and tried to avoid staring at his torn lip, hoping it wasn't as serious as it looked. All signs of violent romance had vanished from Boo — it was hard to believe he had been molesting Cow Paddy just ten minutes ago.

In less than an hour, Austin Equine Associates arrived, our vet superheroes. Boo was sedated, stitched up, and injected with antibiotics, leaving me just enough time to clean up before the reporters arrived. Cow Paddy glared at Boo over the fence, as if to underscore just how much he disliked prison movie scenarios. Boo, still groggy from his pasture vet triage, carefully avoided eye contact, opting instead to sleep off his sedation under a tree far from Cow Paddy's baleful gaze.

Boo's lip healed quickly, with only a faint scar remaining. And I filled in my previous knowledge gaps about equine steroids, finally understanding Tory's insistence on such long periods of "oven time" for her racehorse sales herd.

After a couple more weeks, Boo was at last Equipoise free. As I introduced him back into Cow Paddy's pasture, I noticed Cow Paddy didn't hold any hard feelings. He touched noses with Boo (who wisely chose a nonromantic greeting this time around), then walked off, satisfied that Boo was now harmless. Boo rapidly made friends with the other horses, eventually becoming the calmest gelding in the herd.

Still, I worried about his future. Most equestrians avoid horses with limitations. For example, Damon's clientele often paid for detailed pre-purchase exams on their show-horse prospects, including radiographs of every major joint — ready to bolt from the sale at the first hint of a problem. Boo's old fractures and violent eye scar would have scared them away instantly, not to mention his lack of recent riding or post-track training.

But Boo wasn't exactly in their elite market, anyway — their taste ran more toward giant Warmblood horses, usually imported from elite German farms with long, consonant-filled names and six-figure price tags.

ONE DAY, CLAY EMAILED US, looking for a trail-riding horse. Soft-spoken and in his thirties, Clay worked for the Texas lottery office and loved horses. On his time off, he rode at the state park near his property — he could ride for miles and miles along classic Texas scenery, rugged brush and rocky paths set against big sky and rolling mesquite hills.

The day Clay came to the farm was unseasonably warm for late November. The horses dozed in the humid warmth, with heavy clouds promising rain. Some of the horses trotted in irritation — the heat had brought out botflies, buzzing around the herd, looking to plant eggs on their equine hosts. A botfly looks like a beat-up bee, amber bodied, with a twisted, unsavory shape to its wings. They hover, seemingly harmless, then dive in to glue their parasitic offspring on horse legs. When the horse licks at the egg site, the newly hatched maggots can be transferred to the digestive system.

Horses hate botflies and will bite at them, then frantically try to move away. One filly at our ranch would race frantically around the pasture, ears pinned, kicking at the maddening buzz that seemed to surround her. Blind with annoyance, she'd run over anything in her path — dogs, squirrels, Tulsa, once even my hand.

I showed different horses to Clay, explaining their history and temperaments. Cash was an appealing horse with a prankster personality like Tulsa's — but he had an adoption pending. Crafty, a pumpkin-colored gelding with two hind socks, was a little nervous for trail riding. Cow Paddy had recently left, adopted by a family with a ranch north of Austin. Finally, we came to Boo, who stood quietly in the pasture, looking at us benignly from his Jekyll-and-Hyde face.

Not sure how Clay would respond to Boo's eye and old injury, I started out by describing Boo's gentle disposition (post-Equipoise). Clay patted Boo and admired his athletic build. As Boo seemed to slumber in place, a botfly meandered under his belly, buzzing.

"Hey, let's get that fly away, boy," Clay said to Boo. He smacked lightly at the botfly, trying not to startle Boo. The fly eluded smashing and headed toward Boo's hind legs. Clay slapped at it again, waking Boo out of his doze. Boo turned and watched Clay's hand swatting toward him again — usually an excellent motivation for a racehorse to take off galloping.

Boo didn't move.

Clay stalked the botfly more aggressively, finally crushing it with another emphatic slap against Boo. Boo nodded his head up and down, looking at Clay, seemingly grateful for the insect assassination.

Clay was impressed. "What a good horse! I don't know too many horses that would put up with me hitting them, especially with a botfly buzzing around. What's his adoption fee?"

I laid out Boo's limitations — can't do serious sports, might get arthritis someday, hasn't been ridden since his racing days — but Clay was still interested. "Can he trail ride? It would be lots of steady walking, nothing too fast or strenuous."

After a vet exam, Damon cleared Boo to trail ride. Clay shrugged his shoulders at the thought of possible future arthritis for Boo. "I'll probably get it myself someday. Boo and I will just go slow together then."

Within a few days, Clay took Boo home, picking him up in an open cattle trailer, a roofless combination of horse trailer and flatbed. Boo closed his eyes against the wind, nearly dozing with relaxation, Equipoise a distant memory.

A few weeks later, Clay updated me on Boo's progress, reporting, "Boo is doing great. Last Saturday we made a fifteen-mile trail ride. It didn't even faze him! Boo is very trustworthy and a joy to ride. I cannot tell you how much joy he has brought into my life. I was very fortunate to find him."

Boo was fortunate that Clay didn't first meet him at an auction, right off the track, still on the stuff — and a completely different horse from the one Clay adopted.

SOON AFTER BOO'S ADOPTION, I got a call from Jim, the skeptical race trainer from the Houston track. "I got a horse for you," he said. "He could be a riding horse maybe." Pleasantly surprised, I reached for my notebook. "I can put up a listing on the website for you right away. How old is he? And what price do you want? And where is he located — is he at Sam Houston racetrack?"

Silence. Then Jim said, "He's near Dallas, at my place. But ... I'd like to give him to you, for that adoption deal you got." Jim sounded sheepish. Before I could respond, he added, "And I can bring him to you on Monday. That's my day off."

On Monday, Jim arrived towing a big stock trailer. The horse inside pawed and snorted — he was built like a steeplechaser, long, tall, and leggy. As Jim led him out, turning him loose in the new horse pasture, I took in a sudden, astonished breath.

The big gelding had lumpy ankles and sore hindquarters and moved stiffly — a classic "cripple" by Jim's standards.

Jim spoke rapidly, averting his eyes. "This horse, he's got a real good personality. I always liked him. He's got some problems, sure. But maybe you can still find him a home. Get him adopted someplace nice, better than I could do for him."

We stood together in silence, watching his horse, prophetically named Retirement Joy, jog around the field. Jim climbed back in his truck, revving the engine for the four-hour return trip, his eyes suspiciously shiny. I watched him drive off, pondering a sudden insight.

Maybe it's not just racehorses that need time to get "stuff" out of their systems.

PART III

The Backstretch

You have to give something you never gave to get something you never had.

TOM DORRANCE,
horsemanship guru

CHAPTER SIX

Endofthestorm

B Y LATE FALL 2004, race trainers were calling nearly every week, and our ranch had a waiting list of horses. My cell phone often rang late at night, during racing hours — a sure sign that a trainer wanted to donate a freshly injured horse, possibly hurt in a homestretch sprint ten minutes earlier.

Soon after Clay and Boo bonded over the botfly, John called me. "Got a horse for you. Just got injured. Sesamoid fracture. He's a good horse, great disposition."

This was an epic amount of words from John. A basketball star in Kansas during the 1950s ("Well, that was when people were shorter," was his usual comment on his career), John was a distinguished presence on the backside. Tall (by any era's standards) with graying hair and wire-rimmed glasses, he looked more like a professor than a racehorse trainer. Always in khakis and slightly rumpled plaid shirts, John was also a former veterinarian.

John was the first race trainer to ever list a horse on our website. While I frequently encountered him at the track, his quiet reserve was a barrier — it was hard to get more than a few sentences out of him. As I started to tell John we were full at the ranch, he interrupted with a rare show of animation. "I'll bring him to you. No charge. Can I come Monday?"

Trying to put off saying no, I asked the horse's name. John replied, "Endofthestorm. All one word." I couldn't refuse a name like that.

So Endofthestorm arrived. A deep, almost black shade of bay, he was built like a turbo sprinter, with strong legs and a deep chest. Soon his colorful name would turn out to be sadly ironic.

Storm settled in well, though he remained a tad aloof, preferring to graze alone in a corner of his pasture. His injured ankle was impossible to detect at a walk, and Storm was too sensible to trot or canter with a sore leg.

But after about a month, Storm came in from the field wheezing and gasping, each breath a painful struggle. At first, I thought the rasping sound was the brisk January wind, but it was Storm, his flanks tightening with every inhalation. I quickly haltered him, instinctively understanding that he was in danger. As I led him to a small pen near the house, I grabbed my cell phone, hitting the well-worn speed dial for Austin Equine Associates.

As Damon patiently questioned me — "Is it more of rasp or a wheeze? How many breaths is he taking?" — I reached for my usual film metaphor: "He sounds like Darth Vader, only a little quieter."

Damon was silent, no doubt wondering how to translate my Hollywood analogy into useful veterinary data. Finally he said, "I'll be there right away. Sounds like it could be serious."

DAMON ARRIVED QUICKLY, setting up a long, tubelike device strapped to a lens. As I held Storm, Damon pushed the tube up Storm's nostril. He kept pushing, until its outline was visible under Storm's jaw. Storm sighed but didn't resist — all his energy was directed toward breathing.

Ever calm, Damon squinted at the lens. "Hmmm. That's kind of a mess in there," he commented, making Storm's respiratory system sound like a child's untidy room. I tensed — Damon said "kind of a mess" when other vets would say "disaster."

Storm's nasal scope exam revealed the double jeopardy of a malformed airway besieged by infection. First, he had a paralyzed flapper. Flappers are pieces of throat cartilage that are supposed to open and close over the airway, helping to protect the horse from swallowing food down his trachea. Horses have two flapper pieces — when one is paralyzed, it closes slowly, partially blocking the air passage.

This alone wouldn't have been unusual — many horses have irregular flappers without any serious health problems. But Storm's flapper was so paralyzed that it rubbed against the good flapper, building up calluses on both. Called "kissing flappers," this syndrome creates a larger breathing obstruction, as the calluses nearly touch each other across the airway. That was the good news, compared to the other scope discoveries.

Storm also had an entrapped epiglottis, a congenital defect that occurs when a membrane grows up over the epiglottis, keeping it motionless and prone to deformity. Storm's epiglottis was the worst Damon had ever seen. "That thing looks like an alien crab or something," he said, smiling appreciatively at its distorted contours. But that still wasn't the worst news.

On top of these two congenital defects, Storm had a massive infection throughout his upper respiratory system. Infections in this part of equine anatomy are difficult to treat — it's nearly impossible to take a culture so deep within the horse's neck. So veterinarians must guess which type of antibiotic might work, deploying as broad a spectrum as possible, a medical scatter-bomb approach. Usually, antibiotics need time to build up in the system. If Storm's breathing didn't stabilize, an emergency temporary tracheotomy would be necessary, to ensure a steady source of air while the antibiotics did their work.

"I'm not too hopeful these will work fast enough, but it's worth a try," Damon said, handing me two bottles of different pills. I listened to his instructions about mixing the pills properly, trying to focus. Vet medications always confused me. I rarely remembered their correct names, instead using toddler-style terms such as "pink stuff" or "that dermo thing in the red bottle."

I carefully packed Storm's antibiotic pills into my vet kit, a large plastic container kept in the ranch truck's backseat. A 1992 Ford, the truck represented the last of my DC savings account. I had first spotted it at the rural Texas version of a dealership, parked in a roadside field with a hand-written "For Sale" sign stuck in the windshield. A behemoth of a vehicle, the truck was a four-door, one-ton dually with four rear wheels. The lux-urious "extras" included a long, dented bed, tinted windows, and a stick shift so heavy it made my thigh muscles twitch.

My Saturn, so sensible for East Coast commuting, had failed miser-ably as a farm vehicle. Its cloth seats and suburban-sized trunk had buck-led under the strain of transporting feed, hay, and fencing supplies. An impulse purchase, the truck seemed like the ultimate ranch tool, a steel machine capable of hauling, pulling, and carrying even the heaviest inven-tory from Callahan's store.

WITH MY SAVINGS NOW INVESTED in a dually, the ranch finances were even more unsteady. Tom's well-paid consulting contract had recently ended. He hit the temp circuit again, pulling in dull administrative assign-ments for weeks. Creatively frustrated, he unleashed his artistic talents on LOPE's marketing materials. Within a month, he'd reinvented our web-site, designed a new logo (featuring Zuper), and crafted a LOPE media kit.

Suddenly, our organization looked more professional, like one that a large business or wealthy donor might want to support. Our website traf-fic spiked, as did our adoption rates and PayPal donations. It still wasn't enough to cover our fundraising deficit, but at least we were closing the gap.

In addition, racing people, like Pam and Ruby, rallied support for the adoption ranch. Pam especially took up our cause, actively lobbying everyone she knew for donations and sponsorships. Her efforts soon net-ted us a meeting with a horse feed manufacturer.

The plant director, Roy, walked me through the grain mill, pointing out various huge machines whirring noisily. Men in hard hats were every-where, attired in crisp plaid shirts, pressed jeans, and work boots. Roy paused before a cluster of workers around the biggest machine. "Well," he said, tugging at his blue tie (the only one in the room). "What do you think of our mill?"

Roy and the factory staff looked at me with anticipation, clearly expecting a resounding vote of approval. Desperately, I searched my brain for something thoughtful to say about a feed plant. I cleared my throat. The men leaned forward, eager to catch my words.

"Well, it's...definitely...um...the cleanest mill I've ever seen," I said. "And so...organized."

Roy beamed. "Now, Miss Lynn, you've hit upon it, that's for sure. We are very proud of how tidy our plant is." A deep murmur rose from the men around him, all nodding emphatically. "Most people don't even notice that, and there you are, spotting it right off."

Turning to the group, Roy gestured in my direction. "This is Miss Lynn. She has a LOPE program. We're going to see about helping her." With that confusing edict, Roy escorted me out of the mill and into his office — where he presented me with a full feed sponsorship. Our ranch would receive free grain for the entire year, a donation worth over $5,000.

SEVERAL DOSES OF MULTICOLORED MEDICATION later, Storm showed no improvement. Damon was out of town — his colleague from a neighboring town, Laurie, was overseeing Storm's progress on the antibiotics in his absence. Laurie was always smiling, even when she stuck needles and scopes into horses. Even the supercheerful vet's speaking voice reflected ebullience with its peppy stressed accents and rolling delivery. "Hey, so Storm is still wheezing? *Cool.* It's a *perfect* day for a temp trach, no problem. *Great!* Will you be here at two? You can *assist!*"

Assist? Ewww. Blood, needles, and lacerations made me nauseous and faint. As part of my student curriculum, Tory had tried her best to train the quease out of me — but to no avail. She'd ask me to fetch medicated ointments, wrap horse legs in felt bandages, and prepare poultices. I'd inevitably bring back the wrong creams (often dropping them), twist the bandages instead of folding them, and forget the proper ratio of salve to plastic wrap for poultices.

Even worse, I folded under pressure whenever a crisis erupted. One rainy, dark afternoon, I was walking in Tory's paddocks. Harley, her young two-year-old gelding, ran up to me. Exasperated, thinking he was trying to mug me for food, I threw off my raincoat hood and waved my arms at him, "Go away!"

That's when I saw the blood. His front leg was lacerated in many, many places with flaps of skin fluttering and blood spurting from multiple gashes. Blood was on his leg, on his flank, in the puddles, and even on my jeans as Harley danced around, flinging his corpuscles everywhere.

I screamed for Tory, frantically sloshing my way to the barn. Tory appeared in the doorway, annoyed. "What *is* it?" As I babbled on about Harley, he came trotting up, proudly showing off his gore-splattered leg.

Tory commented, "Wow, that's a good one. Might have to call the vet." Calmly, she caught Harley and began cleaning out the wound, grunting occasionally as she pulled out pieces of debris and random loose flesh.

Tory shook her head at my flinches. "Lynn, get a grip. Try not to be so gutless." When the vet came, Tory watched happily, sipping from a mug of hot chocolate, as he put in about a million stitches zig-zagging up and down Harley's leg. The vet smiled, "Mmmm. This is a fun one to stitch. Look at the bone there." I fled home to my apartment, too nauseous to eat for hours afterward.

So a tracheotomy on a horse didn't sound appealing at all. But Laurie's exuberant smile, beaming at me from its frame of dark hair and John Deere cap, made it all seem all right, like a girl's night out shopping or something.

"Sure, assist. Very cool," I said, trying to sound game.

"*Okay!*" Laurie was delighted — a high five seemed close to happening. I sidled away, just in case.

As two o'clock approached, the temperature dropped sharply — and Storm's breathing became even more labored. It was hard to imagine he not only raced but raced well with his congenital breathing issues. Storm even broke track records, one of which still stands today. He was a turf horse, meaning that he ran best on natural grass surfaces. Most racetracks have a turf course set up in the middle of the track oval, the grass carefully landscaped for maximum traction.

Storm's favorite distance was five furlongs — he was a fierce competitor, displaying aggressive speed especially in tight races. His racing personality was quite a contrast to his mellow demeanor at the ranch, where Storm was known for long contemplative sessions staring at the trees, his eyes half-closed in a meditative gaze. "Storm's Zenning out again," Tom and I frequently commented to each other. He radiated detachment from the material world — the other horses gave Storm a wide berth, puzzled by his preference for solitude.

I haltered Storm as he stood near the house, dozing in his usual Zen trance. Wind and clouds bullied their way across the farm. Ducking back into the house, I did my best to get ready for assisting — donning every item of fleece I owned. My arms pinned by all the layers, I wrapped a wool scarf around my face and went out to meet Laurie.

Storm remained calm and well behaved — even when he saw Laurie had returned to torture him some more. "*Hey!* It's *cold!* That's great — no flies for the *blood!*" Laurie bustled around the portable clinic van, pulling out needles, syringes, blades, and gauze. "So, this is the *Cadillac* of temp trach tubes. Isn't it *awesome?*" She pulled out a big plastic tube — it looked like a gasoline pump.

The wind picked up. I shivered as Laurie injected Storm with a local anesthetic to numb the soon-to-be temporary tracheotomy site. Laurie instructed me to hold Storm's head up while she made the incision and then inserted the tube. Storm was relaxed during the shot, and Laurie decided not to sedate him. "It'll be harder to keep his head up if he's sleepy. If he gets restless, we can always sedate him later."

The big moment arrived. Coached by Laurie, I held Storm's head up and turned mine away. Laurie stood beneath him and peered up. She was quiet, intent on making the incision. Small drops of blood hit her boots. I was getting dizzy. Bundled in fleece, I suddenly felt hot and stuffy, an ominous prelude to queasiness.

Blood splattered on my boots, too. I slouched down, trying not to visualize what Laurie was doing. Storm's head was heavy, stressing my biceps and shoulder.

"*Okay!* The incision is done. You are doing *great!* I just need to pop in the tube." I heard an ugly, sucking sound like a giant boot stuck in mud. It was Storm breathing through the exposed wound in his neck, which was about an inch from my ear. I sagged to my knees, fighting nausea. Now the blood was flying — Laurie was making stabbing motions as she arced the big tube into the incision.

The tube wouldn't go in — Laurie tried over and over again, each attempt spraying bloody mist everywhere. Normally, the tube would simply slide into place, the plastic molding to the contour of the trachea. But the cold air was chilling the tube, making it hard and inflexible. Laurie's petite height, my inability to stand up without fainting, and Storm's growing irritation weren't helping the situation. Laurie started to giggle, "*Wow!* This is kind of a pain. Never had this happen before."

I could hear a splashing THWACK near my ear as the tube hit Storm's neck and then bounced off his open trachea. To add to the overall effect, a powerful odor emanated from the wound — a horse's trachea is full of mucus, a sign of a healthy immune system that I would later label "heinous throat chum."

Laurie ducked her head under Storm and asked, "*Hey!* Are you *okay?*" I blinked — her big grin, pretty face, and dark hair were splattered with blood and tissue (the non-Kleenex kind), her gloved hands soaked bright red, a horror movie moment in my face.

"You look like a freak zombie," I muttered. She laughed and returned to the job at hand, stabbing, chuckling, dripping, thwacking. Finally, the Cadillac tube was abandoned in favor of a streamlined model, a smaller, Honda-type tube. She slipped this tube in successfully on the first try, and the horrible sucking sound finally stopped. Laurie checked Storm's vital signs, then began putting her instruments away. The blood on her hair was starting to dry as she pulled off her gory gloves and wiped away Storm debris from her face.

I noticed for the first time that she was dressed lightly compared to my fleece layer-cake attire — and the temperature had dropped into the forties. Just a long-sleeved shirt, a thin vest, and a scrub coat. Laurie had to be freezing, but she didn't show it. She just kept smiling while she whisked away bloody gauze, reddish lumps, and other surgical evidence from our driveway. Impressed, I fantasized that I'd someday emulate Laurie's grin and cheerfulness whenever I faced a squeamish task. Sans blood in my hair, though — I wasn't quite ready for that level of commitment.

Storm's newly installed temporary trach tube had a simple design, with a latch and rounded faceplate. Laurie demonstrated how it worked — push the latch and pull out the trachea tube first, followed by the faceplate.

As she showed off the mechanism, a blood-stained Vanna White, I focused instead on not vomiting. I wasn't interested in trachea tube engineering — until I heard the phrase "easy to remove for cleaning."

"Cleaning?"

Laurie explained that I'd have to pull out the tube each day and clean off any accumulated debris. "You can use a gauze pad or soak the tube in hot water. But if you use the gauze, be *super*careful not to drop it in Storm's trachea hole. That would block his airway — and there's no way we could get it out in time. That would be *bad*."

Sensing my lack of enthusiasm for the fatal gauze story, Laurie switched over to something more fun, a discussion about antibiotics. Here was a topic I could appreciate. I had by now somewhat mastered the art of crushing pills and mixing them in Storm's feed.

Laurie handed me bottles of liquid antibiotics and several syringes. "So inject him once a day, in the muscle. Two shots. Put one in each side of his neck."

I had only recently learned how to give horse shots. It wasn't my favorite task either.

LIKE SCHOOLCHILDREN, horses need immunization boosters at least once a year. The shots have cryptic names like 4-Way, Rhino, and West Nile. Naturally I was a wimp about needles. I still had to lie down to have my own blood drawn, so the idea of wielding syringes and sticking them into horses didn't exactly inspire me.

Bobbie had once tried to teach me how to inject horses. One April day,

she decided to give the school horses their spring shots, inviting me to follow and watch. Javier, her ranch foreman from a small town in Mexico,
also came along, attired as usual in a big cowboy hat, jangling spurs, and
giant hunting knife strapped to his belt.

Bobbie directed a steady stream of loud "Tex-Mex" dialect his way.
"Javier, no agua-water in trough-o. Agua — understand-o? Si? Fill water.
Mucho grassy." She dropped her voice, turning to me. "Javier is the best
hand I've ever had. But he don't speak English so good."

After several horses, we arrived at Mickey, one of the lesson horses at
the barn. Mickey was a big black gelding with a handsome blaze face. His
utter lack of interest in moving faster than a walk made him ideal for timid,
inexperienced riders.

Bobbie explained her technique. "Okay, so you see that sort of
triangle-shaped depression in his neck? That's where the needle goes.
Throw it at him real fast, so he don't know what's happening, then push
down the syringe like this."

Throwing wasn't my best skill either. Painful memories of junior high
softball rang in my head as I picked up the syringe and needle.

"Throw it in there. Don't wait around, he'll figure out what you're
doing. Go on, throw it."

Nervously, I pitched the syringe at Mickey, aiming it like a dart. It
barely made contact and hung precariously, the attached syringe nearly
parallel to his neck. I smashed down the syringe plunger, tripping on the
lead rope as I pulled out the needle.

Javier looked bored, fingering his mustache and squinting. It was
nearly impossible to ever get a reaction from Javier — his lack of English
and excess of Mexican vaquero cool created dual barriers to communication. Not to mention Bobbie's attempts at Texas-style translation.

Bobbie wasn't pleased with my syringe toss. "No, you can't do it that
way. You got to put the needle all the way in first — otherwise, he could
get an infection. You need to throw it harder in there."

For the next horse, I was ready. As the small pinto gelding dozed, I gripped the syringe javelin-style and flung it into his neck, burying the needle to the hilt. The gelding, Bobbie, and even Javier flinched. "Okay, well, at least you got in there," Bobbie said. "But see, he could get a hematoma from that — you hit him too hard."

I let Bobbie and Javier vaccinate the rest of the school herd, vowing to never inflict my poor needle-throwing skills on another horse.

During the first months of the adoption ranch, I called Dr. Death when the racehorses needed shots. True to form, Dr. Death regaled me with stories of anaphylactic shock and allergic reactions to vaccinations. "Sad thing to see," he intoned. "Out of the blue, boom, they just keel over."

Now Damon was our vet. Scoffing at my stories of needle ineptitude, he set up a lesson one day. As his new vet tech and I took turns injecting the horses, he coached us from the sidelines. Damon's technique didn't involve speed or throwing — rather, he encouraged a leisurely, gentle approach. "They see you coming anyway. No point in trying to trick them. Just go in slow, and most of the time they don't even feel the needle."

It was impossible to blanch or chicken out in Damon's matter-of-fact presence. I felt like I'd be letting him down, tarnishing his perception of me as a competent horse person, maybe even giving him cause to reconsider sponsoring the adoption ranch.

Damon's inability to be flustered was a marvel to me. When Zuper indicated his displeasure with needles, flinging his head and violently knocking the syringe away, Damon took over. "Hello, big fella, how are you?" he said. "Bet you got lots of shots at the track. Don't be silly." He scratched Zuper's nose, then neck — and with cowboy vet aplomb, slid the needle in and depressed the plunger with one hand, the veterinary equivalent of twirling your six-guns before depositing them in their holsters. Zuper flung his head, but too late — he'd been officially vaccinated, the needle and Damon already long gone.

EVERY MORNING, BEFORE BREAKFAST, I'd put together my Storm kit. Armed with a pot of hot water, gauze, paper towels, two syringes full of antibiotics, and latex gloves, I'd head out into the February chill to catch Storm. As Storm stood, haltered, I'd pull out the metal trach tube and its accessories (latch, faceplate), then soak them in the water. Sometimes the latch would be crusted shut with things I refused to look at, requiring aggressive wiping before it would open.

Once the tube was clean, I'd come to the worst part of the process — putting the apparatus back into Storm's neck. His open trachea would exhale clouds of hot air, creeping me out no end. To place the tube properly, a certain amount of wiggling was required — a technique that produced unpleasant squishing sounds as the metal collided with damp trachea tissue.

After his tube was set back into place, I'd give Storm two shots, carefully sliding the big needle into his neck muscles, my face curled into an "eeww" expression. Storm would stand without protest during my nervous nursing sessions, never once dancing away or nipping at me, no doubt channeling the Dalai Lama or some other Buddhist master.

His patience gave me courage, if not skill. Each morning, I plowed through the downright grossness of my vet chores, inspired by Storm's kindly stoicism. When it was over, I'd reward us both with breakfast — a big scoop of grain for Storm and maybe tea or toast for me, depending on my stomach and the amount of disgusting debris on Storm's trach tube.

Storm ate his grain peacefully, his attitude much the same as when I was sticking needles in him. I found myself lingering over my tea, sitting on the chilly porch, watching his contented chewing, a shared sense of quiet between us.

Yet after two weeks, Storm showed only small improvement; the antibiotics weren't working. After another exam, Damon made a big decision — it was time to do a permanent tracheotomy. Although it sounded drastic to my layman's ears, Damon explained that the procedure would guarantee unlimited air to Storm's lungs.

Damon arrived early one Saturday morning, dapper as ever, clearly looking forward to the surgery. Tom and I helped him set up the "operating room" — an open, level area under our tallest tree. Equine tracheotomies are usually performed while the horses are standing upright, so that the veterinarian can have unobstructed access to the throat area.

Nestling Storm's head into a special medical harness, Damon carefully fixed pulley lines to a large, leafless branch. Storm, now sedated, found his head lifting magically on its own — sleepily, he contemplated the sky above him, occasionally snoring. Tom was fascinated, his philosophic mindset giving him the necessary detachment to enjoy Storm's medical spectacle. I was determined not to watch, figuring I'd already earned my tracheotomy stripes for the year, possibly the decade.

"Now, once I make the incision, there's no going back." Damon sounded pleased at the prospect. "I can't touch anything that isn't sterile." Damon held his gloved hands in classic TV-doctor-style, palms up and extended away from his body.

Within seconds, he had cut deftly into Storm's neck.

"That's the sternothyroideus muscle." Damon pointed out a pinkish slab of tissue running parallel to the incision site. "I'll have to remove some of it, so that the muscle won't heal around the permanent trach site." Tom asked more questions, leaning closer to Storm's open trachea. I sidled away, catching a whiff of the infamous throat chum.

As Damon's gloved hands became red with blood, along with his scalpel, I wondered if he would need fresh gloves or clean instruments. Shaking his head, Damon smiled. "Lynn, blood is sterile. It's not a problem."

Storm moved restlessly, his sedation seeming to spark dreams of racing again. Damon and his assistant had their hands full (and sterile). Damon adjusted his knife-wielding technique around Storm's twitching, but I could see it was slowing him down. Certain the answer would be no, I asked if I could help. Surely Damon wouldn't want a squeamish horse handler nearby.

"That'd be good, Lynn. Just stand next to him, and see if you can keep him still. We can give him more sedation, but I don't want him to lie down."

Great — I should have known not to ask.

I stood next to Storm, gripping his harness and petting him. Storm leaned into me and slept deeper. Once again, I was inches from his trachea — a depressingly familiar location.

The surgery took longer than expected, as Storm's powerful neck muscles kept crowding the incision area. Damon pared back the muscles, careful to keep the basic structure of each intact. He then gently spliced the trachea tissue, which has multilayered rings like an onion.

As he peeled back portions of the trachea, stitching them into Storm's neck, he explained the technique — his voice unruffled, as if he were lecturing in a classroom instead of in front of a bleeding horse. "By grafting some of the trachea tissue into the horse's neck, we are fooling the trachea into thinking that it is supposed to have an opening. If I just cut away the tissue, there'd be nothing for the trachea hole to anchor to — the neck muscles would slowly close around it, suffocating the horse."

By now it was early afternoon. Storm stirred again in his sleep, jostling me and taking my mind off Damon's professorial presentation. My hands were tired from holding the harness — and my stomach felt odd.

"Take a look, Lynn. We're almost finished," said Damon. Leaning over Storm's head, I peeked at the surgery site, ready to flinch. The muscles were neatly trimmed back, and the trachea opening was stitched into place. While everything was still way too red for my taste, the overall impression was more like a rare steak than a gory medical scene.

At the thought of steak, my stomach tightened again. This time the pangs were all too familiar. I was hungry — and for something quite specific.

Barbeque.

Damon was very proud of me.

STORM'S TRACHEOTOMY SITE HEALED steadily, its redness fading to a dull pink that barely showed against his dark bay coat. He could breathe now — instead of shuffling at an unsteady walk, Storm trotted around, even playfully bucking sometimes. Night was his favorite time to canter across the pasture, his tracheotomy distorting his whinnies into freakish, *Lord of the Rings* creature sounds.

The rest of the herd would scatter, wild-eyed, trying to get away from whatever was making those demonic squeals. Storm seemed to enjoy the panic he provoked, strutting up to the recently vacated feed buckets and helping himself to their contents. A glimpse of his haughty racing personality resurfaced. Though still mellow, Storm was now selective about the people he bonded with, his Buddha calm more Richard Gere than Dalai Lama.

Not everyone shared my appreciation for Storm's recovery, especially potential adopters. Rosemary, a middle-aged barrel racer and lifelong rancher, recoiled at my description of Storm's tracheotomy. "And just why, exactly, did you decide to put him through all that? Should have euthanized him." Her lips closed tightly around each word, hardening her weathered features further. Clearly, she saw me as inept, a bleeding heart type who didn't understand how to deal with "hopeless" cases like Storm.

Other people confused permanent with temporary tracheotomies, assuming that Storm would have an artificial tube in his throat for the rest of his life. "Aren't you afraid it'll fall out in the middle of the night? How awful that would be," said a Dallas horse mom, aghast. Entirely missing the point of a tracheotomy, a local cowboy asked, "How do you keep the hole covered up?"

Storm's only limitation was that he couldn't swim. Because he now breathed through a hole in his neck, any kind of water sport was out of the question. Other than that, he could be ridden normally. His enhanced air supply gave him an advantage for speedier sports (though his sesamoid fracture did not).

In Europe, they even allow horses with tracheotomies to race. Laurie once did the procedure on a Texas polo pony, who went on to have a long career of post-tracheotomy polo matches, no doubt spooking the opposing team's ponies with demonic neck whinnies.

However, within a few weeks, more maladies hit Storm. He developed abscesses in both front feet, but unlike Zuper, Storm had recurring infections. Per Damon's instructions, I soaked Storm's hooves in Epsom salts, then wrapped them in elaborate booties made of diapers, vet bandages, and duct tape. Rainstorms hit our ranch, soaking the ground and Storm's diapered feet, creating more chance for infection.

Storm's hooves refused to heal, even after multiple doses of antibiotics and weeks of hoof wraps. The infection settled dangerously into his coffin bone, an important, toelike bone inside the hoof. Two surgeries and five months of duct taping later, Storm finally had normal hooves again. His tracheotomy was a minor cosmetic flaw in comparison to such risky hoof melodrama.

Storm had one last surprise for us. Just when he was finally disaster free and ready for adoption, a skin fungus erupted. Impervious to every topical ointment at Callahan's general store, it spread across Storm's shoulders, leaving a wake of baldness behind. Dr. Matt Evans, Damon's vet partner, finally resorted to high-impact IV treatment, dripping steroids and anti-inflammatory drugs into Storm.

Despite Matt's kind intentions, Storm took a dislike to him, curling his lips and averting his head whenever Matt approached. "Don't mind Storm," I said. "Sometimes he can be a little snooty, kind of French, with new people lately." Matt thought that was the best description of equine hauteur ever, and he prefaced all of his follow-up calls with, "How is Storm doing? Is he feeling very French today?"

Soon after, Storm's website listing caught of the eye of Rachel, a retired eventing competitor. She now bred jumping prospects, her decades of experience on cross-country courses honing her keen eye for quality bloodlines. She emailed, "I am definitely interested in Endofthestorm. I have cared for a horse with a temporary tracheotomy and have a young horse of my own who may need a permanent one. We also need a sort of 'enlightened despot' to keep our young geldings in line. Would he be suitable?"

I pondered her question. Storm had a tracheotomy, a habit of Zen practice, and an imperious French manner. A perfect match.

Rachel came to meet him soon after. A trim woman in her fifties, she sported a gray-streaked bob and Darwin decals on her truck. "I really want to give back to the ex-racehorses," she said, petting Storm. "Some of my best eventing horses were Thoroughbreds. They have the most heart of any breed."

I nodded in agreement, thinking of Storm's tenure at our ranch. Storm had been here for two years, slowly recovering his health. I had even ridden him several times, his pain-free steps a delight to us both. During Storm's rehab, I had learned how to give shots, assist at tracheotomies, prepare hoof booties, clean temporary trachea tubes, and handle the sight of equine surgeries.

Most of all, I now understood that stoicism (even faked) is the better part of valor — faced with Storm's patient example during his medical ordeals, the least I could do was stop wincing. By the time Storm left for his new home at Rachel's farm, I felt like a seasoned veterinary graduate — still unenthused about blood, but at least no longer gutless.

CHAPTER SEVEN

Nacho Mann

TIMING AND FEEL, Lynn," Cory, our neighborhood horse trainer, said slowly, drawing out each syllable mysteriously. "You work through the horse's feet to his mind." Cory stood in the pen and wiggled various things (rope, flag, finger) at the horse standing nearby. Cory's ground work, based on natural horsemanship techniques, yielded results. I could see horses relax visibly with him, never being ridden, just being moved around the corral, in patterns I didn't quite understand.

To my shock (and fatigued muscles) nearly forty horses had arrived in the eight months since we'd opened the ranch. I had managed to ride very few of them, my confidence still low in spite of Tulsa's chivalry. But if adoption rates were to keep up, I had to ride and work with the horses more. Not all prospective adopters were like Clay, willing to take a risk on a horse (like Captain Boo) whose last ride was a turbocharged gallop down the racetrack.

Having passed my midterm exams at the Storm school of vet medicine, I now was ready to tackle my riding fears again. Just as I came to this conclusion, Cory drifted into LOPE's orbit.

Recommended by one of our supporters — "I know the most marvelous trainer near you," she gushed — Cory was a car salesman–turned–horse whisperer. Somewhat suspicious of that career combination, I put his phone number in my "might need to call someday" file folder stuffed with farrier business cards and hay-for-sale flyers. Then, one evening after a long day of failure, I called Cory — I needed help persuading a reluctant filly to load into a horse trailer.

Cory looked the part of a horse guru. Always attired in crisp jeans, spotless white cowboy hat, and carefully pressed shirt, he could pass for forty-something instead of his sixty years. Cory had a classic, movie cowboy appearance with his tanned face, lanky physique, and dark hair graying softly at the temples. His quiet voice, slow Texas accent, and habit of repeating your name during conversations added to the cowboy sage effect.

"Lynn." Pause. "It's good to see you." Longer pause. "How can I help your horse today, ... Lynn?"

However, the constant ringing of Cory's cell phone undercut his cowboy aura. The calls were often automotive in nature, as Cory still acted as a sales scout for local dealerships. Cory's end of those conversations was always brief and to the point: "How many miles? Where's it at? Your price? Uh huh. Drop 'er down 15 percent and we'll send a driver to pick it up. Tell Joe-Ben I said hey."

The filly, nicknamed "Phil," was short, stocky, and confident. A pretty horse, copper-colored with a big blaze, Phil was popular on our website. Trudy, a bubbly schoolteacher, quickly adopted her. But Phil refused to step into Trudy's rented horse trailer — and I was sadly inept at coaxing hesitant horses to load. Phil's adoption was in jeopardy if we couldn't get her into a trailer.

Cory came to the rescue, working with Phil in our pasture the next evening, waving his fingers and flag at her. Within a half hour, she was hopping in and out of his trailer easily — a far cry from the two-hour balking and tugging session at Trudy's trailer the day before. Pleased but confused, I peppered Cory with questions, "How did you do that? Why is she loading so well now? What happened?"

"You got to separate the front feet from the back feet," Cory intoned. Pause. "Lynn."

Mystified, but impressed, I later watched Cory's collection of various horsemanship DVDs, hoping some cowboy confidence would rub off on me. Cory had several favorite trainers: Buck Brannaman (Robert Redford's coach for *The Horse Whisperer* film), Tom Dorrance (an elderly, elfin man who specialized in troubled horses), and Cory's favorite mentor, Ray Hunt.

Ray Hunt was a holdover from another era, when horses were valued partners in the dangerous and rugged work of cattle ranching. His imposing height and sardonic humor belied his gray hair — Ray was an impressive physical presence on camera. In his clinic tapes, he barked at the riders, recited poetry, squinted off into the horizon, and gentled every equine rogue, no matter how wild or crazy. Ray was supremely confident in his skills, never once showing worry or fear — he'd just laugh and say something cryptic like, "You got to take the bitter with the sweet."

In one video, he worked with a mare who refused to load into a trailer, bucking and kicking out at his head. Ears pinned, she looked mean and smart, darting her nose toward Ray and baring her teeth. Other trainers had wrestled with the mare, only to label her vicious, a hopeless case.

Ray wasn't worried about her reputation. He deftly pulled her head to one side, standing near her shoulder, foiling all her attempts to bolt or rear or paw at him. "That won't work. Or that either," commented Ray as the mare changed tactics, trying to aim her hindquarters near his hip. He just moved around her, keeping a careful leverage on the lead rope, letting her tire herself.

"She just don't see how the human can be of use to her," he chuckled. "Most times when she does this, well, people just get out of her way. But see, I got a better deal for her."

The mare paused in midleap, taking in Ray's relaxed stance and utter lack of fear. For the first time, she seemed to be thinking, trying to figure out what he wanted.

"Now, that's a nice change," said Ray. Using the lead rope, still standing near her shoulder, he steered the mare toward the trailer's open door. She sniffed the trailer briefly, then voluntarily walked inside, her steps slow and relaxed.

THE TRAINING DVDS WERE HELPFUL, but it was a horse, Nacho Mann, who gave me a true crash course in these techniques.

Nacho was a much-loved seven-year-old black gelding, with a mediocre race record and an old knee injury. Nacho hadn't been ridden in years, donated by his doting race breeder. Kathleen called several times from her Oklahoma farm before shipping Nacho to our ranch. She loved Nacho, telling me many stories about his vivid personality and childhood antics. Despite the distance to our ranch, Kathleen preferred to donate Nacho rather than sell him locally. Oklahoma was a haven for Quarter Horses, Appaloosas, and other colorful Western breeds — plain black Thoroughbreds were much less prized.

"He has such a flashy personality! Knows he's handsome. And oh my! Don't ever ignore him. Nacho pouts if you ignore him." Kathleen's pride was evident. "Best-looking horse we ever bred." She sent me a photo of him, taken at her ranch. Nacho was posed next to a pink azalea bush, his black coat gleaming against the flowers. His elegant head was turned toward the camera, eyes full of expectation for a horse cookie or carrot.

"I wanted to keep him for my riding horse. But then I had my own knee surgery, and Phil, that's my husband, he said it'd be crazy for me to take up riding again. And Nacho, he's so bored, he runs up to the fence every time he sees me. He wants a job, I just know it."

Nacho was set to arrive on a January weekday in 2005, right in the middle of thunderstorm season. Mud was the bane of our existence at the farm in the first year. Record-breaking rain had pounded central Texas. Our driveway, on a "hundred-year floodplain," had flooded twice in three months.

The first time had been a simple spillover of creek across the pavement, no more than a few inches deep. The second flood ominously continued to rise. At eight inches, Tom and I loaded up the truck with the house pets, then drove across the rapidly moving water, heading for the front gate and a local motel. Most of the horse-occupied part of the property was on high ground — except for our largest pasture, the one with Zuper, Tulsa, and Boomer.

This field was half low ground — a growing flood stream now bisected it. Tulsa trotted back and forth over the water, Boomer following. Zuper stayed on the dry side of the pasture, neighing to the others. Grabbing a halter, I headed for Tulsa, who playfully hopped back to Zuper. Boomer stood at the water's edge, uncertain. Splashing through the now thigh-high water, I haltered Boomer, then dragged him across. Damp sticks, leaves, and assorted country trash (beer cans, Skoal containers, Styrofoam cups) smacked into my knees, then swirled away.

By the time we herded Zuper, Tulsa, and Boomer into another pasture, the water was approaching hip height, a narrow, mud-colored mini-river. The flood crested a few hours later, cutting an impressive swath across the pasture, a rush of water with its own current and evolving ecosystem of confused catfish and snakes. Within thirty-two hours, it had receded completely, leaving behind driveway potholes, piled-up logs, and a rank odor of horse manure blending with mold. A swamplike pond appeared in our back pasture, its fetid water attracting several delighted ducks and a disheveled heron.

The unseasonably wet weather continued for weeks. My boots were caked with mud layers, and every pair of jeans had long brown stains on the cuffs, even after repeated washings. During my daily closet rummage for semiclean jeans, I'd wistfully glance at the last of my office wardrobe, remembering the days of pressed, mud-free skirts and pretty shoes. Now my professional footwear was a pair of lace-up work boots. I had to walk all over the farm, leaving the old ranch truck to the safety of the paved driveway. The truck had already been stuck once in our ever-wet grass — it took a winch, a large wrecker truck, and a surly driver to pull it free.

The rains were unrelenting on Nacho's delivery day, making our driveway unsafe for large vehicles. The semi-sized horse trailer instead pulled up parallel to our front gate, ignoring the traffic now rerouting around it on Highway 21. As I signed the damp papers, the driver told me how good Nacho had been on the transport. "That's one smart horse," he said, brushing water off his Stetson. "He must have some cow horse in him, right?" When I told him Nacho was pure Thoroughbred, he was shocked into silence for several minutes.

Unloading a horse in a new environment can be tricky. Most race-horses are so accustomed to trailer rides that they barely react to new places. But others are gripped with excitement and curiosity, prancing, neighing, stepping on their handler in a frenzy of pent-up energy. With a long walk down a slippery driveway in the rain, I was hoping Nacho fell into the first category.

The driver led Nacho down the steep ramp. Nacho concentrated on moving each foot carefully, checking for slick spots. As I took the lead rope, Nacho dropped his head and sniffed my hand. We walked through the downpour, doing our best to ignore the horses in the adjoining pastures. The storm was keeping them much less curious than usual — Avenging Tree, Boomer, and Shaman Chocolate huddled under the run-in shed, barely looking up as we tiptoed by.

Nacho kept his nose pointed at the driveway, every now and then snorting lightly. I could see him looking over at me — his pupils were big and round, like a doll's eyes. I was grateful for his sensible attitude. At the back pasture by the house, I slipped off his halter and watched Nacho check out his new digs for the night. He ambled over to the fence, touched noses with Zuper and Tulsa on the other side, then dropped his weight on one hip, back hoof cocked, and lowered his head for a long post-travel nap. Wow, he's going to be an easy one, I thought, as I splashed back to the house.

All went well until I had to catch Nacho a couple of weeks later. My plan was to move him into Zuper's pasture, now that the rain had finally ended. I walked up to Nacho, halter in hand. But he pranced away, then ran.

Nacho flew by me, mud spraying my face, in full gallop. Patient at first, assuming he was scared, I felt my goodwill fade with each high-speed drive-by. He wasn't afraid, I realized suddenly. What I was witnessing was a playful form of tantrum, not a panic attack. And it was getting danger-ous, as Nacho swooped past me with barely a few feet to spare.

Memories of Lilly rearing and flipping still affected me. On the rare occasions when I mounted a horse other than Tulsa, I'd stare grimly at its mane, certain the horse was about to rear. Even worse, I was sometimes edgy with horses while doing nonriding activities like leading them or shooing them away as I scooped grain into their buckets. Lilly had taught me that anything can happen around horses, even gentle ones. Nacho's frenzied mud gallops seemed further proof of this theory.

I could just walk away from Nacho, give it up for the day. Surely that would be the safe choice, the reasonable response. But what about my goal of riding the horses here? How could I ride Nacho if I couldn't even catch him?

The weathered, laconic cowboys in the tapes had talked about "mak-ing the wrong thing hard" and "going slow to accomplish more." They mumbled these strange mottoes while carrying funny flags on long sticks, using them to direct the horses — and reminding me of my grammar school safety patrols with their orange vests and little traffic flags. One video featured a soft-spoken Wyoming trainer working with problem horses, including an off-track Thoroughbred.

"Typical, spoiled racehorse," he commented as the chestnut sulked around the pen, refusing to acknowledge the cowboy's presence. He waved his flag at the gelding, pushing him into a rapid canter. "Racehorses sometimes get sour about moving forward. Then when they finally do go, well, it's kind of fast and intimidating. I'm here to let him know that I make the decision about how fast to go — not him."

The chestnut gelding's speedy gait slowed down — his ears twitched and his mouth moved slowly, as if he were chewing horse gum. "There's a good change," drawled the Wyoming trainer. The hoof beats in the pen got quieter and quieter, then paused. The racehorse stopped, looking over at the cowboy, then dropped his head, licking his lips.

"See, that's all there is to it. Make the right thing easy and the wrong thing hard." He walked over to the chestnut and petted him on the forehead. The racehorse sighed and yawned, evoking another, "There's a good change. Just go nice and slow."

I watched that tape many times, searching for clues of the "good change" and how the trainer elicited it. The horse looking over and licking his lips seemed to be the key shift. While I wasn't sure, it seemed like the cowboy would first advance closer to the gelding, only to retreat, stepping back several steps, whenever he said, "Nice change." His steps were patient, his voice unflustered at the racehorse's initial commotion of aggressive galloping.

Mulling this over, I decided to try reverse psychology. Walking toward Nacho, I raised my lead rope and spun it over my head, clucking at him to move faster — and away from me. Nacho did a cartoon double take, looking quickly in my direction. My command caught him by surprise and he cantered away, with greatly lessening enthusiasm. It's not as much fun to be *ordered* to run away.

I continued to stalk Nacho at the walk, twirling the lead rope at him, pushing him into a canter again. Each time, Nacho got slower and slower, first cantering off at a near gallop, then loping lazily, then trotting, and finally walking.

Soon Nacho was standing quietly while I haltered him. For the first time, I had used my mind instead of my leg muscles to catch a reluctant horse in an open pasture.

Now that was a good change.

Yet, as the weeks passed, a bigger hurdle emerged — Nacho needed to be ridden. He was prone to nervousness near tack, often tensing and throwing his head high when he thought he might be saddled. A professional show trainer had nearly adopted him, only to decline at his show of temperament.

Impressed with his elegant movement, Cindy had taken Nacho on trial at her show barn near Houston. While Nacho enjoyed the pampered, posh setting, he misbehaved whenever separated from his new equine barn buddies — neighing, charging, spooking. Dismayed at his challenging theatrics on the ground, Cindy never rode Nacho.

I wondered if Nacho's temperamental nature was partially genetic. One of his relatives was War Admiral, Seabiscuit's biggest rival. A tremendous competitor, War Admiral was famous for his prerace tantrums, often delaying his races for several minutes as he raged outside the starting gates, rearing and striking at his handlers. Nacho also shared his ancestor's near-black coat, wide-set eyes, and confident bearing, but unfortunately very little of his speed.

Our budget was small — hiring a specialized trainer like Cory to ride Nacho wasn't an option. And the more generalist trainers, the ones with lower fees and local classified ads proclaiming, "We get 'em rode so you don't get throwed," didn't like working with ex-racehorses. "Them things are crazy" was a common refrain among this group.

Concealing my ignorance under a casual tone, I pumped every trainer I knew for advice. And I zealously returned to watching the horsemanship tapes, replaying key scenes over and over again, trying to get my courage up.

I WAS ALWAYS THE MOST TIMID RIDER at Tory's barn. During my three years there, Tory only complimented me once for equestrian bravery. I was visiting her during the glamorous polo season at Palm Beach. Horse sports there are a tremendous spectacle, like an ongoing equestrian Olympics. The best polo players descend on Palm Beach after Christmas, to play high-goal tournaments and attend charity balls full of tanned women with Eisenhower-era nicknames like Binky or Bunny.

Like most of the pros, Tory had rented a barn and apartment there for the polo season. I was in town for a brief spring break vacation, hoping to soak up some of the more exciting horse sights. Tory offered to give me a tour of the gorgeous stables surrounding the polo club.

When I showed up at her leased barn, ready for a sedate tour of the polo compounds, a line of polo ponies tied to her trailer greeted me. "You're late," barked Tory, handing me a bridle. "Put this on the paint mare. We're going to Rodrigo's place, to show him the sale horses. Do you have your paddock boots with you?"

There were several polo pros named Rodrigo in Palm Beach, all with impressive playing skills, wealthy clients, and a near-constant need for new horses. Why would we be visiting one of their barns? I still didn't get it, even after Tory mounted one of the horses, a feisty bay, bareback. "Hand me the lead ropes for the others. Come on, get on the paint — we're late!"

We were riding, not driving, to the polo stables. Bareback — and leading the other horses.

The paint mare was pretty and seemed kind. My legs gripped her back precariously — horse hair is slippery, especially for bare legs clad in tourist shorts. Instinctively, I grabbed for her mane, but polo ponies have shaved manes. Her long neck stretched before me, without a single tuft to clutch.

"Come on, take this lead rope. Don't worry, this one's quiet. Sort of," said Tory. The brown gelding at the end of the rope looked worried as I slid around the paint mare's back, trying to steer without falling off.

Tory held two other horses. Her bay pranced in place, waiting for me to catch up. "That's a $20,000 horse you're riding, Lynn. You break her, you buy her. Okay, let's go."

We rode down bridle paths that wove the large polo fields and barns together. "Time to trot," Tory announced. Trotting bareback is a true test of balance — you have to be sitting precisely on the one six-inch square of the horse's back that doesn't feel like a pogo stick on diesel.

Tory took off on her gelding, pulling along her other two horses. The bay trotted a little too enthusiastically, prompting a quick tap on the brakes from Tory. To my relief, the paint trotted daintily, giving me at least a 50 percent chance of not slipping off. The brown gelding stepped beside the paint mare, matching her pace politely.

As we rounded a bend in the path, a tall clump of hedges loomed on our left. The paint tensed — the hedges were making noise, something was rustling in them. Tory, still ahead of us by several paces, called over her shoulder. "How about a canter, Lynn? That would be a hoot! And the..." Her voice stopped. The bay had heard the hedge sound, too — he began to leap and spin, throwing his head down, a warning that signaled, "I'm about to buck like a bronco."

My paint mount and the brown gelding stopped, watching the impending rodeo. If they decided to start participating, too, I was doomed. Tory barked, "Quit! Whoa!" and pulled the bay's head up, quite an athletic feat since she was holding two other horses. The bay dipped and dove, an equine version of the Loch Ness Monster, all neck and undulating menace. Morbid but resigned thoughts ran through my mind. Would Tory decide it was fun to play bronc rider, maybe encouraging the paint to buck, too? Was she serious about cantering? I could imagine her kicking her horse into a lope, forcing me to keep up, yelling at me to "ride or die."

I waited to find out my fate, petting the paint mare and hoping she'd maintain her saintlike state of mind. For a few minutes the mare seemed uncertain, jiggling in place and looking over her shoulder at me. But she decided to stand still, perhaps misinterpreting my fatalism as calm confidence. Previous Tory experiences had taught me to keep my fears to myself. Whenever I looked scared during a ride, she inevitably upped the danger ante — usually while laughing or calling out helpful tips like, "Poor Lynn. You look like you need a beer. Relax... or that horse will kill you!"

Tory giggled as she wrestled with the bay and the other horses (who were now spooking and bucking, too). It was a domino effect of equine misbehavior, teetering on the edge of disaster. Just the kind of ride Tory loved (and I hated). In midguffaw, she looked over at me, then went quiet, her face falling in disappointment.

Within minutes, Tory's gelding was back under control, though still snorting at the scary hedge. As we rode off, the bay hopping with adrenaline, Tory smiled. "Guess we'll keep it slow now. We're almost to Rodrigo's place."

Leaning over her horse, looking me in the face, Tory sighed. "Besides, it's just not as fun as I thought it would be. You're getting much harder to scare now, Lynn."

It was the closest I ever got to a diploma from Tory.

CORY AND THE VIDEO COWBOYS had two key tools that our ranch lacked: a cheesecloth flag on a long stick and a safe, large round pen. I soon wheedled a flag from Cory — a bright orange one, mounted on a handle that looked vaguely familiar. "That's an old car antenna," Cory said with pride, his two careers finally in harmony.

The round pen was a bigger challenge. A form of corral, round pens are circular enclosures ranging usually from thirty to sixty feet in diameter. They can be made of several types of materials, such as wood, mesh wire, or steel. The safest models consist of steel interlocking panels, each about twelve feet long, that can be removed or added to change the size of the pen.

Cory and his DVD compadres did their training in large round pens, with plenty of room to do ground work, then ride the horses. The ground work was especially fascinating, with the trainer standing in the middle of the pen while the horse moved freely around its perimeter.

I had only seen round penning once in my DC days. A local horse exposition came to suburban Maryland. Full of training demonstrations and horse breed exhibits, the expo was like a small, portable county fair. Chris, a short, athletic man with an Australian accent, caught my attention — he was cracking jokes with the crowd gathered around his pen, creating a wave of giggles.

The horse with him, a stocky buckskin with big eyes, looked benign enough. Chris announced, "Now the owner tells me, this horse bucks big-time when he canters. She's had him checked for back pain or leg problems — he's clean as a whistle. So let's see what we got here."

I watched Chris stand in the middle of the pen, clucking to the horse and watching his jerky gaits. The buckskin bucked even with just a riderless saddle on him. "Okay, so now I'll ride him," said Chris. "We know he'll buck. And I can help him with that. But I guess you all came here to watch me ride out a buck. Don't want to disappoint you."

With that, Chris vaulted into the saddle, riding the buckskin around the pen. As he kicked him into a lope, Chris grabbed his hat, muttering to himself. "Hold on there, Chris." The horse bucked at every one of the round pen's panels, his bucking so consistent that it seemed part of his canter. Chris never once cursed or yanked at the horse — he let him buck, keeping the gelding's head turned slightly to one side.

He dismounted to applause, a form of praise he quickly rejected. "Let's not worry this little horse with a lot of noise. Plus I haven't done anything to help him yet." With that, Chris began doing complex things with the horse's lead rope, moving the horse sideways like a reluctant dance partner. By the end of the demonstration, the horse cantered without bucking, a relaxed look to his rhythmic strides.

I didn't understand what had just happened; Chris's balletlike movements puzzled me. But the idea of the round pen as a magic training wand was planted in my head. Upon arriving in Texas, land of corrals and cowpokes, I discovered that round pens are very popular here — they are considered a classic Western horsemanship tool.

Like any tool, the best round pens are the most expensive models. The safest design, with lightweight galvanized steel panels, then cost $1,800, a figure well beyond our means. If I wanted to ride Nacho, I'd have to stick with using the truck as my saddle-up station; with Tulsa, I'd rest the tack on the tailgate as I brushed him, then saddle him up for a ride. Our front yard, a smallish open area by the house, served as my unfenced riding paddock — an arrangement that reinforced my reluctance to ride any horse besides Tulsa.

Finally, one day I saddled Nacho at the truck, ignoring his high head and stiff neck. Then I pulled out my orange training flag and tapped him lightly with it, as I had seen the DVD trainers do. Nacho, in true diva fashion, pitched a fit — dramatically flopping around as if tasered. Holding the end of his lead rope, I spun in circles with him, trying to control his wild lurches. Each time I rested the flag on his rump, he fled, tucking his hindquarters beneath him and springing forward in leapfrog maneuvers.

Nacho didn't particularly try to avoid me — I could tell that running me over was definitely an option in his mind. As if to underscore that point, Nacho threw his head up and feinted toward my shoes, his hooves barely missing me. He exhaled in rapid snorts — PSSHT...PSSHT — lifted his tail nearly vertical, and rolled his eyes in *Exorcist* fashion. It was quite a show.

His antics reminded me of the edgy polo ponies from my past. The polo trainers would never put up with such bad behavior. Mostly Argentines, the polo pros were firm with any sign of equine disrespect, whacking the polo ponies with long whips, spurring them into gallops or eloquently cursing at them in Spanish as they yanked the reins. One pro's favorite coaching comment (no matter which rider or horse) was, "Don't let that horse win to you. Be the boss, use your whip."

Another polo instructor, Chad, was a dashing American pro with a slithery charm, his ever-ready grin hiding an imperious temperament. During one group lesson, we were sitting on our horses, listening to Chad's instructions. Tortuga, a sluggish chestnut school mount, suddenly pinned his ears at another horse, Paco, walking behind him. Tightening his hindquarters, he began backing toward the offending Paco, threatening to kick him.

I was amazed at his show of spirit — Tortuga means "tortoise" in Spanish, and Tortuga rarely moved faster than his namesake. His bad temper that day seemed incongruous, like a kindly grandfather pulling a knife during shuffleboard.

Chad's face tightened. "Get down," he ordered the student astride Tortuga. "And give me your whip." With a quick leap, Chad mounted Tortuga, the long polo whip in hand. "How *dare* you? Do it again, see what happens!" Chad whipped Tortuga several times, then spurred him backward toward Paco (who mistook the smacking whip sounds as a signal to run).

Tortuga tensed, then cowered. Chad backed him up to another horse, still hissing, "How dare you?" He whipped him again until Tortuga stood, shaking, with his rump against the other horse. Withdrawn and frightened, Tortuga was docile for the rest of the day, flinching whenever a horse came up behind him.

But adding Argentine profanity, spurs, or a whip to the Nacho situation didn't seem like a good idea. Nacho's emotions were running high — rough treatment might push him over the edge from rebellion to panic. Plus, machismo wasn't exactly my signature style. But the video cowboys weren't particularly macho either. Their low voices and patient body language were a stark contrast to the harsh tactics of the polo pros. I admired their quiet leadership — the cowboys commanded respect, rather than fear, from the horses in their training programs.

Nacho whirled around me, his snorts escalating into squeals whenever the flag touched him. Dirt and clumps of grass flew — Nacho was making the most of the traction beneath his hooves. He was also attracting an audience. Zuper and Tulsa had stopped grazing in the other pasture, popping their heads up to watch Nacho, hay still hanging from their mouths.

Nacho spun his head around, no doubt noticing Zuper's disapproving stare from across the fence. He paused, then glared at me and the flag. It was my move.

Recalling my accidental, poker-faced success with the paint mare and Tory, I decided to bluff, ignoring Nacho's spectacular tantrum. I was already standing motionless, semifrozen with anxiety — might as well fake nonchalance. Nacho half-reared, thrusting his nose into the air. When I didn't react, doing my best to emulate the stoic cowboys, Nacho unexpectedly sighed and did the equine equivalent of shrugging his shoulders. He turned and faced me, licking his lips, a quizzical look on his face.

Nacho was finally ready to get to work. He stood quietly as the flag gently touched his saddle, his legs, and his shoulders. I marveled at the change in him — Nacho had transformed from dervish to donkey almost instantly. What button had I pushed? My hunch was that I had indeed outbluffed him, given his almost sheepish demeanor (as if he'd held only a pair of twos all along).

I pulled on the stirrups and patted the saddle, trying to see if Nacho had more whirling in mind. But after the excitement of the flag, Nacho was thoroughly bored by the saddle on his back. He tolerated my tack adjustments with little reaction. I unsaddled him, surprised and relieved that the session could end on such a good note.

RANCH FINANCES WERE AN EVER-PRESENT STRESS. Each month was fraught with budgetary suspense. Would enough revenue arrive? Which expenses might need to be deferred? One week our bank account dipped to $250, only to be revived again by a timely donation.

In DC, I had worked with many types of nonprofits, from economic think tanks to art organizations. Though they had a wide range of budgets, from $120,000 to $8 million, the nonprofits had one thing in common: tight cash flow. I was adept at juggling expenses and monitoring revenues closely. Armed with these skills, I attacked the LOPE bottom line with vigor. Every dollar was stretched as far as possible under my kamikaze bookkeeper eye. With our veterinary and feed sponsorships, many basic horse costs were greatly reduced up front. In such a fiscally lean operation, all donations made a difference, which endeared us to funders and encouraged repeat gifts.

Sherry was a slim, energetic race breeder with a beautiful ranch two hours west of Austin. A former basketball coach and gym teacher, Sherry always seemed to have an invisible whistle around her neck. Her voicemail messages were quick and command-like. "Lynn. Got a horse to list. Call me." Although we barely exchanged more than fifty words in conversation, Sherry was full of warmth for our adoption program.

She once showed up at our place with a flatbed trailer, tractor, chainsaw, and her best ranch hand, a cheerful man named Ernesto. Within a few hours, Ernesto had chopped up four dead trees and pushed them into large piles to burn (the Texas form of trash disposal). Sherry also personally mowed our largest pasture, sitting high on her tractor as it pulled a giant shredder over our weeds.

When Sherry's mother passed away after a long illness, the family set up a memorial fund for her with the donations going to LOPE. For weeks, checks arrived from all over Texas, totaling almost $2,000. "Mother would be so pleased," said Sherry. "What are you going to do with the funds?"

We could buy lots of hay or stock our vet supply cabinet for years. The truck always needed repairs, too. But none of these seemed right for a memorial fund — something more permanent would be a better tribute, a way to truly honor Sherry's mother.

"Maybe we could get a good round pen with the donations," I replied. "That way, your mother's memorial fund could help all the horses that come here."

Sherry liked that idea. The round pen arrived a week after my saddling session with Nacho. It was the same model as Cory's — sixty feet in diameter with strong, safe panels. Its silver bars gleamed in the sun, encircling an inner perimeter full of dirt and ready for a horse in need of training. I had just the horse in mind.

As I led Nacho into the new round pen, he snorted at its shiny glint. The reappearance of the flag confirmed his nervousness — he stiffened and sidestepped away. But I was on to his bluff now. Nacho soon abandoned his melodramatics, standing quietly for the flag and saddle.

I mimicked Cory's technique, asking Nacho to trot, watching to see if he had any changes, good or bad. Nacho moved obediently around the pen, watching me back. Awkwardly, I stood in the center, waving the lead rope at him, feeling slightly ridiculous and very non-Western in my dainty paddock boots and easy-fit jeans. I wasn't sure how to assess the situation. Compared to Tulsa, Nacho seemed edgy and uncertain. But for a horse that hadn't been ridden in years, Nacho looked pretty relaxed. Which was the accurate picture of Nacho's true state of mind?

There was only one way to find out.

As I hesitantly mounted him, settling in the saddle with a thud, Nacho arched his neck and walked elegantly around the pen. He was a tad nervous, slightly high-strung (just like me), but we somehow clicked well together. I found myself riding easily, with the reins in one hand, looking off into the horizon — kind of like a cowgirl, maybe even one being videotaped.

Within a few rides, Nacho settled into a calm, personable mount. Molly, a local dressage student, was smitten with him immediately. Her bond with Nacho was obvious, as she deftly guided him around the corral. Nacho lengthened his strides, relaxing into a refined saunter, his eyes proud. Molly's velvet helmet, tan breeches, and tall boots complemented Nacho's elegant form, accentuating his graceful movements.

Delighted with Nacho's aptitude for dressage and his vibrant personality, Molly adopted him. There was only one thing about Nacho she didn't like. Shortly after he arrived at her barn, she decided Nacho was too ordinary a name for a prospect of his talent. "Such a noble horse deserves a more fitting name. So I'm leaning toward Phoenix — since he is getting a second chance to shine."

And that was a good change, too.

CHAPTER EIGHT

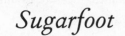

Sugarfoot

THANKS TO NACHO (and the cowboy tapes), I was riding all of the horses at the farm at least a couple of times. Adoption rates went up, along with my confidence — I now could tell potential adopters more about the horses and their personalities under saddle.

Although my rides were usually short and simple, nothing like Tory's intense training sessions, the horses gave me plenty of information. I could tell which ones missed racing; they moved restlessly at the walk, exuded mild boredom, and were rarely frightened by anything. These were the horses that would go on to jumping or barrel-racing careers, a zest for performance still in their characters.

The nervous horses, the ones who had lost confidence at the track, would scuttle sideways with anxious hopping strides, feeling like giant neurotic crabs under me. I'd work extra slowly with them, trying to figure out what job would scare them the least.

Then there were the easy, quiet horses — like Sugarfoot.

Sugarfoot was known for two things at the racetrack: an endearing habit of licking her groom's bald head and her incredibly slow speed. A small red filly with gentle eyes, Sugarfoot was oddly put together, like a toy assembled in a rush. Her front hooves turned out, her knees were crooked, and her drooping hindquarters didn't match her long back. But her kind face, with its big dripping star, made up for all those imperfections.

She was donated to the farm as a three-year-old in the spring of 2005. Most experienced horse people wince at the thought of a chestnut filly or mare. Like red-haired women, they are assumed to be difficult, high-strung, and moody.

Sugarfoot put all these myths to rest, with her mellow disposition and willing attitude. She was easy to ride and loved the outings when we rode around the farm, a contented look on her face as she ambled through the tall grass. Sugarfoot followed Tom and our dog Sophie on their morning walks, her head bobbing in rhythm to Sophie's canine strides. After breakfast, I'd often spot Sugarfoot near the porch, draping her head over the railings, peering into the windows, her eyes bright with curiosity and affection.

Sugarfoot's poor conformation would have kept her out of Tory's barn on principle — another "useless" horse, too weakly built to jump high or run fast. But her gentle disposition made her beginner-safe, a real surprise in a filly so young and inexperienced. Sugarfoot impressed me — she was the quietest horse I had ever ridden at the farm.

Her race trainer, Michelle, had trained Sugarfoot from the start, even breaking her to saddle as a two-year-old. Michelle, a former jockey, wanted to keep Sugarfoot for a pony horse, but she wasn't big enough, her slight frame not much of a deterrent for misbehaving racehorses. As the mounts of track outriders, pony horses must be stocky and powerful. They walk racehorses to the starting gate, escort two-year-olds on their maiden work-outs, and help calm bolting or bucking horses at the track. Pony horses exhibit both leadership and linebacker traits, often taking body slams from the unruly racehorses they guide.

"When we got her she was pretty small, but we started her and gave her an opportunity to grow up," she told a local newspaper. "Sugarfoot did everything perfectly, but it didn't look like she was going to pan out as a racehorse. Some of them just don't have it in their nature."

Laughing, Michelle related how Sugarfoot became fascinated by the shining, bald head of one of the grooms. Every day, he would come into Sugarfoot's stall to meticulously clean out the used shavings. This can be a dangerous shedrow chore if the stall's resident racehorse is antisocial, maybe prone to kicking out at the worker. But Michelle's groom faced a different hazard.

"Sugarfoot would follow him around, trying to put her tongue on top of his head. We'd all be cracking up, watching her." The groom was good-natured about the damp greeting, sometimes leaning over and letting Sugarfoot nuzzle his head like a puppy.

Michelle started young Thoroughbreds on their race careers by trail riding them on a large ranch. Her years as a jockey gave her a keen understanding of equine psychology. By the time the horses came to the racetrack, they were confident about riders, saddles, and open spaces. Michelle's shedrow was full of personable horses with fit physiques and calm eyes.

Like Tulsa's old trainer, Keith, Michelle believed that only happy horses could win races. Her philosophy soon proved to be sound. Within three years of getting her license, Michelle became one of the top race trainers in Texas, her well-rounded program producing consistent winners — and the occasional cheerful loser like Sugarfoot.

I WAS IMPRESSED THAT MICHELLE had once been a jockey. One of our racetrack volunteers, Deirdre, was also a jockey. A lithe, pretty woman with delicate features, Deirdre helped LOPE by taking photos of track horses, planning fundraisers, and networking with the race trainers. She regularly entertained me with tales of buck-offs and spills, her tone light, referring to her harrowing falls as being "dropped."

"I had a two-year-old last night spook in the post-parade and get loose from the pony horse. He almost hit the inside rail but ducked at the last second. I lost both my stirrups — while he ran off at top speed. I eventually got both my feet back in the stirrups and pulled him up. How I stayed on, nobody knew — but somehow I did."

Deirdre had experienced difficulties with this young horse before, commenting, "At his last race, he bucked me off in the paddock when I tried to mount him. Knocked me in the head while dropping me, too — I had a shiner for over two weeks."

Sadly for Deirdre, the rambunctious two-year-old placed fourth, qualifying for a $150,000 stakes race. She rode him in that race, too, the chance to compete for a big purse outweighing the risks, the type of nerve-wracking choice that epitomizes the jockey lifestyle.

I WAS CERTAIN SUGARFOOT would find a new home quickly. Many people were interested in adopting her — my email in-box filled with inquiries from all types of riders. Now that adoption rates were rising, I began to detect certain patterns in potential adopters, which have held true.

The hunter/jumper show competitors arrive late in expensive vehicles, toting video cameras, barn friends, and small, pampered dogs. They like to film each other riding the horse, from every angle and in every possible gait. The appointment takes twice as long as normal, culminating with several phone calls to their trainer and a frantic search for at least one runaway dog.

Dressage riders arrive promptly on time, typically sporting black breeches, clean boots, and styled hair. They stare intently at the horse's conformation, with the shoulders, back, and stride length given especially close scrutiny. They rarely ride the horses, preferring to watch their movement instead, asking, "Now do a collected trot. Now do an extended trot. Can you do a more collected extended trot?"

Western trail riders always ride the horse. They pull up in rumbling trucks, festooned with decals of cowboys kneeling at giant crosses, bring their own saddles, and invariably comment, "I can't believe these horses are Thoroughbreds. Thought they were all crazy and hyper." Zuper seems to enjoy busting their racehorse myths, strolling up to their trucks in a photogenic doze, refusing to leave until petted. By contrast, Tulsa prefers to nibble at the truck decals or steal tack from the tailgate.

Polo players are the most entertaining. If a horse catches their eye, I receive numerous calls, usually while they are riding ("Hold on, my horse is spooking at something."). Polo people prefer phone calls to email, as most aren't internet savvy, typically still using their AOL addresses from 1996. Farm visits are handled with a flair for drama, the players arriving hours late, days early, or without appointments at all.

The most elite members of the above groups always inquire about my credentials. The trail riders ask if I break colts or rope. The polo players want to know where I play polo and in which tournaments. "Who did you train with?" and "Where did you compete?" are common questions among the show riders.

I used to dread those last two questions, as they immediately exposed my lack of expertise — especially to prestigious potential adopters, a difficult group to impress. And if they aren't impressed, they don't tend to adopt — no matter how ideal the horse or reasonable the adoption fee.

At first, trying to figure out the right fee was a confusing process for me. Unlike shelter dogs or cats, horses can have genuine market value as competition mounts or breeding stock. Setting the fee too low could accidentally encourage "quick flip" auction resales. Even though our adoption contract specifically forbade such transactions, many horse welfare groups still advised me to avoid nominal or free adoptions.

On the other hand, fair market pricing for sport-horse prospects (typically ranging from $2,000 to $5,000) also didn't seem appropriate. Most of our horses had injuries or other limitations. Most of all, the ranch was a nonprofit rather than a commercial operation. Our goal was to find the horses good homes, not make sales profits.

After many consultations with experts, I structured each horse's fee to be above meat dealer price (about $400 then), but also well below the current going rate in local horse sale classifieds. This strategy seemed to work well, creating an average fee range of $500 to $1,000 (all put toward our feed, hay, and vet care budget). More limited horses, like Storm, would be on the lower part of this range, while sound, flashier mounts, like Nacho, would be on the higher side.

AS I SCHEDULED MULTIPLE APPOINTMENTS to show Sugarfoot, I remembered watching Tory and the polo pros sell expensive horses to wealthy, high-maintenance customers. It was such an elegant process — the meticulous grooming of the horses, the careful staging of the arena, the delicate balancing of hard- and soft-sell techniques. Their horse dealing was lucrative compared to our modest adoption program — a well-trained polo pony or jumper could easily sell for $20,000 or $30,000.

Tory had a master salesman's flair for showmanship. When a prospective buyer came to look at a horse, Tory had already prepared the setting. She would set up jumps in her pretty front paddock, with its views of the neighbor's ploughed fields. The sale horse would be washed, groomed, and brushed, its mane sometimes braided elaborately. Tory also often timed the appointment for when the posse would be riding, creating a feminine backdrop of long hair, fringed chaps, and polished equestrian skills.

As the potential buyer, nearly always a woman, mounted the horse, she'd look out over scenic pastures full of pumpkins ready for harvest. The posse lent a touch of Jackie Kennedy to the paddock, jumping their handsome foxhunters while exchanging pleasantries with the customer. Tory knew that, just as in Pottery Barn catalogs, associating sale items with a chic lifestyle was half the battle.

Unwittingly, I was once part of the background scenery. The posse wasn't around, and Tory had a sales appointment on the way. "Lynn, saddle up Brown and go ride in the front paddock . . . and hurry, please," she ordered. Before I could get more explicit instructions, the potential buyer arrived. A chunky brunette unwisely attired in tight breeches and tall riding boots strode into the barn.

"Oh, hello, Carol," Tory said, quickly pulling out a sleek black gelding from his stall. "This is Riley." As Carol went back to her Lexus to get her saddle, Tory turned to me. "Go out and ride around the jumps to warm up Brown. Once we're out there, jump a couple of the low jumps. And relax!"

I trotted Brown in the paddock. My only jumping lessons with Tory had consisted of hopping over logs during our trail rides. Nervously, I eyed the smallest jumps, harmless-looking poles perched over brightly colored standards. Brown, clearly anticipating what was to come, pinned her ears and bit at my boots in the stirrups.

Carol and Tory began riding in the paddock, Carol on Riley, Tory on her favorite mare. Tory made clever equestrian jokes, pointed out Riley's smooth movements, and effortlessly jumped her bay over the largest fence. Carol looked impressed, then cantered Riley around the paddock, her dark braid flying in rhythm with his strides. Tory glanced my way, nodding her head at the low jumps.

Sighing, I kicked Brown and headed for the fence. Brown lurched over the poles, her neck bouncing. I grabbed at her mane and aimed Brown at the next jump. We clomped through it, taking a clattering pole along with us. My helmet slipped down ungracefully, squishing my attempt at a posse ponytail, a one-inch tuft of blondish wispiness.

I could feel Tory's glare from the far end of the pasture. As I looked her way, she rolled her eyes to the sky — then slashed at her throat in a classic "Cut!" gesture. "Oh, Brown," she trilled as Carol rode into earshot. "Some days you just don't feel like jumping well. Poor old girl. Take her back to the barn, Lynn. Now."

I must have been a very bad catalog accessory, a pink beanbag chair placed in a sleek Art Deco living room. Carol didn't buy Riley. And I never was asked to be backdrop scenery again.

WHILE OUR RANCH WAS A FAR CRY from Tory's lush East Coast farmette, I made an effort to tidy up the round pen area for adopter visits, removing the fallen leaves, small branches, and monster weeds that flourished in its perimeter. My horse-grooming skills were sketchy, but I brushed down each horse's coat and mane, pulling out tail burrs and other signs of pasture living.

The effect was more Kmart than Pottery Barn — but it was the best catalog I could muster. Our round pen was bordered by tall pecan and cedar elm trees, their thick-branched greenery more decorative than any man-made landscaping. While our fields were never fully mowed to perfection, the horses grazed in them happily, the long grass moving softly under their bellies. White cattle egrets in search of bugs wandered with the horses, their delicate orange plumes providing splashes of accent color in the pasture. The ranch's natural beauty always outweighed any attempted makeover on my part.

Cathy, an amateur polo player from California, was drawn by Sugarfoot's short stature. She flew from the West Coast to meet Sugarfoot, the first potential adopter to ever visit from out of state. Petite and bubbly, Cathy spent quality time with Sugarfoot, marveling over her sweet face and good manners. A typical Californian, Cathy had a decidedly New Age explanation for the filly's mellow nature.

After looking up Sugarfoot's pedigree, she emailed me her theory: "March 1 foaling date. No wonder she's a sweet little wimp — she's a Pisces. I know, I know it's silly but I swear it works. Aquarian horses untie knots and open latches. Pisces horses are quiet and easy. Aries horses like to run. Geminis are hot. Taurus horses buck and are stubborn. Try it out and see if I'm not right!"

I liked Cathy, astrology and all — but Sugarfoot was sore-footed on the day she visited the ranch, nixing an immediate adoption. The farrier had trimmed Sugarfoot's hooves the day before Cathy's arrival, her long toes in need of shaping. Like many horses, Sugarfoot was a little tender after her trim session — her hooves needed some time to get used to their new shape. Cathy flew back to California, urging me to send a video of Sugarfoot when she was no longer sore, her voice warm with appreciation for the filly's good nature.

Other prospective adopters were still interested, eager to overlook temporary tender-footedness. Anna was a classic horse-show mom. A former competitor herself, she now focused on the promising show career of her teenage daughter, Brittany. With a younger daughter, Caitlyn, clamoring for a horse, Anna was in the market for another family mount. After many emails and calls, Anna sent in an application to adopt Sugarfoot. "Please call my references right away," she urged. "I can't wait to be approved and come meet Sugarfoot. She'll fit in perfectly here. Caitlyn will be so thrilled to have her first horse!"

Delighted with Anna's enthusiasm, I began calling her references. The second person on the list was Sheila, the show trainer of her older daughter, Brittany. Once a professional jump competitor, Sheila now owned a sprawling lesson and boarding barn near Waco. In addition to multiple barns and two covered arenas, the facility boasted its own saddle shop and summer camp dorms. As I dialed Sheila's cell phone number and settled comfortably in my favorite porch chair, I smiled with anticipation, imagining Sugarfoot in a family of posh show horses.

"Hello, what do you want?" said a gruff, raspy voice. Wondering if I had dialed the wrong number, I asked for Sheila. "This is she. Who is this? I'm at a horse show, so keep it quick, would you?"

I could hear horse and crowd noises in the background. Fumbling over words, I explained why I was calling: "Um, Anna gave me your name as a reference? She is thinking about adopting a horse from us, an ex-racehorse. We're LOPE, and..."

"Oh, for Christ's sake. What's she getting into now? Tell me about this so-called racehorse."

Sheila listened to my description of Sugarfoot. Within a few seconds, upon hearing the dreaded term "chestnut filly," she exploded, cutting me off in midsentence again. "No! I won't have *anything* to do with this. I don't approve at all. Rescue? Forget it!" With an emphatic beep, the cell phone equivalent of a slammed receiver, she broke off our connection.

Lisa, my hunter/jumper friend, later told me that Sheila's nickname was "Sheila Tarantula." She was known for vigorously discouraging her clients from buying horses from anyone but her. There was only one designer label allowed at Sheila's barn — her own. "She's one of the most abrasive trainers in Texas," confided Lisa.

This was a spectacular statement, given the high-maintenance types that I had found populating most show barns.

WHEN I FIRST ARRIVED IN TEXAS, desperate for a horse-related job, I interviewed for a barn assistant position at a posh farm near Dripping Springs. The stable was a fabulously luxurious eventing facility, full of arenas and cross-country jump courses.

The owner, Jackson, arrived late for the interview. An equestrian star in his twenties, Jackson was now a somewhat paunchy midfifties athlete — but still capable of dazzling jumping and dressage performances. Witty, charming, and rarely sober, Jackson split his time between chewing through barn staff and seducing the prettiest of his college-age working students.

Exuding whiskey and other unhealthy fumes, he insisted on taking me on a tour of the grounds. Escorting me to a battered "gator" (a four-wheel utility vehicle), Jackson pointed to the passenger seat. I barely had time to slide into it before he gunned the motor, driving the gator full speed along bumpy, wooded trails, lurching precariously around hairpin turns. "Over here, thash where we'll put our treehouse for campers. And maybe a wet bar? Whaddy think? Great idea, right?" Jackson laughed at his own bons mots, certain my silence reflected awe.

I turned down that job offer, but I still learned a great deal about show-horse handling there. Prior to Jackson's belated interview, the barn manager asked me to follow her around for a couple hours — so I could understand the stable's routine. A dour girl with a fireplug build, Dory explained the morning routine. "So we turn the horses out in the arena every day for two hours. That's their only time out of the stalls, so you have to watch out. They get pretty excited."

As Dory explained, show horses must be blemish free, with shining coats, in order to catch the eye of the judges. No nips or love bites, like the ones Tulsa gave Boomer, were allowed. The horses were never turned out in pastures together like our ex-racehorses — instead, they spent most of their day cooped up in luxurious, but confining, stalls.

Dory put on a huge, reinforced suede glove, like something you would use to carry an angry cat. "Now, the worst part is not the walk to the arena," she said, stopping at a big chestnut horse's stall. I tried to guess his height, mentally sizing up his sea monster presence. Horses are measured at the withers in four-inch increments called hands. The gelding flung himself around the stall, kicking at the walls, pawing the cedar shavings. "Duffer, get *back*," she bellowed, snapping a chain shank to a halter and opening the door.

"The most dangerous thing is actually releasing the horse at the arena gate." By now, she had slipped the halter on the chestnut and jerked the chain several times to get his attention. Duffer, all of 17.2 hands tall, towered over Dory, trying to run through her and out the open stall door. My eyes were getting big. Dory marched the gelding out of the barn and down to the arena.

Dory's strategy was "walk fast and yank the chain hard" — so the horse couldn't figure out how to escape. Duffer was flinging his big head and sidestepping; Dory's repeated pressure on the chain around his nose was barely registering. Dory clutched the lead rope and chain in a death grip, straining the suede glove's seams to the breaking point.

The cobbled walkway to the arena was pretty, lined with trees, flowers, and tortoiseshell barn kittens sunning themselves. A flock of grackles, the pushy dark songbirds of Texas, perched nearby, chirping loudly. As the sounds of screeching chain and smacking hooves reverberated up the path, the birds and kittens scattered before us, rapidly fleeing for cover.

We reached the arena gate, and Dory's voice tensed. "Okay, now, you open the gate. *Careful!* Don't get between him and the gate like that, he'll kick you." I pulled open the white metal gate, keeping my body behind it; once Dory and the horse were inside the arena, I closed the gate again. Duffer was coming out of his skin with excitement, smacking his lips together nervously and clenching his teeth. His powerful body skittered one way, then the other — a kick seemed imminent.

Dory stood on her toes, straining to unclip the lead rope from the halter. Duffer was leaping, even with Dory still on the other end of the lead rope. "*Quit*, quit *now*," she shrieked. Startled, he paused in midbuck, looking to see what made that freakish sound. Dory seized the moment and hopped up, unclipping the lead with a desperate swipe.

"Hurry! Open the gate, now," she panted. I obeyed and Dory catapulted out of the arena. Duffer spiraled upward, a huge chestnut-colored projectile, then landed violently — only to lurch skyward again. His hooves brushed the gate, nearly clipping Dory.

Dory was out of breath and quivering. "Okay, then, so that's all there is to it. Just take out every horse for two hours in one of the arenas." She tried to hand me the lead rope and glove. "The next horse is Branson. He is the tall gray horse in stall four. Now he can be tough, so be careful. I'm going to lunch." She flapped the glove, waiting for me to accept it.

Backing away, I told her I hadn't been hired yet, that Jackson still had to interview me, and I was supposed to meet him at noon. As I retreated to my car, pretending I had a cell phone call, I caught a glimpse of a gray horse dragging Dory down the path, her body bent nearly backward trying to slow him down. "*Quit!* No, *quit!*" wafted over the parking lot.

I CONTINUED TO FIELD INQUIRIES about Sugarfoot. Jimmy, a jovial Western rider, came to meet her next, his wife and trainer in tow. The trainer, Paula, was tanned, stocky, and in her sixties. A thick, silver ponytail flowed from under her Tractor Supply cap. "Jimmy might want to show one day, maybe Western pleasure or ranch horse versatility," she pronounced, looking at Sugarfoot closely. "I think this filly might be too small for him. Plus he'll probably outgrow her soon, with the way he's learning so fast."

Jimmy's friendly attitude outweighed his weak riding skills. Though he bounced painfully in the saddle and sometimes dropped the reins, Sugarfoot was well behaved during the ride. "Trot faster, Sugarfoot," said Jimmy, his enthusiasm evident and his balance highly suspect. Sugarfoot politely ignored his request, keeping her trot slow as Jimmy slid in his saddle, clutching the saddle horn.

Jimmy's wife, Carrie, was next. She was even less experienced than Jimmy. "Here, I'll walk beside Sugarfoot," I offered. "That way, if you feel worried, I can just reach out and hold her bridle."

Carrie was nervous but smiled gamely as Jimmy snapped photos of her. Sugarfoot walked slowly around the pen, overlooking any mixed signals from Carrie — such as when she kicked Sugarfoot's sides, then pulled on the reins. Sugarfoot kept up her steady stroll, gently carrying Carrie in more ways than one.

Paula was impressed, but for the wrong reasons. "See — that filly is more for a novice. Look at how quiet she is. Jimmy needs something with more pizzazz. And Carrie's not ready for a horse yet."

Soon after, Pam called me, full of excitement about Sugarfoot. "Lynn! The most wonderful trainer is going to call you about that red filly. She competed in the Nationals years ago. We rode together on the circuit, when I studied under the Major. You remember me telling you about Major Buddha-Chi?"

"Um, no." I'd remember a name that sounded like a Zen sorority — at least when pronounced in Pam's Georgia-Texas hybrid accent.

"Well, anyway, Abbie is top flight, still an important show trainer today. She's looking for a quiet prospect for a teenage girl. Abbie lives in Florida this time of the year, but she's very interested in the filly."

Stung by my experience with Sheila Tarantula, I reminded Pam that Sugarfoot didn't have show style conformation. Abbie would no doubt be looking for a more glamorous horse. Pam brushed aside my concerns. "Oh, Abbie just wants something quiet and sweet for this girl. It's not like she's trying to flip the filly for a big profit or something."

Abbie called me later that week. After describing her clientele and sales operation for several minutes, Abbie finally was ready to hear about Sugarfoot. "Tell me about this *adorable* filly," she commanded.

Abbie's teenage client was the daughter of a friend. "I'm not even charging her a commission to find a horse for her. They are a lovely family. The horse would have a wonderful home."

We made plans for a former student of Abbie's, a Houston resident, to assess Sugarfoot. When she arrived, Erin looked the part of a college horse-show princess turned affluent stay-at-home mom. Attired in stylish casual wear, Erin was pretty, sporty, and well coifed. She mounted Sugarfoot and assumed her best show position — head up, heels down, legs perfectly positioned behind the girth, body tilted forward, and reins wrapped around her manicured fingers.

Erin delicately tapped Sugarfoot's furry flank with her heel. No reaction. Erin tapped again, raising her reins slightly and pointing her chin higher. "Let's go," she said. Sugarfoot walked one step, then paused, uncertain about Erin's dainty requests. "She's not jumpy or nervous," I said. "You can ask her to move faster. She's not going to bolt."

Erin shot me a withering look and continued with her Tinkerbell-like foot taps. I clucked to Sugarfoot, "Go ahead, girl." She trotted off slowly, as Erin flexed herself into classic two-point position. Erin was coiled and ready to jump a course or smile at a judge, both worthy activities for the show ring, but definitely out of place in our overgrown pastures. Sugarfoot did her best to please Erin, strolling quietly along, standing still for her post-ride grooming. Her placid nature was obvious — I was proud of her.

Later that night, Abbie called from Palm Beach. "Well, Erin was *quite* concerned. Sugarfoot barely responded to her aids. And of course Erin's a *marvelous* rider. Won *everything* on the circuit in high school."

I listened, stunned — was Abbie actually saying that Sugarfoot was too quiet?

"Poor filly must have a physical problem. Is she *anemic?*"

It was an effort, a teeth-gritting grind, to keep my voice polite. "No, she's not anemic. Are you thinking she's too calm for your teenage client?"

"Well, actually — some things have changed there. She's not my client anymore. Now, I do have *another* client looking for a horse, but it's not a done deal that she'd like this little filly. And I'd have to pay shipping and maybe not get enough of a commission, so you know how it is. Maybe if her adoption fee were lower, say $300 or so, but even then, I don't know..."

The rest of Abbie's monologue faded into "blah, blah, blah" background noise for me.

Sugarfoot had performed so earnestly, riding in the hot summer sun, walking over logs, standing patiently for conformation exams, nuzzling each potential adopter hopefully. I couldn't believe they all had rejected her. My annoyance grew each time I heard Sugarfoot's flaws detailed in pretentious voices using technical, snooty terms.

Sugarfoot's talents were too modest to be of true value — she was ordinary in their eyes. Plus she wasn't coming from a well-known "finishing school" trainer like Tory or Sheila — there was no brand-name glamour attached to Sugarfoot, with just my unpolished rides on her post-racetrack résumé, the equine equivalent of a Kmart label.

Neither of us merited respect in their show world — and I was beginning to wonder if that was to our credit.

A FEW MONTHS EARLIER, the ultimate designer-label trainer had visited our ranch. Dana, a Dallas professor, was a legend on the national show jumping circuit. The other show equestrians all wanted to emulate her precise jump techniques and flashy riding style. They referred to her as "Professor Dana" in hushed tones, nearly bowing their heads in reverence for her many show wins.

I later discovered Dana also had a reputation as a bulldozer — you didn't want to oppose her in any business negotiation or equestrian competition. Despite her wealth and undisputed success as a rider, Dana approached every horse deal like a young Trump making his first real estate killing.

Dana adopted a flashy mare recently arrived at the ranch, Ruckus, a dappled gray with black legs, an especially long tail, and a kind disposition. Ruckus was made for the show ring, with her floating trot, impressive height, and gorgeous head — not to mention her utter lack of speed. Ruckus had the slowest workout times in her race barn.

Dana's freckled face, wide grin, and disheveled curly brown hair seemed out of alignment with her elite image. She looked like any other nice horse lady, dressed in loose jeans, colorful rubber boots, and grass-stained shirt. The only sign of her academic life was a pair of reading glasses hanging from her neck, librarian-style.

"What a sweet horse," she declared, petting Ruckus. "I want her. She's lovely." Delighted with the reasonable adoption fee, Dana whisked Ruckus away in her expensive trailer. Ruckus was heading off to the major leagues, to become a top-notch show horse. Thrilled to place a horse in such a pres-tigious home, Tom and I celebrated that night, toasting Ruckus with our favorite wine, a bottle of "vintage" pinot grigio sporting a $6 price tag.

But Dana returned Ruckus several weeks later. "She's lame, off at the trot," she pouted. "It's an old racing injury. A torn suspensory. I had her ultrasounded at my vet." Shocked, I took Ruckus back immediately, hop-ing that Dana wouldn't be angry about the unknown injury.

There was just one problem. Ruckus didn't have any suspensory injuries, according to her former race owner. Puzzled, I scheduled a vet exam, which revealed a fresh tendon strain, the type a young horse might get from being jumped too hard, too soon. Thinking I must have misun-derstood, I called to get Ruckus's ultrasound record from Dana's vet. But it had vanished — there wasn't a copy in the office files.

When Dana had left, our refund check in her pocket, she had paused and rolled down her truck window. "Now, Lynn," she said, pitching her voice over the diesel rumble. "Please do think of me *first*, before anyone else, if you get another horse like Ruckus. I'd love to get first crack at any nice ones you have here. I know it wasn't your fault about Ruckus, you just didn't know. No hard feelings."

But now I did know — and there were a few hard feelings.

DISCOURAGED, I considered keeping Sugarfoot myself — just to avoid watching her get rejected again. But one day, a couple contacted me. They were looking for a gentle horse for their daughter, Desirée. She was twenty years old, but developmentally disabled with Angelman syndrome, a neurological disorder that impairs motor skills and cognitive function. Desirée couldn't speak and gestured wildly to communicate. Riding helped her coordination and soothed her troubled nervous system.

For the past few years, Desirée had ridden her own horse, a palomino gelding named Domino. But sadly, Domino had been put down due to illness a few months ago, and Desirée was inconsolable.

Sanjuanita, Desirée's mother, and I talked for a long time on the phone, discussing possible ideas for a new horse. She explained that Desirée had always been exposed to horses but that her condition kept her from understanding danger. It was critical that Desirée ride only gentle horses, preferably ones with special training for carrying disabled riders.

After our talk, Sanjuanita emailed me. "Desirée, my husband Ronald, and I have a big soft spot in our hearts for horses. We believe that the reason Desirée walks today is because we have exposed her to horseback riding since she was five. We're ready to open our hearts to another special horse."

They came to see Sugarfoot shortly afterward. Desirée had brown pigtails and striking, almond-shaped eyes. Dressed in jeans and a T-shirt, she looked like any other teenager from a distance. As I came closer, I could see Desirée's unusual, fast-moving gestures. Sanjuanita and Ron were calm and matter-of-fact with her, easily interpreting her special language of body movements and non-worded sounds.

"Desi, look," her father said. "This is Sugarfoot." Desirée seemed confused, then happy — she whacked the filly's neck and head, a form of enthusiastic hug. "Not so hard, Desi," said Sanjuanita, tossing me an apologetic look. But Sugarfoot wasn't offended by the bombastic greeting. She stood still, looking at Desirée with curious, friendly eyes.

Within minutes, Desirée's saddle was on Sugarfoot, followed by Desirée herself. Desirée sat on Sugarfoot while her father led the filly in our round pen. Excited, Desirée waved her arms and cried, perhaps thinking of Domino. Suddenly Sugarfoot stopped dead — no amount of tugging on the lead rope could convince her to move forward. First her father, then I pulled on the halter, urging Sugarfoot to walk. Politely, but firmly, she refused, her face placid but her feet fixed.

Her mother went to comfort Desirée and discovered she had slid off center in the saddle. As soon as Desirée's position was adjusted back in balance with the saddle, Sugarfoot walked forward again — with one ear tipped back, listening for Desirée.

It was clear that Sugarfoot was protecting Desirée, that this little red filly with the funny build had a true, deep vocation to be a therapeutic riding horse. Awed, we watched as Desirée and Sugarfoot walked together, with Sugarfoot always listening, always careful to keep her steps slow for her special rider.

The next day, Sanjuanita gave the official thumbs-up. "Sugarfoot is everything you described her and then some. I think she was exceptionally sweet (her name is perfect) and sensitive to Desirée's special needs. We felt like we can trust her not to act crazy. Also, I can develop my skills as I train her more, to understand leg aids and verbal commands. We can grow together."

Sanjuanita reassured me that Desirée's emotional outburst wasn't a sign that she was frightened of Sugarfoot. On the contrary — Desirée was smitten. "On our way home, we were talking about Sugarfoot, and Desi would stare out the window, looking for her."

Sanjuanita and Ron adopted Sugarfoot, impressed with her sensitivity to Desirée, an innate, unschooled trait that could only be called talent. When they came to pick her up a few days later, Desirée stayed in the truck, excited and agitated. As they drove off, Desirée turned her head, gazing at me through the back window, her shyness put aside for a moment. She suddenly grinned, giving me a flash of the undamaged child inside her, a girl thrilled with her new pony, a sweet pet she will always love and never outgrow.

I grinned back, for once pleased with my Kmart-level training proficiency.

PART IV

The Unbroken

It is not enough for a man to know how to ride;
he must know how to fall.

MEXICAN PROVERB

CHAPTER NINE

Spider, Part II

MONTHS HAD PASSED without a frightening vet crisis or a challenging horse to handle. Most of the new horses were on rehab — my last steady riding project had been easygoing Sugarfoot. Finally, I could settle into a more peaceful routine at the farm, maybe even take a short trip somewhere pleasant and hay free with Tom.

The horses and I weren't the only ones changing careers. After creating our new website, logo, and marketing materials, Tom amassed a small, but attractive, design portfolio. His last temp assignment, in the marketing division of a software company, had given him an opportunity to showcase his creative skills. The department head took notice and offered Tom a full-time job as a web and graphic designer. This past month, several bottles of budget pinot grigio had been consumed in celebration (and relief).

There was just one nagging worry at the back of my mind. No one wanted Spider. Since his snakebite, all of his equine family had been adopted. He was now the last of Debbie's horses at the ranch. Even worse, his favorite pasture buddies, such as Big John and Windy, had been adopted, too.

Spider had recovered quickly from his rattlesnake attack in summer 2005. His nose was scar free and his neck bore no signs of the temporary tracheotomy site, now fully healed. Within a week of the snakebite, he was back to normal, splashing troughs and following visitors around the ranch. But three months had passed since then, and still no one was interested in adopting him.

Spider was cute, sweet, and personable — but he wasn't started under saddle. People prefer their riding horses to already know how to be ridden, and there was little market for unbroken geldings. Especially Thoroughbreds — even ones with regal pedigrees like Spider's.

Spider was bred by Debbie, a vivacious Texas transplant from Michigan. Over time, Debbie's farm had gradually become her full-time job. She was a dedicated breeder, with a thoughtful approach to pedigrees. "I did a lot of research and discovered which bloodlines produce sound, sane horses — ones that tend to be well built and very athletic."

To top off Spider's good breeding, his dam was Alice, the head mare in Debbie's broodmare herd. With her superb conformation and near-human intelligence, Alice was a formidable mother. Debbie bought Alice as a weanling, a surprise purchase and her first mare.

"I actually went to the farm to look at a different mare. But while I was there, a little filly, about nine months old, was in the next paddock. She came up to the fence to say hi and we exchanged greetings. Then she whipped around, tried to nail me with her hind feet, and took off at breakneck speed. I just fell in love with her. Who can say why?" Debbie laughed, Alice's youthful hostility now a nostalgic tale.

Back then, Debbie's main experience with racing had been as a fan. When it came time to have Alice trained to race, she picked a trainer because his farm was nearby. "The day the trainer came to pick Alice up to start training, my mom and I were very excited. We decided to 'pretty her up' for the trainer. I am embarrassed to say I bought a bunch of hair barrettes — little pink plastic bows — that we clipped down her mane after spiffing her up with a bath. The trainer thought we were complete idiots. And he was right."

Over time, Debbie became more savvy, studying racing and Thoroughbred bloodlines carefully. She came up with a very specific breeding plan, one that would have taken twenty years to complete. Unfortunately, her strategy was cut short by unforeseen circumstances, poor health forcing her to end the breeding program prematurely.

And so Debbie donated Spider and eight members of his equine family to LOPE, unwilling to see her prized homebreds and broodmares sold to the general public at auction. All of them (except Spider) had found homes quickly, their good looks and pedigrees a powerful draw for adopters.

My stomach tightened whenever I saw Spider standing forlornly in his pasture, trying to make friends with the new horses. Unless I helped him, he might never find a new home. Unfortunately for Spider, my experience with young, unbroken horses was pretty minimal — and not very pleasant.

TORY HAD ONCE PRESSED ME INTO HELPING her break one of her horses, a sulky teenager type named Bonita. I wasn't much of a training assistant — my only goal was to avoid being mauled by the malevolent Bonita, a priority that didn't sit well with Tory.

"Lynn! Pay attention — don't get me killed!" Tory sounded annoyed, no doubt regretting my presence in the stall. That morning, she had assigned me to be part of the "saddle and ride Bonita" project. My orders were to get in the stall and lead Bonita, while Tory sat on her back for the first time.

Bonita was a hellacious youngster. A three-year-old chestnut Thoroughbred draft cross (or mix), she had a broad back and stocky hindquarters. Her ears were sometimes pinned in annoyance, sometimes friendly and forward — and always unpredictable. Sometimes Bonita pinned one ear while simultaneously pricking the other up in a jaunty position. I learned to always believe the pinned ear.

"She *must* move forward. *Lynn!* Wake up, you're asleep at the wheel."

Not asleep — petrified with fear. To me, unbroken horses were like huge feral dogs, scary and primal. Especially while crammed in a small stall with me. I held the end of Bonita's lead rope, nervously dropping it whenever Tory snapped a new command my way. I had no idea what to do, and Tory's impatient, cryptic comments confused me even more: "Walkies, Lynn, walkies!" "She can't plant, okay? It's dangerous." "Lead her *away* from my leg." "Faster! Can't you see she's propping?"

Tory's narrowed eyes and edgy tone warned me not to ask questions. But none of her statements made any sense. Propping? Planting? Walkies? My ever-fertile imagination conjured up an image of a walkie-talkie, leaning Pisa-like in a garden patch.

In spite of the cool morning, sweat wound its way between my shoulders. A large filly can be tremendously intimidating — especially when a rider mounts her for the first time ever. My sole objective was to avoid being bitten or kicked by Bonita, whose ears were now flying backward every few seconds.

Bonita and I already had a troubled relationship. She liked to walk into me in the pasture, shouldering me frat-boy-style, often going out of her way to intersect my path midfield. Having me trapped in a small space was a special bonus treat — Bonita pondered my shins with malevolent pleasure, lurching toward me aggressively.

Tory had already hopped on her back gracefully, a riding crop in her hand. As I did my best to drag Bonita around the stall, Tory tapped her rump with the crop, creating instant flinches in my shoulders. I was certain Bonita would jump away from the crop and into me, a good target with my proximity and slow reflexes. Unlike Sugarfoot, Bonita epitomized the stereotype of a chestnut filly — smart, mean, and inclined toward ambush.

The barn ceiling wasn't terribly high. Tory's head seemed perilously close to it, her thick, red hair no substitute for a helmet if Bonita decided to rear up and whack her into the beams. Tory barked a steady stream of orders, my hands stiffened in the cold, and Bonita planted her front hooves on my heels, bringing me to near-disastrous trips twice.

Tory kept up her patter of near insults. "Why are you nervous? I'm the one in danger here. Lynn! Pay attention!"

My lips and shoulders tightened simultaneously. I marched in the stall, hauling Bonita and Tory around, my fear overcome by juvenile rebelliousness. Tory's head whipped from side to side. Bonita looked surprised at my sudden energy.

I stalked through every inch of the dark stall, hauling Bonita through the cedar shavings as chicken feathers wafted down from the rafters. The farm hens perched on the ceiling beams, their bright eyes staring down at us. Tory hunched in the saddle, holding the crop up like a talisman.

I could see my breath in the chill and sped up, trying to keep warm. Surely Tory would approve of my tempo now, call it a day, maybe even invite me into the barn office for coffee and donuts.

"Don't *yank* her, Lynn — Jesus, poor Bonita, getting your head ripped off."

Poor Bonita? Glaring down at my boots, I shook poultry debris out of my hair. The training session ended soon after, with several dirty looks flying between Bonita, Tory, and me.

MY SECOND (AND LAST) COLT TRAINING experience hadn't been much better. Soon after I started teaching lessons at Bobbie's stable, I was hired to work with a mare named Rocket, a friend of a friend's horse at a local boarding barn. Rocket's owner had called me. "I hear you exercise horses. Can you break mine to saddle again? She got broken a year ago but hasn't been ridden since." Strapped for income, I couldn't turn down the offer of $600 for "rebreaking" Rocket. Poverty fueled my hubris in those early Austin days.

A pretty buckskin who shared Bonita's hostile personality, Rocket sized me up quickly. Instead of trotting sedately around the perimeter, she liked to charge me in the round pen, sometimes throwing in a rear or two for good measure. I learned to wave my arms and fling the lead rope, to discourage her from plowing into me.

Rocket had a long, black mane that flew in all directions when she shook her head angrily. She'd follow up the rock star hair display with a series of vicious faces, baring her teeth and curling her lips into werewolf scowls.

I round-penned her for weeks, well past the usual thirty-day deadline for basic colt training. Thanks to her previous training, Rocket was relaxed about carrying a saddle, rarely bucking. Instead, she'd threaten to kick me while I tightened the girth, deftly smacking at my hand with her hind foot. But once saddled, Rocket trotted and loped around the pen without much fuss. It was me, not the saddle, that annoyed her.

Every session ended the same way. Donning my helmet, I'd put my foot in the stirrup, then hop up and hold myself against her left flank, clinging to the Western saddle horn. Rocket would turn her head and lift her upper lip, showing one or two teeth. I'd hastily jump back down, too cowed by her dental display to swing my leg over and mount her.

I did eventually ride her, uneasily, both of us certain that she had the upper hand (or hoof). She felt like a table on wheels under my legs — her body wobbled in unexpected directions as she tried to adjust to my weight. Even off balance, Rocket still managed to convey contempt for my presence, glaring at me over her shoulder and snaking her head back and forth.

THE MEMORIES OF BONITA, Tory, and Rocket were more discouraging than helpful. Clearly, Spider needed a real trainer, someone skilled with colts and first-time rides. He'd already been through enough, with his snake trauma — it didn't seem fair to inflict my training ignorance on him as well.

But our budget was still too small to hire a colt specialist like Cory or AJ, the Mormon cowboy. Their rates were several hundred dollars per month, a figure wildly out of reach for the LOPE checkbook. Our budget relied heavily on donations from the general public. Since my fundraising skills weren't much better than my colt-starting talents, I had to be careful about any unnecessary expenses. Hay, grain, and vet care were essential costs — colt trainers were luxuries we couldn't quite afford. And so far I'd crossed paths with only one trainer who was open to discounting his services.

Jed was the most colorful cowboy I had ever met. He called one day, asking about mares to adopt. Although we didn't have any available at the time, Jed suggested we meet in person anyway, "just to be neighborly" — even though he lived three hours away. Enticed by a possible good home for future mares, I agreed to visit his property and confirm it was suitable for LOPE's adoption requirements.

The following weekend, I met Jed at a large cattle ranch deep in the Texas Hill Country. A large, beefy man with a long red beard and Mad Max–style sun goggles, he epitomized apocalyptic sci-fi film chic. Ushering me into a dilapidated, brown truck, Jed announced he was going to give me a tour of his breeding operation.

"Careful there, don't jostle the beer." Jed gestured at the truck floor. Wedged between the gearshift and overflowing ashtray was a twelve-pack of Bud Lite. "You like Jimmy Buffet, don't you? Everybody does." Jed didn't wait for my reply, twisting his volume knob to high. "Cheeseburger in Paradise" blared, Jed hit the gas, and we were off, slamming through mesquite and scrubby underbrush.

Out of the wooded foliage scattered several multicolored horses: duns, grullas, buckskins, roans. "These mares of mine are top quality. They were all born hunting a cow," shouted Jed. "And my ol' roan stallion is Easy Jet bred. Then I got another young stud colt, straight son of the Dash lines with a speed index that'll blow your mind." Balancing a beer on his lap, Jed steered between two chunky paint mares as they darted from the sound of truck axles whacking into grass-covered gullies.

My head hit the truck roof — thunk-thunk — every couple of minutes. Jimmy Buffet blasted and Jed talked nonstop, his voice drowned out by the music and frequent beer chugs. He looked over at me every few sentences, clearly expecting a response — I nodded weakly, clung to the decaying seat, and hoped it would all end soon.

After what seemed like hours, Jed turned off the ignition, ending a deafening bray of "I blew out my flip-flop, stepped on a pop top." As I waited for my ears to regain function, Jed explained he wanted Thoroughbred mares to cross with his stallion. "I want to get into that eventing horse market. They'll pay top dollar for a good-looking horse with solid bone and speed."

All too soon, Jed started up the truck's engine again — it was time to head back. The trip culminated with Jed abruptly pulling over in the middle of a residential access road. "It's time," he announced, his speech slurring as he stumbled out to answer the call of nature on the side of the truck. Fortunately, not the passenger side — where I sat, determinedly averting my eyes.

It was a memorable afternoon.

Jed called me several times afterward, offering his horse-training services. He also had lots of advice about ranch management, usually delivered in long monologues on my voice mail, accompanied by the sounds of pop tops cracking open.

SCARRED FROM THE JED EXPERIENCE, I was leery of hiring bargain trainers. Instead, I studied more of Cory's horse-training tapes about colt starting and tried to work up the nerve to start Spider myself. The videos were fascinating but also confusing.

"Pet him!" Ray Hunt's voice boomed off camera. He was shouting at a young cowboy on a dun-colored colt. The young horse was starting to buck, his rider balancing precariously with each lurch. The cowboy shot a look of dismay at Ray — why would he pet a horse that was misbehaving? The colt then flung him off, galloping to the other side of the paddock. "I'm glad he bucked you off, Bill. That's been coming all morning, no surprise at all," chuckled Ray. Bill picked himself up, dusting off his chaps, trying to convert his grimace into a rueful smile.

In another scene, a group of cowboys were paired with unbroken horses at a large cattle ranch. Ray's clinic was an annual event — the season's two-year-old colt crop was saddle trained under Ray's tutelage. Each ranch hand performed the same ritual — put a rope halter on the colt, then twirl and gently pull out the lead rope, encouraging the young horse to follow its movements.

As I watched each pair go through the same strange dance, Ray shouted out encouragement from atop his husky chestnut gelding. "Careful, Jim. You got the slippery one." Jim's small black filly darted evasively from the rope, flicking her tail rapidly. "Nice job, Buddy. That's a nice change." Buddy, a slight boy who looked no older than eighteen, glowed under Ray's praise, his paint gelding following him quietly.

"Okay, they've had enough of this stuff. Go get your saddles," Ray ordered.

I wondered how they would get the saddles on the colts. There must be some special technique, a precise series of steps, to convince the unbroken horses to accept forty pounds of leather on their backs. Eager to learn, I leaned forward and watched the screen closely.

The cowboys led their colts to the corral fence, where they had stashed their big Western saddles. Several fumbled around, hesitantly hefting the saddles near their colts, but not lifting them very high. "What are you waiting for?" came Ray's voice. "Saddle them up!" And then they did.

The older ranch hands calmly placed the saddles on their colts, then deftly drew the cinches snug. The newer cowboys took longer, which seemed to make their horses nervous, maybe giving them too much time to think about the saddle headed their way. "The horse is ready, are you?" Ray was an omniscient presence, his comments wafting over each cowboy-colt pair.

Soon every colt was carrying a saddle — and a cowboy. With little fanfare, the riders simply climbed aboard the colts, stopping on the way to pet their necks and bounce in the stirrup a few times before settling into the saddle. "Just let them go where they want. Don't let them stop for too long. And *pet* them," said Ray.

Jim's slippery filly took off, trotting rapidly, then loping. "Hang in there," laughed Ray. "You'll make it. Pet her!" The filly slowed, licking her lips, as Jim rubbed her neck, then turned her head around, her nose touching his knee. "That's the way, Jim. A good change."

Frustrated, I rewound the tape again and again. What was the technique?

What did the cowboys do — besides put the saddles on and mount up? I wondered if Ray prepped them before the video somehow, maybe giving out instruction sheets on how to ride the colts. "Pet them!" seemed to be Ray's most repeated command. Followed by "What are you waiting for?"

None of this made sense, although it was clear that Ray's approach worked. By the end of his video, the colts were all riding quietly with their cowboys. But Ray's technique ran counter to what I had heard about colt starting from my Texas sources.

Our long-gone ex-neighbor Jesse had volunteered his colt opinions on our first meeting, proud of his twenty years of horse experience. His round pen included a wooden stake cemented into the center. Called a "snubbing post," it was used to subdue less-cooperative colts: the trainer would tie the young horse tightly to it, on a short lead, in order to force obedience and submission. "You gotta learn them good who's in charge" — this was Jesse's philosophy, taught to him by his father. Such outdated techniques were ineffective but still entrenched in traditional horse training.

Woody, our farrier, used a two-man approach. "You need someone on horseback, on a quiet, old gelding, to pony you on the colts. Keeps 'em from bucking and makes 'em move forward. You gotta keep them moving forward. Be sure his horse is quiet, though — otherwise they both start bucking and you're up a creek. And wear spurs."

AJ, the Mormon cowboy who promised "We eat broncs for breakfast," liked to work with colts by himself, one-on-one. Supremely confident of his skills, he preferred handling difficult horses — the easy ones bored him. I once watched AJ work with a big roan gelding. The horse was young and rambunctious, fighting the reins and bucking, then bolting out of the ring. AJ smiled and sat back in his huge roping saddle, pleased by the roan's challenge. Unruffled, he rode out the gelding's thirty-minute-plus tantrum. By the end of the session, the roan was tired but compliant, his taste for bad behavior exercised away. "It ain't his fault," drawled AJ. "He's just young and full of himself. No one ever told him that he wasn't the boss."

I quickly ruled out Jesse's snubbing post, and AJ's solo colt wrangling was not for the faint of heart, like me. Yet Ray Hunt's "pet them and get on" approach seemed like it wouldn't work for me either. I wasn't quite ready for such a bold, relaxed technique. Noting Woody and Tory's preference for using a colt-starting helper, I pondered my options. Maybe I could hire a day laborer?

SOMETIMES THE RANCH ATTRACTED VISITORS in search of work. Battered trucks pulled into our driveway, their occupants rasping, "These horses for sale? How much? I got cash. I can trade work for 'em."

I was regularly accosted at our highway mailbox, 1970s-era cars halting by the gate, brakes squealing, followed by questions shouted through rolled-down windows.

"You want any farm help, lady?"

"You got a farrier yet? I'm one. Got cheap rates. Cash only."

"Need horses broke?" This from an elderly Latino man with a long knife strapped to his belt and a tattered shirt open to the waist.

A Jamaican cowboy offered his services, loping up our driveway on a skittering, sweaty, foam-covered palomino. "My name's Elmo," he grinned, displaying several gold teeth. "I ride my horses along the highway — helps 'em get over being spooky." His filly panted beneath him, too tired to glance up.

Tom and I began locking our big front gate shut with a chain and padlock. Towering about fifteen feet high, the gate merged into white stone walls on either side. The system wasn't perfect — the chain was long, bulky, and easy to drop while adjusting the padlock. But as long as the gate remained chained, drive-by intrusions by the underbelly of rural Texas faded significantly.

With this in mind, a one-day worker seemed like a bad bet for my colt-starting needs. I considered enlisting a volunteer, someone who was interested in helping a charity training project. But I wasn't too sure about that either, based on a recent encounter with a would-be helper.

The ranch chores were tiring; we never had time to do them all. Tom put a plea for volunteer help on our website. Gracie contacted me soon after, her email full of excitement at the prospect of volunteering. She described herself as in her forties and physically fit. Something in her email raised a faint warning bell — she was so eager, almost insistent on setting up a visit as soon as possible. Still, I appreciated her desire to help. We set a tentative date for one summer afternoon, but a flu-filled household foiled the plan — I was under the weather that day, nixing the visit.

After napping fitfully, I woke up with a start as Sophie barked loudly. Looking out the window, expecting to see Sophie's nemesis (an obese squirrel who patrolled our porch with impunity), I instead spotted a stranger on our ranch. Even worse, the trespasser was with one of our horses — and appeared to be dancing around the young filly.

My flu headache pounded. Something else pounded, too, as I remembered that our front gate was locked. I jogged down the driveway to the pasture.

A woman dressed in vaguely yogalike garb, all loose folds and pinkish purple pastel colors, was crooning to the annoyed filly, hovering around her. The woman laughed as the filly pinned her ears; she was having some kind of bizarre New Age moment with a horse that was seriously contemplating kicking her.

"Oh, helllooo!" The yoga lady beamed up at me, completely misunderstanding the zeal of my approach. "I'm Gra—"

"What are you doing with that horse?" I growled, interrupting her with a short speech that ended abruptly with, "You need to leave. Now."

Gracie's fantasy faltered, her shocked face reflecting the ferocity of my greeting.

It was a short, but tension-laden walk to our gate, as I accompanied her down the driveway. Gracie's compact car was illegally parked on the shoulder of Highway 21. Our gate was still locked, but opened to the full length of the chain. Gracie had pushed the gate as far as she could, then shimmied her slim frame through the narrow opening, completely disregarding our lock, trespassing in the name of equine mind melding.

As I related the story to Tom over dinner — my tale full of phrases like "How dare she," "Should have let the filly kick her," and "Crazy lady" — I realized I didn't sound like a respectable DC accountant anymore. Instead I was talking like a farm owner, a protector of my herd, a rancher who gets mad, not scared, when a trespasser appears — you know, like a Texan.

Could raising meat goats for fun and profit be far behind?

PERHAPS INSPIRED BY MY BUDDING INNER COWGIRL, I got tired of waiting for the right helper or discount trainer. As Cory would say, it was time to "git 'er done." One day I led Spider to the round pen. He was cheerful as usual, happy to be the center of attention. His big eyes took in the round pen, my saddle sitting on the fence, and the other horses grazing nearby. Zuper stood by the fence, watching us both, no doubt prepared to dial 911 if needed.

Zuper's "I got your back" expression boosted my morale — at least I had a helper now. I began working with Spider in the round pen, asking him to walk, then trot, then canter while keeping away from me in the center. Spider was willing if somewhat uncoordinated, his puppy legs still getting used to his growing, three-year-old body. After a few revolutions around the pen, we were both getting bored.

Holding my breath, I put my old polo saddle on him and tightened the girth. I hopped back quickly, certain Spider was going to buck at the weight of the saddle. Spider watched me hop, a playful look in his eyes — clearly he thought this was some kind of game.

I led him around, so he could feel the saddle on his back. No reaction. Baffled, I let him loose in the pen again and shooed him away. Spider trotted around, looking like a seasoned saddle veteran, without a single sign of bared teeth or wild mane shaking. Still, I was wary. One of the track trainers, Shawn, had recently recounted a near-fatal encounter with a young horse.

Shawn had a mop of white hair, permanently tanned skin, and kind blue eyes. A devout Christian, he laced his conversations with many

references to Jesus and God's will. But Shawn retained the racetrack's
carnival-style speech patterns, his rapid-fire delivery sometimes overpowering his pious language. He ultimately reconciled his religion and
career, donating a hefty percentage of his best horse's winnings to the local
church.

He said, "All those old church ladies, they'd shake their head and tsk
tsk at me for being involved in racing and gambling. But then when my
horse would win and bring a big donation to the collection plate, well —
they came around, know what I mean?"

Shawn was especially pleased that his horse's name was Bold Reply.
"Whenever someone asks me if race gambling is a sin, I just give them a
Bold Reply."

Shawn's colt-related incident had been unexpected. The two-year-old
had been standing in his stall when Shawn came in. His intention was to
clean out the stall, a normal shedrow chore that rarely troubles the racehorses. But the colt was having a moody day, typical of any male teenager,
and decided he wasn't happy about Shawn's presence.

"He just up and kicked out at my head. I wasn't even looking at him,
didn't see it coming. But something told me to duck — his hooves hit the
wall right where my head had been a second earlier. The good Lord was
taking care of me that day. I'd have died on the spot otherwise. These
young colts, they're real unpredictable sometimes. Seem like they're going
along fine, then all of sudden, boom, they blow up on you."

Shawn's dramatic story still fresh in my mind, I stared suspiciously at
Spider's back feet, ready to duck if needed. But Spider and his hooves were
relaxed and nonthreatening. Even after I hopped in the stirrup and held
my torso over the saddle, there still wasn't any reaction from Spider. Other
than a yawn or two. Still, I was wary and didn't ride him, despite the
positive signals. Never one to be self-delusional, I knew this outcome
couldn't be due to my flustered technique.

I called Debbie later that day, asking her if she had started Spider under
saddle and just forgot to tell me. She laughed. "No. But he used to watch

while we trained his brothers. He seemed really interested in the whole deal. Maybe he taught himself."

Debbie home raised all of her racehorses, handling them from when they were foals and exposing them to halters, lead ropes, and saddles from an early age. By the time they were old enough to be ridden, her horses already trusted people and were familiar with tack. She created confident, relaxed young horses from the start — proving Ray Hunt's often-repeated point that "the long way is the short way."

Also, Debbie's horses had a genetic head start, thanks to her breeding strategy. "To me, all good horses are sound, well put together, and sane. It doesn't matter if you're talking about riding horses or racing horses. I've purchased horses that didn't meet those criteria and always regretted it," explained Debbie. As she delved deeper into Thoroughbred pedigree history, an older sire named Prince John caught her eye as the epitome of her ideal horse.

"My stallion was a grandson of Prince John and great-grandson of Princequillo, one of the greatest racehorses ever. One big issue with me was all the chatter about how horses aren't sound now and have such short careers compared to in the past. I wanted to counter that by going back to older bloodlines, the ones that delivered soundness and stamina — as well as speed."

Debbie was ahead of her time, painstakingly developing her breeding philosophy over several years. Later, the tragic injury of Eight Belles at the 2008 Kentucky Derby would create intense scrutiny of the same Thoroughbred breeding practices she disdained. Compared to Seabiscuit's era, the best performing racehorses today run fewer races for higher purses. And the most lucrative phase of a racehorse's career can come well after his last race — if the horse is able to stand at stud.

This trend tends to produce blazing fast, precocious young runners — but it does little to prove their pedigree's endurance, according to breeders like Debbie. A predisposition toward bone chips and cysts can be common in these bloodlines, creating more chance for serious injury under athletic stress.

Debbie chose well with a Princequillo descendant. Princequillo was an iron horse, often called the best long-distance horse in American history. Princequillo was the leading overall sire in North America for 1957 and 1958, but he also was a leading broodmare sire, his daughters foaling the most winners for eight years. Prince John, grandfather of Debbie's stallion, was clearly a chip off Princequillo's block, with an impressive set of progeny.

Although he died in 1979 at age twenty-six, Prince John was still the leading broodmare sire in 1979, 1980, 1982, and 1986. Earlier he had been the leading juvenile sire, fathering two-year-olds with the highest earnings in 1969. Prince John's offspring included 55 stakes winners, and he was the broodmare sire of 172 stakes winners — including Spider's grandfather, Blushing John (a winner of over $1.5 million).

"His bloodlines were fading and I didn't think they should," asserted Debbie. "His progeny were good-looking, fast, sound, and known to have good minds. When I say fast, they were fast over distance — not the sprinters. I liked the longer races, so I never was aiming for sprinters — I wanted distance horses. Contrarian all the way, I guess."

Spider's gene pool was rich with racing heritage and classic sport-horse pedigrees. He represented much of the best of Debbie's plan, with his intelligence and sensible temperament. Under his gangly teenage frame peeked the bones and substance of a well-built, mature horse, the horse Spider would become with time. However, unlike the elegant, statuesque Princequillo, Spider would always fall on the cute, rather than handsome, side of attractive.

Even amateurs like me could start Debbie's unbroken horses because she prepared such a solid foundation in them, covering both the "nature" and "nurture" sides of the equation. Spider's ability to homeschool himself let me off the hook — he was easy to train and did most of the work without me. The first time I rode him was anticlimactic, without any Bonita or Rocket theatrics. Spider seemed pleased to have me aboard, his steps slow and contented. Within a few minutes, we both forgot that it was Spider's first ride ever.

By the tenth ride, Spider and I were trotting over poles spread out in the pasture, a precursor to jumping. Spider's springy strides and pricked ears signaled a jumper in the making — he seemed to genuinely enjoy the pole exercise. I consulted with Lisa, my hunter/jumper friend. On her advice, I set up more poles on top of buckets, my inelegant method of creating jumps, and asked Spider to hop over them while cantering riderless around the pen.

His eyes lit up as he headed for the first makeshift obstacle. Spider cleared it with a foot to spare, a delighted look of "Hey, can we do that *again?*" on his face. Excited, I updated his website listing, describing his new "started under saddle" and "shows aptitude for jumping" status. Tom took photos of me riding Spider, capturing his cheerful expression and long stride length.

Finally, Spider's calm riding, smooth gaits, and happy disposition caught the eye of a family hunter/jumper show barn. The entire stable came to visit Spider. A big van and stock trailer pulled into our driveway, rocking with noise and excitement. With a cascade of giggles, a pack of girl students burst from the van, ranging in age from ten to sixteen.

Spider was fussed over immediately. "He's so *adorable,*" pealed one girl. "I like his hip," said a teen, trying to be objective. As Spider nuzzled her, she added, "And his kind eye. What a sweet face." As the oldest girl rode him around the pen, grinning, I smiled, too. He would never win the Kentucky Derby or be a leading broodmare sire, but Spider's lineage still had guaranteed a successful career.

Spider was adopted to become a show horse in training, and he has since excelled wonderfully. "He is so *easy* to work with," a recent email gushed. "We think he is going to have excellent form over fences." And Spider's new barn soon discovered his secret obsession — bananas. The girl student cadre carefully fed him whole ones, peel and all, laughing at his blissful expression.

I can't truly say I started Spider under saddle — Debbie and his big brothers deserve the credit for that. But I did get to ride him first, the highlight of my dubious (and now happily defunct) colt-starting career. No more unbroken horses for me — that was a challenge better left to more skilled, "real" horsemen. At least, so I thought at the time — but the horses had something else in mind for me.

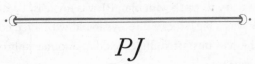

CHAPTER TEN

PJ

THE PEACEFUL STREAK OF LUCK at the ranch slammed to an end with PJ, one of our young geldings. Late one night, I walked around the ranch, enjoying the scent of hay and contented horse. My good mood vanished as PJ kicked his heels up over the fence. I didn't see the kick in the dark, just felt the hair lift on my neck — then heard cable screeching against something, a something that turned out to be PJ's hind leg hitting the fence on the way down.

Never one to think his way out of a problem, PJ yanked his hind leg harder — I was witnessing an ugly violin recital, with PJ's leg as the bow, the cable fencing as strings. It didn't end on a good note, with a large gash on PJ's hock.

My flashlight revealed a big pocketlike tear on his inner hind "elbow." This is the worst place for a cut — near the large hock joint, an infection-prone location notorious for its difficulty to bandage. In the mud, at midnight — and on a young gelding renowned for his low levels of coordination and intelligence.

As I grabbed the hose to wash the wound, it began to rain. PJ spooked at the drops splatting on him. Closing my eyes, I envisioned the long days ahead wrapping his leg. PJ was scared of the water hose, and contrary to normal horse physics, he would spook *toward* things that frightened him. As I rinsed his leg, PJ lurched at the hose (and me), slipping in the mud.

When in doubt, panic and run into things — this was PJ's philosophy on life. It was scary to work with him; PJ was my least favorite horse on the ranch. He was a big, stocky three-year-old with a red coat and blaze face — and he was unstarted under saddle, another unbroken gelding donated by a race trainer.

In his two months at the farm, PJ had frustrated me with his commitment to silly behavior. No matter how patient the handler, PJ was always on the edge of a minor freak-out. It seemed almost defiant, this utter inability to learn or process new information. After numerous experiences with PJ tromping on my feet, yanking lead ropes from my hands, and sidestepping into me, my concern had morphed into active dislike.

PJ not only didn't race; he had never been fully trained to ride. About a week into his under-saddle training, he came up lame. His race owner and trainer took him to the vet — X-rays revealed a congenital bone cyst in his ankle, which ended PJ's racing career before it started. PJ could be a trail or pleasure horse, but he would never do hard sports like jumping or barrel racing.

Bone cysts are usually formed during the first year of a horse's growth. In normal development, the cartilage tissue gradually calcifies into hard bone. If a portion of cartilage doesn't calcify, due to poor nutrition or a congenital defect, the bone forms around it instead. An island of soft tissue remains, creating athletic weakness, especially if located in joint areas.

PJ's owner was a young race trainer, just starting out. A clean-cut, Norman Rockwell–looking fellow with blond hair and sunburned cheeks, Justin took his hard luck matter-of-factly. He donated PJ instead of sending him off to auction — he was kind to his horses and wanted PJ to find a good home.

"The only thing I'm mad about is the breeder," said Justin. "PJ is the second horse we got from him. The first one we bought had the same kind of problem. No way I'd get another horse there — either his stallion passes down leg trouble or he's not taking care of the foals right."

Although PJ had the build of a dairy cow, he was turned out like a show horse when he arrived. Justin and his wife had carefully groomed him for his new home, even trimming his mane and brushing out his long tail. PJ's red coat was spotless, his huge white blaze standing out dramatically against the deep auburn.

PJ's big, soft eyes looked benign yet blank. Tory called this type of gaze the "my brain chip got wet and all I can hear is a hissing noise" look. I didn't notice this particular expression till the farrier came. PJ stood placidly, needing only some cud to complete a heifer look, until the farrier picked up his hoof. Then PJ simultaneously lurched sideways, reared up, and fell over — he couldn't figure out how to balance on three legs.

By this time, we had a new farrier, Craig, a tall, strapping cowboy who used to ride bulls in his youth. Woody, our previous blacksmith and spitter extraordinaire, had become consumed by his hay business and cut back on his other services. Recommended by a neighbor, Craig was patient, gentle, and tremendously strong — no horse ever worried or bothered him. But by the end of their first session, PJ's antics had worked even Craig to near exhaustion.

I decided it was the complete disconnect between PJ's behavior and his appearance that was so maddening. You expect lanky, taut-muscled horses with high heads and white-rimmed eyes to act nervous — not round horses that always seem to be in a placid doze.

MY NEXT SEVERAL WEEKS were indeed an ordeal.

Per our vet's midnight instructions, I had taken the precaution of borrowing one of Bobbie's stalls next door for PJ. As Damon had said, "Hock wraps are tough to keep in place, especially if the horse is moving around in the pasture. Can you put him in a stall till I see him tomorrow? I can come in the afternoon."

Fortunately, Bobbie's place was between tenants, the barn empty and ready for PJ. I put Ivy, a laid-back black gelding with ankle injuries, in the stall next to PJ — to keep him company and perhaps inspire him to a calmer life philosophy.

The next morning, PJ's cut was worse. The bandage had slipped during the night and now constricted the ankle, the plastic gauze winding tighter as PJ paced restlessly. Berating myself for my poor wrap job, I went to halter PJ in his stall. He spooked and ran past me into the barn aisle, heading for the pasture.

Finally catching him, I tried to pull off the bandage. PJ danced away, leg cocked high Bruce Lee–style, dangerously close to my shoulder. I tried sedating him with Ace, a mild drug that relaxes nervous horses, but PJ seemed impervious. The Ace only made him twitchy and even *less* coordinated about his kung fu kicks. I was sweating, out of breath, and worried about his uncovered cut. After an hour, I gave up and called Damon again. He listened patiently, then rearranged his appointments to come right away, bringing stronger sedatives and vastly superior wrapping skills.

Damon had no better luck with PJ. His usual deft, "easy there, big fella" exam techniques were powerless against PJ's philosophy of panic. After avoiding two near kicks, Damon went for the big gun — a syringe with butorphanol sedative. He emptied the contents into PJ, commenting, "You weren't kidding. He's a tough one."

PJ's nose immediately dropped toward the ground. His legs remained upright, if wobbly. Some sedatives, like Ace, can make some horses uneasy and more likely to kick out. Others, like butorphanol, produce a more sleepy overall effect. Yet another vet favorite, detomidine, is designed to sedate the horse while also suppressing the kick and bite instinct. Within seconds of injection, horses tend to lean forward with their head down — often wandering straight into corners, for convenient nose parking. Damon's partner, Matt, called this the "downhill skier" syndrome.

Damon cleaned out the wound, then created a bandage confection of vet wrap, cotton Gamgee, and Teflon pads. His hock wrap was anchored by wide strips of Elasticon, a sticky, thick medical tape. PJ's entire rear leg was encased in multiple layers of cotton and plastic, like a giant papier-mâché cast.

"Okay, Lynn, you'll need to change the wrap twice a week for about ten weeks. Maybe more. And be sure to hose the cut for about ten minutes each time, too."

I sighed, thinking of PJ's kung fu and water-related antics.

"I can tell you'll need to sedate PJ for every bandage change. The IM [intramuscular] shots take longer to deliver the sedation, maybe as long as thirty minutes. But if you inject directly into the bloodstream, PJ will be instantly sleepy."

Sensing my dismay, Damon explained how to give intravenous shots. Using Ivy as a guinea pig patient, Damon injected harmless saline solution into his neck, probing for a vein first. "Now, you put your thumb and forefinger here — see that line? That's where the jugular vein usually sits. Just put pressure on it, to pump the blood up, so you can see the vein more easily."

I clutched Ivy's neck, watching a swollen vessel grow under my grip.

Damon instructed, "Slide the needle into the vein slowly, then draw back the syringe plunger, to make sure you're still in the vein."

The image of PJ's kicks inspired me past my usual needle phobia. I got the vein on the first try, earning a "good job!" from Damon. A bright cloud of blood poofed into the syringe, muddying the saline contents.

"Go ahead and inject the saline." Damon smiled as I depressed the plunger, squirting saline into Ivy without incident. "Now go ahead and inject him again, on the other side of his neck — for practice."

The next day, PJ somehow scraped his front ankle, even though his stall was full of soft shavings. The abrasion was superficial but his ankle was puffy. Shaking my head at PJ's talent for mayhem, I doctored the scrape to draw out any inflammation and hopefully reduce the swelling. Then I smeared a goopy ointment called Magna Paste on PJ's ankle. Finally I wrapped his entire lower leg in cotton, followed by a polo bandage. At least I could relax for this task. PJ was always cooperative about his front legs. He stood calmly as I slathered smelly, green gel on the scrape.

The next morning, I led PJ to the barn aisle and bent down to remove the polo bandage. I tugged gently at the blue felt, unwinding it from his ankle. PJ dozed, his eyes half-shut and face hanging low.

Suddenly, his head snapped up. A bird flew by, one of approximately ten thousand that PJ saw every day. Before I could react, PJ spooked

toward the scary bird, knocking me flat. On my back, I looked up at a terrifying sight. PJ's belly and hind hooves were floundering less than an
arm's length over my face.

After pitching me to the ground, PJ realized that I was now between
him and the bird. Rather than step around me or perhaps take the more
rational course of spooking away from the ferocious wren, PJ made a bold
choice: He jumped over me.

I cringed below him. There was plenty of time, too much time, to con-
template his underside — PJ was a very slow, very clumsy jumper. He
hung in the air, not sure where to put his feet for the landing.

I closed my eyes until I heard a big whack. PJ successfully cleared my
prone form but sideswiped the hose rack on his way down.

PJ's great-great-grandfather would have winced at that sound. King
of the Tudors was a British champion racehorse, descended from the great
English sire Hyperion. In 1954, King of the Tudors won the prestigious
Eclipse Stakes, held each year in Surrey. He went on to become a stud,
fathering many successful runners. One of his Irish-born sons, Tudor
Royal, also stood as a stallion in the 1960s and 1970s, stamping many of his
foals with large blazes on their faces — just like PJ.

King of the Tudors must have been an elegant, poised mover. His
grandson sired Clearly Canadian, a world-class dressage horse. Of all the
horses who had come to our ranch, only PJ was related to both racing and
dressage champions — his distant cousin was a grand prix competitor, a
possible Olympic contender in his day.

Clearly, PJ took after the more Texan side of his pedigree, as he completely lacked the graceful gene.

I stood up and followed the trail of unwinding blue bandage. PJ was
at the end of it, nervously watching for winged menaces while standing in
his own manure. Not exactly a "look of champions" kind of moment.

A FEW WEEKS LATER, new tenants moved in at Bobbie's place next door,
taking over after Jesse's departure. A heavyset man with graying hair

appeared, hauling tack and horses into the barns. "My name's Jack Kemp-man," he rasped. "But just call me 'Kemp,' everyone else does." Kemp was a race trainer, mostly of Quarter Horses. In addition to his string of active runners, Kemp also owned breeding stock. His current crop of young horses was small, just two gangly colts.

One was about a year old, a dark bay with long legs. The other was younger, maybe six months old, with a red coat and a big blaze. His liquid eyes had a familiar, damp look — the infamous "my brain chip is wet" expression. Detecting a possible genetic link, Tom greeted him by calling out, " Hey there, little Baby PJ," whenever the colt wandered close to our fence.

Kemp's operation also boasted several sullen Latino grooms, who lived in the same house vacated by Jesse. Spanish curse words, still familiar from my polo barn days, wafted regularly across our fence line — along with the smell of improvised barn campfires. Each night, the grooms cooked their dinners over trash fires despite the presence of an oven in their bunkhouse.

Fortunately, PJ had just graduated from barn to round pen confine-ment, no longer needing Bobbie's stall.

AFTER THREE MONTHS, PJ healed beautifully. It had taken hundreds of dollars in vet wrap, cotton bandages, and sedation, and about forty ban-daging sessions in total. The jagged wound had shrunk to a thin line of scar tissue. PJ would always have a small, bumpy scar, but not too much of a blemish.

Thanks to our shared growth experience, I was now adept at giving IV shots, constructing hock wraps, and — more importantly — decon-structing hock wraps using a surgical blade. Because of PJ's near immu-nity to sedation, I had to give him large doses. PJ would sway slightly, head down, eyes closed, but still capable of lurching sideways or trying to kick. While PJ was sedated, speed was of the essence — he didn't stay groggy for long. Hence, I developed a rapid-fire wrapping and unwrapping technique. I would bend over the bandage, wrapping materials stuffed in my pockets, and frantically fly my hands over PJ's leg — looking like some kind of bizarre calf roper.

PJ discovered that the water hose wouldn't kill him (though he remained wary) and that he could stand on three legs without falling over. He still spooked into things that scared him, but he was slower and more thoughtful about it.

Finally, the big day arrived — PJ no longer needed bandages and could be turned out in the big pasture. As I ceremoniously let him loose, I realized I had become fond of PJ. He looked so content, dipping his white nose deep into the grass for a twelve-hour snack session.

Then, two weeks later, PJ came running up to his bucket for morning grain. Sleepy from caffeine deprivation, I squinted at him — something looked wrong, yet familiar, with his rear leg. PJ turned toward me and I let out a truly impressive string of epithets, startling Kemp's rough-edged staff across the fence.

PJ had cut his leg again — in the same place. His painstakingly healed scar now flapped open again, only not as deeply as before. There was little blood, but a new wound gaped next to his fresh scar tissue.

I called Austin Equine Associates, possibly for the millionth time that year. Matt agreed to come out right away, his cheerful, professional tone boosting my morale. Within an hour, he was at the ranch, examining PJ's latest attempt at slow suicide.

"Hmmm. How did he manage to do that? Interesting," mused Matt as he examined PJ's leg — from a safe distance. PJ was already cocking his leg in martial art style. "Right above the previous cut. But I think I can put in some stitches. They may pop out sooner than I'd like, but even a week's worth will save you some wrapping time."

I kept my tone deadpan. "Can't we just amputate?"

Matt paused in mid–gauze unrolling, his face blank. I immediately regretted my flippant comment. After all, Matt was a dedicated vet and animal lover — my sarcasm had probably offended him. I opened my mouth to apologize.

Matt's jaw twitched, then he nodded. "Well, actually, you might just want to consider euthanasia. Save both of us a lot of trouble in the future." Matt erupted into laughter, shattering his professional demeanor. I wasn't the only one tired of PJ's antics.

Matt quickly recovered himself. "Okay, seriously, I'd like to sedate PJ fully and lay him down here. If his leg's relaxed and non–weight bearing, I have a better shot at putting those stitches in. Let's walk him there to the shade. That way, I can work on him away from the sun."

I led PJ under the shade of a small tree. He seemed rooted until the instant Matt injected him with the heavy-duty sedative. Then PJ lurched away, heading with drunken purpose for the sun, which was radiating about 98 degrees of pure Texas heat. Matt and I couldn't deflect his 1,200-pound bulk, and as soon as his hooves hit the brightest, most shade free part of the field, PJ dropped to the ground. He was out for the count.

Matt sighed and got to work, baking in the heat as he meticulously stitched PJ's hock. Predictably, PJ had fallen in a graceless heap — Matt had to twist himself awkwardly to reach the injured leg. Stitching is delicate, slow work; by the time Matt finished, his face was sunburned. PJ's new cut was now sewn into a tidy line.

Thanks to Matt's stitches, PJ's second cut healed much faster than the first. He was soon back in the fields grazing, the picture of equine peacefulness. Now able to eat grass nonstop, PJ filled out rapidly, nearly crossing the line from "stout, good-looking gelding" to "broodmare about to give birth."

A WET-WEATHER CREEK flows behind our house and around the back pasture. In some spots, its banks are deep, nearly eighteen feet down. In rainy seasons, swirling, fetid water fills up the minigorge, sometimes spilling over to our driveway. During drought months, the creek bed is completely dry, covered with crackling leaves, old tires, and assorted reptiles. Dozens of teenage trees cling to the steep banks, a curtain of green foliage obscuring the creek bottom below.

I often walk our dog Sophie along the tree line, its quiet shade providing a soothing path. One day, as we navigated around an especially leafy bend, we stopped in midstep at the sight of a dark-coated animal cavorting twenty feet ahead of us. Blinking through the sun flickering between the branches, I tried to make sense of the creature. Bigger than Sophie's Aussie Shepherd mix, it leapt playfully after a squirrel, the movements oddly feline. Suddenly, with a comic double take in our direction, the animal froze in shock, his face turned toward us, telltale ears now visible.

A bobcat, the first I'd ever seen outside of magazine photos. And he was a big one, with a wide head and tall, tufted ears. Before Sophie could bark, the animal was gone, bounding down to the creek bed, weeds and tree leaves shuddering in its wake. Although the encounter was more mystical than threatening, I made sure our slower, injured horses stayed in the upper pastures as a safety measure. The only bobcat attack I'd ever heard of involving horses was of a young foal, recently born. Pondering that, I decided to move PJ as well — just in case his maternal-sized belly prompted bobcat stalking.

SOON AFTER THE BOBCAT ENCOUNTER, Tara came to our ranch looking for a trail-riding mount. A willowy girl in her midtwenties, Tara had a truly Texan upbringing. Growing up with horses, she broke her first colt in high school, the first of several young horses she had started since then. Tara and I walked the pastures, stopping to meet each horse on our ranch.

As we approached PJ, Tara commented on his handsome looks. PJ was bursting with health and about two-thirds of the grass in the pasture. He glowed with contentment, his jaws ever chewing, pausing only to touch Tara's hand with his white nose.

Tara was charmed, and she decided to adopt PJ. As he stepped into her trailer, I felt proud of him — and of myself — since we had both come a long way together. Also, I was relieved that I would never have to ride PJ. Gentle Spider was about my limit for unbroken horses.

The trailer pulled out of our driveway, with PJ's red rump peeking out. I smiled as I closed the gate, silently blessing Tara and her colt-starting skills — she was a perfect home for PJ.

However, my relief didn't last long. Within a month, Tara was back in touch. She said that PJ was panicking whenever she tried any kind of premounting ground work, which usually consists of throwing an arm or a rope over the horse's back or jumping up next to him. Tara said, "I haven't ridden him since he has been here. I haven't felt he was ready for it. And I won't get on young horses until they have gotten over most of these issues ... for my own safety."

I offered to extend her trial period with PJ, hoping he would settle in with time. But time didn't help, and Tara contacted me again within a few weeks.

"I haven't been able to make much progress with PJ as far as riding goes. He is still spooky at things. Even when I just walk up to him to give him a good rub or scratch, he shies away. He accepts the saddle and blanket with mediocrity. He doesn't freak out at them, but you can tell that he is very worried about them. He gets wide-eyed, doesn't react, but looks as though he might at any second."

After three months, Tara decided to return PJ. From our house, I watched her trailer pull back through our gate. My mood low, I walked up the long driveway to meet her. But when I arrived, there was another problem. PJ refused to leave the trailer — Tara pushed gently against him, clucking softly. Big-eyed, PJ took two steps backward and balked. Then he took three steps forward into Tara, then one back — and balked again.

"He's just scared and needs time," said Tara. Or, I thought, he's the most annoying horse in Texas. It was sad enough that Tara had to return him — could he do us a favor and step off the trailer like he had done dozens of times before? Sighing, I watched PJ repeat his one-step-back, two-steps-forward dance over and over.

Forty-five minutes later, I grabbed my trusty training flag and hopped into the narrow stock trailer with Tara. PJ filled most of the trailer — he looked happily at me, as if to say, "Hey, what are you doing here and do you have food?"

Waving the flag in his face wiped that expression away pretty quickly. He lurched backward for a couple steps, then looked speculatively up at the roof. Uh oh — the flag was inspiring him vertically, not backward. Tara, a nice girl who relied heavily on kindness and carrot sticks with horses, looked defeated. Suddenly, inspiration tapped my shoulder.

"Well, if he won't unload, you'll just have to keep him, Tara," I said cheerfully.

Tara's slender frame stiffened — I had pushed the right button. She threw herself into PJ's chest with a new vigor. "*Back* up now, PJ!" she hissed, popping the lead rope at his feet. A huge clatter, a scraping of hair against steel, slipping sounds, and several curse words whispered in nice girl tones, and there was PJ, back at the LOPE ranch.

NEXT DOOR, Kemp's operation was deteriorating rapidly. His groom staff was down to just one vaquero barely out of his teens. He stayed in the bunkhouse most of the day, only occasionally emerging to do barn chores. An ill-advised barn cookout set off a miniature bonfire near the stored hay bales, shaking my confidence. I began watching the property, nervously alert for any signs of smoke.

Two broodmares, full figured and sassy, appeared in the pasture next to Baby PJ and his yearling sidekick, whom I nicknamed "Big Brother." While Baby PJ ignored the mares, Big Brother showed extreme (and unwise) interest in their every movement.

One evening, I heard a commotion during my feeding chores. The stoutest mare, a palomino, had backed up to the fence, teasing Big Brother. He reared up, trying his barely pubescent best to mount her. In his testosterone haze, he failed to notice a key barrier to his plan — the pipe fence.

In midflirtation, Big Brother caught his armpits on the fence top. Helplessly hanging, his hind hooves barely touching the ground, he squealed sadly as the palomino mare wandered off, unimpressed with his seduction technique.

After several calls, I reached Kemp, who grudgingly emerged from the barn area, scowling as he rescued Big Brother. Within a few weeks, both he and Baby PJ were gone, followed by the mares — then by Kemp himself.

We were neighborless once again.

I WAS DISMAYED AT THE SIGHT of PJ's bovine bulk back in our pastures. After his misadventures with Tara, I knew he'd somehow have to get started under saddle at our ranch; otherwise, he'd never leave. Plus, if the gaps in his training persisted, PJ might turn more dangerously temperamental — like Tory's Bonita.

After Tory had first mounted Bonita in the stall, it was several months before Bonita's education was resumed. By then, I had become a barn boarder (instead of a student), with the purchase of my first horse, a small, middle-aged mare named Pepe. Due to Tory's full schedule of polo tournaments and horse-training gigs, she hadn't been able to keep working with Bonita much.

Meanwhile, Bonita grazed in the pastures, getting bigger and stronger. Tory sometimes muttered to herself when she spotted Bonita galloping playfully, building more muscle daily. The unfinished breaking of Bonita was weighing on her mind.

One day, I arrived at the barn to ride Pepe. Tory and Dee were bustling around the barn, cleaning their saddles, chattering nonstop. "Lynn, ride with us," Tory ordered. "We'll need another quiet horse out on the trail with us."

Dee was tacking up Brown, who looked less than pleased and pinned her ears. Dee was one of the boldest posse riders — she used to timber race in college, a wild form of cross-country competition over giant log fences. Usually, she rode the green horses at Tory's barn rather than the beginner-safe Brown.

As Dee and I mounted our horses, we heard skittering clip-clops from the barn. Tory emerged leading Bonita — who looked much more mature than during my last encounter with her in the stall. I commented something to this effect, and Tory said confidently, "Bonita is a made horse now — she just doesn't know it yet."

Confused, I glanced at Dee, who was throwing her hair back while simultaneously adjusting her stirrup length. Absorbed in this feat of balance, she hadn't heard Tory's optimistic assessment. No chance of edification from that direction.

Off we rode to the trails. Dee stayed ahead of Tory, with Brown acting as a tour guide for Bonita. I brought up the rear, listening to Tory and Dee's banter. Pepe was fun to ride. She loped gracefully along the trail, happy to hop over stray logs blocking the path. With her tan coat and sure-footed movements, Pepe resembled a deer as she scrambled through the woods.

To my surprise, the ride didn't end after a long lap around the pumpkin patch, with its sloping descent to Tory's back paddock. Instead, we rode down a bank, crossing a paved road, and bounded up the other side — where the woods led to several open fields.

Dee kept up a rollicking commentary, sometimes at the expense of trail leadership, wandering into tree branches and mud puddles. Tory's head swiveled every few steps, looking ahead for obstacles, calling instructions to Dee, glancing back at me to make sure Pepe wasn't tailgating Bonita. But I had a healthy respect for Bonita's hind feet and needed no prodding to keep a large gap between us.

After about thirty minutes, we turned back, retracing our steps through the woods. Tory was silent. In spite of her ride, Bonita wasn't out of breath, trotting along easily, her ears twitching, with one starting to drift backward.

The day tipped from afternoon to early evening, the air cooling. I could tell Tory wanted to get back home. She stared ahead, looking for the clearing before the paved road, the one that led back to the pumpkin patch and her barn.

"She's not even *tired*," Dee blared, pointing to Bonita. Tory looked at her with an expression usually reserved for me.

We reached the clearing. Bonita balked at a log in the path, slowing our progress to the road. Tory was full of sudden alertness — I saw it in the flex of her back and the quick tilt of her head, helmetless as usual.

I reined Pepe back as we ambled toward the bank, which dipped down to the asphalt road. The street was driveway sized, with shadows criss-crossing it. The sun dropped behind the trees, a melting red ball signaling dinnertime back at the barn. Dee and Tory, riding in front, headed down the bank. I decided to wait until they crossed the street before following. I didn't want to be crowded with two other horses on the narrow road — especially when one of them was Bonita.

Bonita balked again and Tory kicked her firmly. "Must always move forward, Bonita," she said. Bonita lurched across the bank's slope, then stopped in the middle of the deserted road. As Dee and Brown followed, clattering down the bank, Bonita exploited their noisy distraction. She vio-lently reared vertically and then, before her front feet touched back down to the pavement, leaped forward in a spectacular buck.

Tory was unseated and flung sideways, the ambush taking her by rare surprise. Tory had iron legs and decades of bronc-riding experience — it took something epic to get her off balance. If Bonita had only reared, Tory would have recovered her seat easily. But Bonita's leaping buck doomed Tory. She ended up falling on the pavement with a sickening thwack, right under Bonita's hooves.

Dee shrieked into action, jumping off Brown. She waved her hands at Bonita, shouting, "How dare you" and "Get away — oh my God," which only spooked Bonita closer to Tory's sprawled form. Brown looked des-perately at Pepe and me for assistance. Tory glanced up, catching my eye and shaking her head, as if to say, "Here I am, helpless on the pavement, watching Dee and Bonita try to kill me."

Tory was hurt, but she managed to crawl away from Bonita's hooves. Finally, Dee got control of Bonita, holding her and Brown by their reins. I remained back on the bank, convinced I couldn't help. Another horse and rider would only escalate the excitement. All I could do was stay out of the way and keep Pepe calm, a possible beacon of equine good behavior for Bonita.

Tory stiffly remounted and rode Bonita home to the barn. She was in pain, mumbling many cruel things to Bonita and to Dee — but she still rode. "Because Bonita will be so much worse the next ride, if I don't get back on now," muttered Tory, her bruised ribs keeping her voice low and breathing ragged.

ONE LATE AFTERNOON, soon after PJ's return, I started working with him in the round pen. I saddled him and made him trot around the pen, the stirrups flapping down against his round sides. My plan was to assess PJ, then hire Cory to train him. Although Cory's cost would strain our tiny budget, I didn't feel ready to handle an unbroken problem child —especially one that had been returned as "too spooky" by an experienced colt rider.

I walked off to the center of the round pen. PJ followed, like a school-kid going to the blackboard. I shooed him off into a trot around the pen. Expecting a buck or wild lurch at any moment, I watched PJ clop around the corral. PJ trotted obediently — even with the stirrups bumping him. I stepped backward. PJ stopped immediately and turned to face me, head down, slightly sheepish.

No sign of fear. But Tara had said he was scared of being mounted: "He seems really worried about me throwing my leg over the saddle. He hasn't bucked or done anything bad — but I'm afraid he will."

This didn't fill me with confidence. However, before sending him to Cory, I needed to get some idea of PJ's reaction to mounting. Although Cory was a seasoned trainer, he was pushing his sixtieth birthday — he'd appreciate some insider information before getting up on PJ. Sighing, I put my hand on the stirrup and wiggled it, waiting for the appearance of the flaky PJ I knew so well. I thought wistfully of Spider, PJ's opposite in every respect.

Putting the rope halter on PJ, I took turns pulling on each of the stirrups, slapping the saddle, and twirling the lead rope softly. He was immobile, head down, big blaze pointing toward the ground. Standing at his left shoulder, I gathered the lead rope in my left hand, leaned on his mane, and put my left foot in the stirrup, then bounced up. PJ lifted his head and looked at me.

Even after Spider, riding young horses wasn't my favorite pastime. And of all the unbroken horses in the world, PJ would be my last choice — I had seen too many of his youthful indiscretions. My stomach tightened at the thought of being on his back.

Random excuses flitted through my mind. I could just skip riding him today — Tara didn't want to mount him, and she was an experienced colt rider. I'd be foolish to risk an injury. Or I could pay Cory extra to ride him without any preflight assessment — after all, he was the expert.

These were feasible, sensible ideas, and I mulled over all of them as I bounced up in the stirrup. The saddle looked small on PJ's thick, bulky frame — my bounces were really more like power hops, as I struggled to stretch my foot up into the stirrup. I braced for a sudden spook.

But PJ wasn't lapsing into his usual fugue state. Surprised, I looked closely at him. PJ was quiet, receptive — he was ready. Plus, young horses have their tipping points — he might not be so ready tomorrow. If I chickened out, it could set him back mentally. And neither of us (or LOPE) could afford that.

"Get on him, what are you waiting for?" the video cowboys whispered.

I closed my eyes, clamped my fear down, and mounted PJ. Sitting precariously on his back, I held my breath and waited for him to buck or rear or let loose with whatever wildness he had in mind.

PJ yawned.

Then he looked over at my right leg, surprised to see it there against his flank, and yawned again. I tapped his rump and clucked softly to him. PJ took one uncertain step, then another, then stopped, turning his nose again and nuzzling my right boot.

Up in the saddle, I marveled at the view from PJ's back. I had gone further than I ever thought possible with him. I looked around at the muddy footing in the pen, the low-hanging branches brushing the panels, and at PJ himself — all potential grounds for disaster.

Headlights appeared in the driveway; Tom was home from work. I realized suddenly that I'd been riding PJ in rapidly dimming twilight, with my weak colt-starting skills, alone on the property — all because PJ was ready.

And to my surprise, so was I.

After several more rides, PJ was adopted out to become a family trail-riding horse. Renamed Tristan, he is much loved — and has finally learned that the water hose is his friend.

PART V

The Dark Horses

Believe in your horse so your horse can believe in you.

RAY HUNT,
horsemanship guru

CHAPTER ELEVEN

Bridge Place

O FTEN, HORSES WILL SEEM TO COME IN CLUMPS at the ranch. One spring we had almost all bay geldings (prompting many weak *Baywatch* jokes from Tom); another fall, only chestnuts littered our pastures. Sometimes the ranch is full of sound, uninjured horses, only to be followed by a herd of knee chips and torn suspensory ligaments.

Our current clump seemed to be of colts, a term that can mean "young stallion" or "unbroken horse," or sometimes even just "young, green horse." As I was putting the first rides on PJ, another memorable colt arrived.

"Can you fit another horse at your place?" The race trainer, Bret, sounded casual, but I detected a pleading note under his laid-back North Texas accent. He knew we were sending a trailer to pick up a horse at his Sam Houston shedrow, and he was hoping to add a second horse to our transport. "He's a really good colt, easy to handle. Not studdish at all." The pleading note was stronger now. "I'll even pay to get him gelded for you. He'd make a great riding horse, if someone would just give him a chance."

Bret epitomized Texas racing with his Dallas roots and courteous presence. However, his kind demeanor in no way hampered his fierce competitive drive. In ten years, he had saddled over a thousand winners, a benchmark reached by few race trainers nationally. With dozens of horses under his training, Bret raced in several states, his operation a complex juggling act. His grooms and gallop girls were well trained and chosen carefully for their skill with horses. Captain Boo's former gallop girl, Laura, vouched for Bret and his barn with enthusiasm — it was she who had arranged the donation of Singularity, the horse in his barn already headed our way.

Laura had recommended our ranch to Singularity's race owner and breeder, Thomas, who said to me, his voice hoarse with emotion: "This horse is very special to me. He was an orphan foal; we raised him with a bottle. And he got sick real bad, right as a weanling. They thought he was going to die. But he was a little fighter and pulled through. The whole vet clinic turned out to watch me pick him up, too — they were all crying, they were so happy to see him go home healthy. Now that he's done racing, I want to be sure he finds a good home. He's a big, tall boy — someone will want him for a riding horse."

Laura was going to bring Singularity to us, happy to give LOPE a discount for horse transport. As she pulled her roomy trailer up to Bret's shedrow, asking for Singularity, one of the grooms casually led a second horse out, perhaps hoping Laura wouldn't notice. After a flurry of calls between me, Laura, and Bret, both horses were heading our way two days later.

Bridge Place was a gorgeous bay, with superb conformation and a cheerful look in his kind eyes. Bred in Britain, he was shipped to the United States with high hopes for a big racing career — he was regally bred, expensive, and full of talent. Sadly, he developed a slab fracture in his knee at age three. His owners sent him for surgery to pin the knee, hoping to save Bridge Place's racing career. Slab fractures are vertical fissures, usually in a joint. They can range from mild hairline cracks to large bone chips. Peanut, our first adoption horse, had the hairline version. Bridge Place's slab was on the bigger side — he required surgery to secure the cracked bone.

Despite a successful surgery and many months of rest, Bridge Place's knee couldn't take the pressure of running. When he returned to race training, his knee became sore after a few weeks of mild workouts. Bridge Place had been a high-priced yearling, but his value as a racehorse was now close to zero. So he found his way to LOPE, slipped into a transport at the last minute.

Not sure what to expect, I watched Laura's rig pull into our driveway. First she unloaded Singularity — he was even taller than his owner described, with a long elegant head. Then Bridge Place swaggered off the trailer, ready for attention and treats. A deep shade of chocolate bay, he carried himself like a football star, seeming to look for admiring fans as he eyed our pastures. Clearly, he thought highly of himself — the only problem was that he was all of 15 hands, about sixty inches tall at the withers. Beautifully conformed, athletic, cocky, and, well . . . kind of short.

Laura approved of him. "That's a nice-looking colt. He traveled real quiet, too. They liked him a lot at Bret's barn. I could tell they were happy he found a spot here." Bridge Place was perky for a recently castrated horse, nickering to a filly two pastures away, a rumbling "Hey, baby" greeting.

I should have been reluctant to take Bridge Place. We were full at the ranch, plus Bridge Place fit the profile of trouble for most barns. He was young and fresh off the track and had just been gelded. It can take several weeks for equine testosterone levels to drop down to "no longer stud muffin" levels. But after Tawakoni and Captain Boo, I wasn't fazed by Bridge Place's recent stallion status. He'd have to start screaming or molesting geldings (probably simultaneously) to get my attention now.

Bridge Place also cribbed, a habit that involved gripping a bucket or fence post with his teeth and sucking air with a hiccupping sound. Many equestrians consider cribbing an ugly and destructive vice, a deal breaker in any horse purchase.

I remember once when Tory was shopping for young polo prospects at a breeding facility. Jill, the farm owner, was proud of her three-year-olds.

"From the beginning, we always expose them to polo mallets and balls. Polo gear becomes part of their routine even as babies." One filly caught Tory's eye, a dainty chestnut with the short back and wide hindquarters of a future polo star. Tory admired her quiet demeanor and drew closer to pet the filly.

"We call her Shasta," said Jill. "I love her! How much?" Tory asked, ready to pounce on the purchase and already patting her pocket for a checkbook. Before Jill could answer, Shasta reached for the fence, gripping it delicately with her teeth. She pulled back on the wood, a distinct belchlike sound erupting from her sweet face.

"Oh my god. How tragic. She *cribs*." Tory sighed, her hands abandoning the pocket search and settling on her hips. "Too bad. She's a lovely filly. But no resale value. My customers hate cribbers."

Bridge Place was a dedicated cribber, mouthing buckets and fence posts with gusto. With half-closed eyes and a dreamy, satisfied look on his face, he radiated endorphin overload. To me, cribbing is just an unattractive but fairly harmless hobby — like Tom's habit of social cigarette smoking at parties.

Singularity and Bridge Place made an entertaining pair with their wildly disparate heights and builds. Even though Singularity towered over Bridge Place, he wasn't the head honcho, however. Bridge Place bossed him constantly, stealing his food and chasing him through the fields when bored. It was Bridge Place who decided where they should graze, which hay bale to nibble on, and which water trough to tip over.

Equine leadership rarely has anything to do with size or strength. Zuper took command of our herd while still limping from his injury, and the mooselike PJ was timid with other horses, often bullied by the smallest filly in the field. My first experience with horse leadership dynamics was back in my DC days, when I began riding at the polo stables.

ON MY FIRST DAY I ARRIVED EARLY at the polo school barn. One of the polo pros, Dan, greeted me with a yawn, his Australian accent thicker than usual. He eyed me skeptically, as I explained why I was there — to be a working student for Ellie, the head instructor. Ellie wasn't there yet, and Dan seemed at a loss as to what to do with me. After several minutes of awkward silence, he told me to go catch the polo school horses. They were turned out in the sprawling fields behind the barn, where they grazed each evening.

"Go on and catch 'em," he said with a barely concealed smile. "They usually come in all at once — it's easy, at least for me. Of course, I'm usually a'horseback. With a big lasso." Dan guffawed, then waited for me to pepper him with questions or express doubt at the assignment. I felt my inner teenager rise.

"Fine, then. I'll go get them." I walked away before I could see him smile again.

The twenty-acre pasture crisscrossed in a looping zigzag formation of fields. There were scrubby bushes, leafy trees, and about fifteen polo school horses scattered across its hilly terrain. A bent metal gate separated the pasture from the barn paddock area — it stood open, to give the horses access to the barn in case of rain.

Spotting a path, I marched away from the barn, annoyance giving an extra smack to my steps. The trail wound up and around several clearings. Here and there, groups of horses grazed together, their shaved manes marking them as polo mounts. I counted seven horses; the rest were hiding somewhere among the bushes and trees. The horses looked up at me, curious and expectant expressions on their faces.

I had grabbed a single halter and lead rope (all the others were missing from the school tack room) — it would take forever to catch and lead all of them down the long pathway to the barn, one at a time. As if sensing my thoughts, Mentirosa, an edgy mare, sidled away from me, her eyes staring balefully at the halter.

Perplexed, I stood for a minute, imagining how it would feel to walk back to the barn and admit failure to Dan. Ellie might have arrived by now, waiting impatiently for the horses, maybe beginning to regret letting me trade work for lessons.

A horse walked a step in my direction, the expectant look more urgent on his face. He was one of the fatter school horses, slow and lazy, the kind who never skips a meal. Another horse drifted closer, too, grazing but keeping an ear cocked in my direction. It was Junebug, a gazellelike mare, slender like a fashion model.

Hunger. That's what these two horses had in common, the fat gelding and supermodel mare wandering near me. It was morning, the horses had been out all night, and they were hungry for their morning grain.

Junebug was on the trail now, standing in front of me, all pretense of grazing abandoned. I looked down at the trail, saw how wide and well traveled it was, with hoofprints etched over its surface. I remembered the open gate back by the barn paddock, the gate that was usually closed during polo lessons.

"Hah!" I ordered, swinging the lead rope and halter around my head and pointing back to the barn with my other hand. "Git!"

I wondered from what deep part of my brain the word "git" had come from — it certainly wasn't an accounting term. Junebug and Fat Gelding looked up happily and trotted off down the path, heading back to the barn together.

That was two down — I turned my attention to the other thirteen. Mentirosa retreated farther into the bushes, her face sullen. Not all the horses would be as easy as Junebug and Fat Gelding. I could tell Mentirosa was going to be the type to evade, to head to the gate, then double back at the last minute. She needed to be part of an equine group decision. Scanning the hills ahead, I saw JP, a buckskin gelding, edging his way toward me. JP was a favorite polo school mount — he enjoyed the lessons, especially if he could intimidate the other horses away from the ball. Although he was short and somewhat elderly, JP was an undisputed herd boss.

I slipped down the trail until I was behind JP, between him and the bushes. Then I shouted, "Hah! Git there," while maniacally flinging the lead rope and halter over my head. JP headed for the barn at a gallop, sweeping Mentirosa and the others ahead of him like a wave.

The stragglers came tumbling over the bushes behind JP, the sound of the group hoofbeats too enticing to resist. Morning habit, hunger, and herd manners compelled all the horses through the gate together. I ran breathlessly after them, just in time to slam the gate shut in Mentirosa's face as she wheeled back.

Ellie arrived about fifteen minutes later. I was sitting on a hay bale in front of the barn. After a hurried conversation with Dan, who reappeared at the sound of her jeep, Ellie strode up to me, looking apologetic. "Sorry I'm late! Dan said you went to get the horses." I nodded, watching as Dan ambled up behind her, a look of anticipatory amusement blooming on his face.

Ellie asked, "Okay, so how many could you catch? Did you get at least a couple in?"

I could see Ellie was distracted, thinking of the time it would take to catch the horses, then feed and saddle them before the other students arrived. Dan was carrying a lead rope, poised to step in and save the day with his round-up skills.

"All of them," I replied.

"ALL?" Ellie and Dan stopped in midstride, looking back at me with shock.

"Yep, they just came on in. It was easy," I said, turning to Dan, pausing so he could see my grin. "Just like you said."

Ellie smiled and asked if I could come every Saturday morning. Thanks to JP's equine leadership (spurred on by my creative use of "git"), I was officially established as the polo school's working student.

I SOON BEGAN RIDING BRIDGE PLACE, now nicknamed "Billy." He rode well and seemed to love the attention. With his breeding and speed, I was expecting sass from him, but he seemed content to go slow, picking his way through tall grass and over logs like he was an old lesson horse. If anything, Billy was lazy — I had to kick him into the canter, setting off a sigh and pout. My standards for green and spooky had been set high by PJ — Billy was a delight to ride.

I loved Billy's "short guy" ethos — he truly seemed to believe he was the size of a Clydesdale. He would carefully walk around hanging tree branches (that were several feet over my head), clearly concerned that his mighty height would put my head at branch-whacking risk. Billy was also a bit of a dandy — he hated getting muddy and always managed to be the cleanest horse on the farm.

Bridge Place took after his sire, another diminutive yet charismatic racehorse. Polar Falcon raced well in Britain and France, especially on the turf. After winning over $375,000 in fourteen races, he was turned out to stud at Cheveley Park Stud, one of the oldest breeding farms in England. Racehorses have been bred there for over a thousand years — several of Cheveley Park's buildings date back to the sixteenth century.

Before his untimely death at age fourteen, Polar Falcon was a zestful and successful stallion. He produced a crop of competitive, fiery race-horses with combined earnings of nearly $8 million as of 2001. Many of his progeny were winners abroad, capturing stakes races in France, Britain, and Italy.

Polar Falcon was a memorable personality, sorely missed by his han-dlers. In a magazine article at the time, the director of the stud farm lamented his passing, commenting, "Although only small in size, he was large in stature. He was a kind horse with immense character who offered us many magical moments on the racecourse and through his progeny."

Before Bridge Place was injured, he displayed fierce speed and cocky competitiveness. I could see Polar Falcon's stamp not only on Bridge Place's racing talent but also on his confident, cheerful personality. With all his entertaining attributes, I pictured a future for Billy as the beloved pet of a young girl, perhaps an aspiring English riding equestrian, who would take Billy to schooling shows, carefully braiding his mane and feed-ing his vanity for each competition.

Sugarfoot had taught me that not everyone sees what I do in our horses, particularly the young ones with "dings" like knee pins and cribbing habits. I reminded myself that any nice home would be a great ending to Billy's story — I shouldn't be picky. But still, the image of Billy in sleek show tack surrounded by girl riders persisted in my mind. To me, it seemed like his calling — and sometimes horses, like people, can do their best work only at something they love.

Like Marcos, the polo school horse.

MARCOS COILED HIS HUGE HINDQUARTERS and sprang toward the calves — his ears flat, head thrust forward, he dared them to dart past his chestnut bulk. Two tried anyway; twin blurs of baby bovine streaked to the right, heading straight for the announcer's platform perched by the bleachers.

Marcos whirled, his arthritic ankles forgotten, heading the calves off. One calf turned back, the fight out of him. The second kept running, determined to call Marcos's bluff. Marcos closed down his escape with inches to spare — as the calf skidded to avoid us, Marcos spun, matching the calf's evasive feints. Marcos was a fierce opponent, rearing up as he swiveled to block the calf.

I clung to the saddle, doing my best to stay out of Marcos's way. He was edgy about too much bit pressure, even in the slow-paced polo lessons. I sensed any rein interference now would anger him intensely.

When Ellie offered to take some of her polo students to the local team penning competition, it was just for fun — and to give the polo school horses a break. We showed up in our breeches, tall boots, and helmets — to the vast amusement of the team penning regulars, Maryland cowboys attired in Stetsons, fringed chaps, and Wranglers. But Marcos, the polo school horse assigned to me, was taking the competition seriously.

Somewhere deep in Marcos's troubled Argentine childhood, he had been taught to work cows, probably as a two-year-old, before his polo career began. It seemed likely that he had been treated roughly soon after, given his brooding nature, strong opinions about who could ride him (only women), and reluctance to show affection. His legs and ankles were scarred with old tendon injuries and calcified lumps, showing a hard, long career at the hands of indifferent owners.

In the arena, Marcos was deeply in the moment, engrossed in the calves. He flew up and down the fence line, sliding to rapid, hock-popping stops, turning like a cat, with vehement, unstoppable speed. As Marcos contorted his body nearly inside out to turn back the rebellious calf, I instinctively kept my hands low, doing my best to stay with his movements. Otherwise, I was going to be heading to the ground — Marcos liked me well enough, but he wouldn't wait for me. He was on cows.

Murmurs rose from the bleachers, as Marcos shoved his bulk between them and the calf, rearing up again, menacing the calf back to the herd. "Good cow pony," one lady said, from under her cowboy hat. "Yeehaw, look at that English horse," said an elderly man, chuckling at the sight of Marcos reliving his pampas roots. "That lady better hold on to the saddle!"

After our turn was over, we headed back to the trailer. Marcos strutted, pride in his eyes. I praised him and petted his neck. He touched his nose softly to my shoulder, a rare display of emotion for Marcos. I sensed his delight in reliving a carefree, adolescent moment — clearly, his true vocation was to work cattle, not play polo.

For Marcos, polo was about as appealing as accounting was to me.

I FOUND MYSELF SUBTLY DISCOURAGING male Western riders who inquired about Billy, emphasizing his diminutive height, creating a vague impression that Billy was a tad delicate for rugged cowboy riders. One look at Billy's stout hindquarters and bodybuilder muscle tone would have exposed that fiction immediately — but none of the men pursued their interest beyond an email inquiry.

Besides, some working cowboys weren't particularly enamored of their mounts. They considered horses to be valued tools of their trade, nothing less — but nothing more either. Our rural county boasted several large cattle ranches. I often saw their stock trailers parked at the local gas stations. Usually two or three saddled horses peered through the slats, their heavy Western tack full of dust and drab colors.

Once, a trio of local ranch hands visited our farm. Their dually was white, smeared with grit and road base. Heavy roping saddles were strewn across its bed, mud-colored saddle blankets clinging to them. The foreman of the group, Larry, sported a handlebar mustache and a battered Stetson. The two junior cowpokes were nearly identical, short and wiry with tanned faces, faded chaps, and dirt-smeared work shirts.

Larry got to the point. "We're looking for a ranch horse, maybe two." As I showed them a couple of the taller horses, Larry shook his head. "No, we like small ones. When you have to get on and off a dozen times a day, to open gates and rope calves, you get pretty tired of big horses."

A stocky filly caught his eye. "How much for this little Bubba?"

"She's kind of high-strung," I said, careful to emphasize the "she." "Maybe not a good match for cattle roping."

One of the junior cowboys snorted. "She seems docile enough. All we need to do is be able to catch her. After she's been rode eight hours in the brush, she'll get over being high-strung, that's for sure. Won't you, momma?" The filly looked at him skeptically, then returned to grazing.

Larry appeared to be searching for cash, pulling out his wallet as he sized up the filly. Eager to deter him, I filled him in on our adoption process, pulling out our approval questionnaire. "Once you complete this form, I can check your references. Then we can figure out what horses might match up with your needs."

As I rattled on, Larry shot me a look of baffled dismay. "No, we don't have time for all that fuss," he sighed. "Guess we'll look somewhere else."

Walking back to his truck, Larry confided, "I get so tired of horses sometimes. My buddies will call me, the ones that don't work on a ranch, asking if I can come trail ride on the weekends. Trail ride? Last thing I want to do is get on a horse on my day off. Rather watch TV."

BLUSTERY WEATHER IS COMMON at the ranch, especially in the spring. Windy days are always pretty, the big gusts stirring the pasture grass and tree leaves into ever-shifting designs. I like the cheerful rowdiness of the wind, even if it does spray dust in my eyes and hay all over my hair. The horses share my enjoyment, often prancing or galloping playfully around the fields, trying to outrun the breezes. When big weather fronts move in, with powerful gales, the sky turns extravagant shades of blue and purple, contrasting dramatically with the vivid green of the treetops.

Billy and Singularity would race each other on gusty days, their mismatched heights giving an entertaining twist to the competition. Singularity covered twice as much ground with a single stride as Billy — but Billy was scrappy, making up the distance with rapid, eggbeater steps. Plus he wasn't afraid to bend the rules, sometimes nipping at Singularity if he was close to taking the lead.

Billy soon developed an unfortunate new blemish, one guaranteed to put off macho Western types. One morning, as I blearily scooped feed into Billy's bucket, I noticed that wind was blowing his tail into strange patterns. The gusts seemed to flip his tail over, giving the illusion that it was half as long as it really was.

But it was a calm day — not a single breeze in the air.

Squinting harder, I realized that Billy's tail really was half-size. The hair stopped just below his tail's bone instead of midhock as usual. For a second, I thought someone must have cut it off, the lines seemed so neat and clean. A clump of hair near Singularity gave the key clue. Sometime in the night, Singularity must have chewed off Billy's tail, a form of revenge for all his bullying.

Billy now looked eerily like a giant weanling. With his muscled, round body and tiny, foal-like tail, he could pass for a Warmblood or draft horse baby — at least at a distance. Over the following weeks, several visitors commented on him, asking, "Is the draft cross foal for adoption?" Or, "I didn't know they raced Warmbloods." Or, "Are you *sure* he's full grown?"

After a few months, Cheryl came to the ranch to look for a lesson horse and pleasure-riding mount. She now liked to trail ride, but had once been a show competitor. Cheryl shared her barn with many young girls, all in need of lessons. During her show days, Cheryl had a history of buying off-track horses, training them to jump, and then finding them homes as junior hunter mounts.

We had met previously over email, when Cheryl had sent me photos of her latest success story, a Quarter Horse ex-racer named Heza He Mac. Renamed "Mack," the five-year-old had racked up numerous ribbons in the highly competitive Houston show circuit. His photo showed a gorgeous bay horse, with show ribbons festooned on his bridle. A grinning teenage trainer stood beside him in full show apparel, velvet helmet, spotless fawn breeches, and tailored jacket.

Cheryl's pride was unmistakable. "When I first went to see him, Mack was about a hundred pounds overweight and stubborn — but moved beautifully and free-jumped two feet with his body round and tight. I decided to buy him on the spot — what a natural at jumping! After five months' hunter training with a local pro, he is now a champ. At his first Houston show, Mack was Champion in the Green as Grass class [for novice show horses] and he was Reserve Champion in his second show."

Now Cheryl was content to pleasure ride, to go slow on the trails near her farmette. Yet the giggling preteen girls at her barn often asked Cheryl's advice on proper equitation and show protocol. A trail mount that could also pull duty as a lesson horse would be ideal for Cheryl's barn.

Cheryl and Billy hit it off right away. As he dozed in the round pen, his eyelids flicking open at the sound of our voices, Cheryl admired his stocky conformation and handsome head. After a short demonstration of Billy's sleepy gaits in the round pen, she was ready to saddle up. A slender woman with a sleek, short hairdo, Cheryl was a perfect match to Billy, her petite height balancing nicely with his 15 hands frame. They meshed well in appearance — both looking like they had just stepped out of a spa, well groomed and nonsweaty, even in the Texas heat.

Cheryl rode Billy around the pen, marveling at his laid-back attitude, his responsiveness to voice aids, and his happy, beaglelike personality. We laughed together about "wild ex-racehorses," while Billy snoozed along, trotting slowly in the ring. "Can I ride him out in the pasture?" Cheryl asked. With a nod from me, she and Billy headed out for the fields. Billy roused himself enough to trot faster at Cheryl's urging, then settled back into a lazy walk.

Cheryl's relaxed attitude was refreshing. Many equestrians had a bias against young off-track Thoroughbreds, a belief often encouraged by their riding instructors or trainers. I often had to combat the perception that ex-racehorses were somehow equine pit bulls, dangerous, erratic, and bred to be hostile. My experience at the ranch had taught me that horses, like schoolchildren, are sensitive to authority figures, their performance often rising or falling to match expectations.

TUCKER WAS A GENTLE THREE-YEAR-OLD GELDING with a Sugarfoot disposition. Similar to Billy's build, his athletic conformation was packed into a short frame. With his seal brown coat and the sharply etched star on his forehead, Tucker was easy to spot in the fields. Originally purchased at a yearling sale for a hefty price, Tucker had seemed like a good investment.

"My only worry was that he was a little small for his age," said Robert, Tucker's racing owner. "But I let my partner talk me into buying him. And then of course, he never really grew much. Plus he was slow."

Though he was bossy with other horses, chasing them around the pasture with Napoleonic glee, Tucker was quiet under saddle. I rode him on his first day at the ranch, a rare exception to my rule of waiting at least two weeks before riding new horses.

Shortly after we posted his photo on the website, Dean emailed me. A Lubbock dentist, he was looking for a horse for his thirteen-year-old daughter. Lauren had been riding since she was in first grade and she was ready to own her first horse. She had been showing and jumping for two years, displaying confidence and talent.

Her instructor, Janice, had a lesson and show barn near Lubbock. After I talked with Janice, it seemed like Tucker might be an ideal horse for Lauren. Dean scheduled a Saturday visit. He said, "If it's okay with you, I'd like to bring Janice or her husband, Ben, along. They both know more about horses than I do."

That Saturday turned out to be blistering, well into the upper nineties by 10 A.M. Dean and Lauren arrived in a shiny SUV; following them were a truck and horse trailer. A trim cowboy emerged from the truck — it was Ben, Janice's husband and co-trainer at their facility. "Janice, she does more of the English riding. I'm the Western rider," he said. "Been working with horses my whole life."

Tucker stood in the round pen, watching Lauren, Dean, and Ben with interest. I demonstrated his willingness to do ground work. "I just twirl the lead rope and cluck to him. And off he walks or trots. See, I have to really jog with him to make him canter," I panted. Tucker was laid-back as usual, his gaits smooth and slow in the sun. I concluded the session by riding Tucker in the pen, showing off his calm temperament under saddle.

Ben stepped up to the pen panels, his face skeptical. "Let me see how he goes," he said, spitting and turning back to his trailer. Unsaddling Tucker, I looked up to see Ben return with the biggest whip I'd ever seen. It seemed to be six feet long, towering over Ben's wiry frame as he carried it into the round pen.

He cracked the whip several times at Tucker. Trying to stay polite, I reminded Ben that Tucker was used to just a lead rope and a clucking sound from me. "Uh huh," mumbled Ben. He snapped the whip again. Tucker jumped in place, then loped around the pen, eager to please Ben and his oversized whip.

After several laps, Tucker still hadn't impressed Ben. He placed a pole in Tucker's path, pushing him to jump it. "Tucker's never jumped before," I said, prompting another "Uh huh" from Ben. Tucker hopped over the pole, confused but game.

The temperature had inched up. Dean, Lauren, Tucker, and I were ready for the session to end. But not Ben. Tucker still wasn't delivering something that he was looking for. He said, "Reckon I'll ride him now. Lemme get my roping saddle."

Ben pulled out a huge Western saddle, a sofa of leather with a back cinch bigger than my English saddle. "I don't think Tucker has had a Western saddle on before," I cautioned. "You might want to go slow with that."

"Uh huh." Ben slapped the saddle on Tucker, who looked worried.

With a jerk, Ben tightened the front cinch, then he grabbed the back cinch and pulled it taut with a rough, quick movement. Scared, Tucker flinched — not only was his belly covered with leather; it was being pinched, too. He looked over at Ben, hoping for some help. Ben didn't notice Tucker's distress or appeal for leadership. Instead, he smacked the stirrups down and picked up his whip.

Tucker couldn't take it anymore. He sidestepped, desperate to get away from the giant back cinch and whip. Ben advanced toward him, his body clenching in a machismo strut. Tucker fled, bucking for several steps.

With that, Ben threw up his hands and walked over to Dean. "See? This horse bucks. I knew he would." Shaking his head in disgust, he spat again, his worldview of Thoroughbreds confirmed. Tucker huddled in the far corner of the pen.

Dean and Lauren wanted Ben to work with Tucker some more. "Maybe he'll come around," said Lauren. She sounded hopeful, no doubt confident in Ben's skill. By now, I too was confident about Ben's abilities — I ushered him and his saddle out of the round pen.

Despite his bad day, Tucker was happy to see me return right away, allowing me to put my saddle on his back. I mounted Tucker, doing my best to reassure him, petting him as he trotted uncertainly. Within a few minutes, he relaxed into his usual quiet mode, Ben and his monster gear rapidly receding to a distant memory.

AFTER THEIR RIDE TOGETHER IN THE PASTURE, Cheryl adopted Billy on the spot, loading him into her roomy trailer. Within a couple weeks, I had my first update from her.

"I've ridden Billy several times now. He's every bit as quiet here as he was at your place. His gaits are very smooth — especially his trot. And he is totally unafraid of ground poles. We're not planning to do any jumping with him (trotting over poles is all he'll have to do for the level he'll be working with). All the little girls *love* him — he's so sweet and easy to handle."

After another month, Cheryl sent a second glowing report: "I'm in love. We took Billy on a trail ride Sunday. What a guy! Absolutely *no* jitters, spooking — nothing. We'll soon be using him for lessons, so I'm going to take some pictures of him with little kids riding him in lessons."

Finally came the email I had been waiting for. Cheryl wrote: "Billy is doing *great* and is much beloved by all the kids out here. Billy is now a lesson horse for the beginner riders who have developed a little skill. He is totally safe and calm; he just needed to learn the basics."

Just as I had hoped, Billy now teaches little girls to ride in Houston — instead of one doting rider, he now has several fighting over the chance to groom him, comb out his mane, and compete him in school shows.

Today, I sometimes visit Billy and Cheryl, enjoying the sight of Billy surrounded by his giggling entourage of preteen fans. Instead of racing tack, he now wears a pink saddle pad and matching leg wraps. "He likes pink the best," Cheryl confides with a laugh.

I smile, too — without my odd, thoroughly unprofessional assessment "system," Billy could have easily ended up a cowboy horse, trapped in a masculine forest green saddle pad and bulky Western saddle, with an unstyled mane and an owner who spits and calls him "Hey there, Bubba."

Finally, I feel like a true racehorse career counselor.

CHAPTER TWELVE

Your My Baby

WHENEVER MY CONFIDENCE WOULD START TO RISE, after a successful horse challenge or satisfying adoption, some new surprise was always lurking, ready to pounce. One cold, raw morning, Halo Selecto and A Secret Toast came running to the feed buckets, drawn to the siren call of my truck pulling up to the fence. But something was wrong — where was Babu?

Your My Baby — or "Babu," as we called him — was a beautiful dark gelding, with the shy air of a bookworm. He always was last to the buckets, preferring to walk slowly instead of racing like his pasture mates. I looked over to the run-in shed — Babu was there, flipping his head desperately at me, nickering for help. Uh oh. I sloshed through the frosty mud to him — he was shivering violently, a look of panic in his eyes.

Babu had been donated just a month before. He was fast, really fast, but like Storm, he had a paralyzed flapper, a congenital weakness in his respiratory system. As he flew around the track, pounding for the finish line, and just when he needed air the most, his flapper would drag, creating a barrier to his airway. Babu became withdrawn and worried — he couldn't understand why he was so fast, but then never could win.

His owners arranged for surgery, creating a permanently unobstructed airway. But the psychological damage had been done: Babu continued to slow down in the homestretch, certain he was about to run out of air again. His self-esteem battered, he came to our ranch shy and uncertain but gentle. He was one of my favorites.

As I led him to the round pen (aka "the sick bay") near the house, Babu shook, his muscles twitching in wavelike spasms. A rank odor hovered around his face. Passing my hand over Babu's neck, I could feel his body heat from six inches away. Babu had a fever. Imagining Damon or Matt's first question ("How high is his temperature, Lynn?"), I sighed. Time to bring out the equine rectal thermometer from my disorganized vet supplies bin.

Taking a horse's temperature was another recently acquired skill. Matt had demonstrated the technique, a simple maneuver that consisted of a) lifting the horse's tail, b) inserting the thermometer into the obvious place, c) waiting for the digital timer to beep, and d) removing the thermometer. However, there were a couple of tricky elements to the process — in particular, avoiding an indignant kick from the ailing horse.

Another: not "losing" the thermometer. "You got to watch out. Sometimes the horse will sort of suck it into his rectum," Matt cautioned cheerfully. "And, well, that can be a mess. You don't want to have to go digging around in there looking for the thermometer. So always keep hold of it, no matter what."

Matt's vivid combination of "rectum" and "digging around" still haunts me every time I have to check a horse's temperature.

Babu was waiting, looking at me miserably. I grabbed the thermometer from its resting place, a plastic syringe container, and approached Babu. Feeling like a pediatric nurse, I waved it at him, "This will all be over soon, I swear. Sorry, Babu."

Minutes later, the deed was done — Babu had a fever of 103 degrees. Armed with this data, I called Damon. He said, "Sounds like a possible respiratory infection. Give him a shot of Banamine now. I'll be out to see him by noon."

I stayed near Babu, petting him. He dropped his head and sniffed at strands of hay on the ground, the shot easing his discomfort. Damon arrived soon after, pulling his scope out of his vet van. Recognizing the device from Storm's many exams, I knew it would soon be up Babu's nose. Between the thermometer and the scope, it was shaping up to be a very invasive morning for poor Babu.

Halfway through the scope examination, Damon frowned. "Looks like they removed the flapper instead of tying it back. I don't like that procedure. Babu has been aspirating his feed — and now he has a nasty infection."

The tie-back surgery is basically just that — tying back the flapper so that the airway is unobstructed. The procedure doesn't have a high success rate, as the sutures often give out over time, allowing the flapper to go back to its presurgery configuration. The removal of the flapper is a permanent surgery. With the flapper completely excised, the horse's trachea has constant airflow. But this comes at a price — the flapper is also designed to keep important things out of the airway, such as grain, insects, and water. Horses without flappers are much more susceptible to breathing in their feed and developing respiratory infections, such as pneumonia.

Damon left antibiotics and detailed instructions. Babu made rapid progress. An excellent patient, he never once objected to his daily antibiotic shots or random thermometer insertions.

Impressed with Babu's gentlemanly behavior during his illness, I looked up his pedigree. He had a collection of racehorse relatives with entertaining, Lewis Carroll–like names such as Miss Cougar, Cindy Lou, Bowl of Flowers, Sweet Tooth, and Plum Cake. And he had a very famous grandsire — Seattle Slew, winner of the 1977 Triple Crown.

At his foaling, no one would have ever bet that Seattle Slew would be a Triple Crown champion. His pedigree was unremarkable, his conformation athletic but similar to that of hundreds of other colts. As a yearling, he was consigned to the Fasig-Tipton auction sales service. A stellar sales venue, Fasig-Tipton hosts auctions of Thoroughbreds all throughout the United States.

Then just an unnamed one-year-old colt, Seattle Slew caught the eye of Mickey and Karen Taylor. Mickey was a logger from the Pacific Northwest. He and his wife had a dream — to buy a young Thoroughbred and be part of the glamorous racing world. But their budget was modest; $15,000 was the most they would spend. In the racing industry, even during the 1970s, the top-class yearlings sell for hundreds of thousands of dollars. The Taylors could only buy the equivalent of a minor-league horse, like Tulsa or Nacho, in partnership with another couple, Jim and Sally Hill.

Seattle Slew strutted around the auction walkway with exuberant pizzazz. The couples spotted something in his eyes, in his jaunty arrogance — and busted their budget, paying $17,500 for him. There was nothing unusual about the colt's pedigree or conformation that signaled a future champion. Just that flash of cockiness in his bearing. Once in training, Seattle Slew proved that individual drive and heart are the most important factors in racehorse performance. Even in his early workouts, he loved to run and to beat the other horses.

Seattle Slew was the first undefeated Triple Crown winner. A kind, gentlemanly horse off the track, Slew was a fierce competitor in his races. During the Triple Crown races, he liked to break out of the gate fast, take the lead early, hold it and then, just as a horse or two might be closing, open up in the stretch, usually winning by four lengths or more.

I watched footage of his races, struck by similarities to Babu. Both horses were dark, almost black bays with intelligent faces. And like Slew, Babu preferred to race in front, shooting ahead of the field quickly. But at the final turn, when Slew would push forward for the win, Babu would gasp for air and fade back, his weak respiratory system unable to match his competitive drive.

Soon Babu had recovered enough to return to his pasture, though I waited another few days, keeping him near the house where I could watch him from the living room window. Finally, I let him go back with A Secret Toast and Halo Selecto, certain it was silly and neurotic to wait any longer. But the very next morning, Babu stood uneasily near his bucket. The other horses had finished their breakfast long ago, heading out to doze in the far corner of the field. Babu didn't follow them, standing stiffly next to the fence, his head held in an awkward pose.

As I ran to investigate, I spotted something dripping from Babu's clenched jaw. He was drooling copiously, with thick strands of goopy saliva hanging from his lower lips. Too worried to be disgusted, I haltered Babu, gently probing his cheeks and mouth, looking for a laceration or maybe an abscess site. Babu tightened his lips, his eyes anxious.

My fingers were quickly covered in horse drool and mucus. Wrapping my cell phone in my fleece sleeve, I managed to dial Austin Equine without shorting out the SIM card. An hour later, Damon's exam revealed nothing. "Hmmm, there must be something in his mouth that bothers him. No sign of choke, so that's good. But I can't quite see anything. Or feel anything."

To my surprise, *choke* is an actual veterinary term. When partially chewed food gets stuck in the esophagus, a horse will cough violently, trying to expel or shift the blockage. Because the horse can't swallow, food particles and saliva will sometimes ooze from the nostrils. A potentially dangerous condition, choke must be treated immediately, usually by flushing the esophagus with fluids via a long, unpleasant tube.

Certain that Babu's new ailment was due to his recent bout of pneumonia, I peppered Damon with questions. "I don't think it's related, Lynn," replied Damon. "He's not running a temperature and his lungs sound clear. It's just a coincidence, two different problems back-to-back." A freakish coincidence, though, I thought to myself.

Babu refused to unclench his jaws until encouraged by sedation. I held his head up while Damon peered into his mouth with a flashlight, then slid his gloved hand along Babu's tongue. "There's got to be a foreign body in there somewhere." Damon wrestled with Babu's tongue, a foot-long mass of muscular, undulating tissue. "But I can't find it."

"Foreign body" was a phrase that conjured up many unpleasant

images. I associated it with ominous veterinary mysteries, like the one I
encountered during my polo lesson days.

"SEE THE PUS? You see it, yes? The pus is good, see the pus." Dr. Ivanov's
heavy Russian accent distorted his diagnostic explanation into punk rock
lyrics. He pointed at the draining ooze sliding down the brown mare's
hind leg.

I kept my distance. The sight of Dr. Ivanov simply pulling out his
sharp-edged tools was enough to turn my stomach back then. Across the
street, a polo practice was finishing up, the sounds of hoofbeats mixed with
player yells carrying over to the barn.

Pepe, my mare, had developed a running sore on her leg weeks earlier. No amount of topical ointments or antibiotics was effective — the
sore widened and dripped noxious fluid. Dr. Ivanov, an avid polo player,
had set aside time between his weekend tournament games to examine her
again.

"This mare, she has a bad problem, down in the leg. I can try this
thing, this procedure, maybe to give her one more chance." Thinking he
meant a formal surgery, I asked where I should take Pepe — to the local
clinic or a specialized equine surgeon?

"Ah, no, Lynn. I can do this here, after my match. At the barn. It will
be not so much expensive."

In spite of his habit of scheduling casework around his polo matches,
Dr. Ivanov had a reputation as a good vet. Tanned and confident, he
exuded competence. He had set up his medical kit, sedated Pepe, and made
the first incision within fifteen minutes of his arrival at the stable.

More pus dripped, accompanied by another refrain of "See the pus, it's
good. See it?" But not enough fluid drained from Pepe's leg — Dr. Ivanov
frowned, then shrugged his shoulders. He'd done his best. An airhorn
blasted from the polo field, the traditional signal for chukker's end. Dr.
Ivanov twitched reflexively at the sound, then put away his equipment,
explaining follow-up care over his shoulder as he headed toward his truck.

Days later, Pepe's leg continued to ooze. Tory advised me to ride her, to help circulation in the limb through mild exertion. I'd ride Pepe in slow circuits around the fields, her gaits as sound as ever, then carefully hose her leg afterward. The strange wound, less than an inch long, shrank somewhat as weeks passed, but it continued to drip intermittently.

Dr. Ivanov was puzzled and counseled a wait-and-see approach. His tournament roster grew heavy, requiring frequent travel to out-of-state clubs. I began looking for another vet, maybe one with a less-active sporting life, and came across a new vet, Dr. Wagner, with a mobile practice — I resolved to call her and set up an exam for Pepe.

One early evening, Pepe and I went for our regular canter. She loped along, her ears pricked forward, a relaxed cadence in her steps. As I reined her in, turning back for the barn, I wondered if her leg mystery would ever be solved. At the barn, I hosed the sweat off her back, then turned to her hind leg. Something looked different. Crouching down, I peered at the wound in the dim light. An object was protruding from her leg, a piece of wood the size of my thumbnail. Pepe shifted her weight, stepping to one side. The wood slid back into her sore, then reemerged with her movement, accompanied by a thin stream of blood.

Horrified, I pulled the new vet's number from my purse, placing an urgent call. Dr. Wagner sounded intrigued. "Hmmm. Sounds like she's had a foreign body in there all along. I'll be there as soon as I can."

In twenty minutes, a large van pulled into the barn parking lot. An Amazon-like woman with a curly brown ponytail jumped out, pulling a vet smock over her denim shirt. "Hi, I'm Lydia. I mean, Dr. Wagner." Striding across the barn aisle, her hiking boots leaving thick tread marks behind, Dr. Wagner smiled. "Let's see the patient. My, what a cutie." Humming to herself, she probed Pepe's wood piece, then produced a large syringe. "Let's get her into a stall. I can't tell how long this splinter is, so I want to lay her down with sedation, then extract it. Just in case it turns out to be something unusual."

I thought about that last statement. Wasn't a chunk of wood floating around Pepe's leg unusual? Reading my unspoken question, Dr. Wagner grinned, "You'd be amazed."

With Pepe in a sedated doze, Dr. Wagner got to work. I hovered outside the stall, afraid to look. After about ten minutes, I heard an "Aha," then a gloved hand appeared in the doorway, waving a jagged, four-inch slice of wood. "I got it," declared Dr. Wagner.

I stared in shock — the wood looked like a fat pencil. "How did *that* get inside her?"

Dr. Wagner said, "We'll never know for sure. But most likely, she was playing with some other horses, maybe got spooked into the fence or side of the barn. When there's an impact injury, sometimes the body will absorb a piece of shrapnel, so to speak, very quickly. The tissue will close over the foreign body and seal it off from sight."

Dr. Wagner pulled off her gloves, happy with her successful extraction. She put the wood in a syringe case, handing it to me for a souvenir. "That reminds me of another story. One night, I got a call to check out a big foxhunter. Pretty horse, a draft cross. He'd slipped and caught his leg in their wood fencing. Nasty cut. As I was cleaning it out, I saw the edge of a wood chip in there. I gave it a tug and out popped a six-inch square of wood fence. Dang thing was nearly the size of a paperback book. The owner almost fainted on the spot."

EVEN BABU'S BULKY TONGUE couldn't be hiding a wooden paperback. Damon and Matt both came to our ranch the next day, eager to figure out Babu's ailment. Damon was sure something was caught in his throat or tongue, but even after several exams they couldn't find anything. Babu couldn't eat unless I injected him with a muscle relaxant, poking him in the vein every morning. Frustrated, the vets kept returning, looking for some kind of obstruction.

Their progress was hampered by equine anatomy. A horse's head, mouth, and throat are notoriously difficult to X-ray or ultrasound. The sheer breadth and tissue mass of these areas challenge diagnostic equipment. A horse's jaw is long, narrow, and very heavy. To X-ray the interior of the mouth often involves sedation, a vise, and sometimes pulleys. Even then, results can be mixed, especially with traditional film radiographs. Film is prone to showing "artifacts," a form of afterimage left from previous use of the X-ray plates.

The situation was growing dire. Babu was losing weight, and he couldn't be kept on premeal injections forever. Surgery was the next option — but without an accurate radiograph, that could be a risky, exploratory procedure. As Damon explained, there could be a foreign body anywhere from Babu's tongue to his esophagus, a very large area for random surgical searches.

Later that day, Matt called back. "Hey, I want to come out today and try one last time to find out what's in Babu's mouth." Matt explained that this would be a full-assault diagnostic treatment — involving ultrasound equipment, scopes, and radiographs. "I'll need to lay him down with heavy sedation, like PJ — so let's do that near the house. It will be level ground there, plus I want to be near electric outlets. Maybe have some blankets ready."

An emergency call delayed Matt's arrival, and his "vet-mobile" pulled up to the house near 4 P.M. The temperature had dropped, leaving a damp crispness in the air. Amber, the Austin Equine vet tech, tied her smock over her ultra-hip skinny jeans, then grabbed a coat from the backseat. A cheerful vet student intern carried out bulky pieces of equipment, carefully setting them up on the ground.

I rummaged through our tool kit, toting every extension cord we owned out to the porch. The sun was just starting to set as Matt sedated Babu, then laid him gently on the grass. "Brisk, isn't it?" Matt rubbed his hands together, then slipped on very non-warm-looking latex gloves. "Let's get to work."

Despite the chilly air, Matt stretched out on the ground, painstakingly pushing a special scope down Babu's throat. He was determined to find the problem, even as darkness fell and he had to strap a flashlight to his head.

Amber manned the ultrasound station, shivering under her fashionable jacket.

Matt was now flat on his stomach, probing intently with his scope, then glancing at the ultrasound image. "I have a good feeling about this," he declared, ignoring the uncomfortable conditions and low-odds diagnostic gamble. His khaki trousers were damp from the winter ground, his arms exposed above the elbows, but he never complained.

Matt's benign, dadlike countenance and fondness for goofy jokes hid a steely side. Damon, the most unflappable person I knew, once described Matt as "having grit," the ultimate compliment from a Wyoming native. Like Damon, Matt had attended A&M University vet school, but his goals had been much different. At first, Matt had been interested in conservation work. He wanted to become a wildlife veterinarian, perhaps one day working on a nature preserve.

As part of the normal course rotation, all vet students study equine medicine — even those who intend to only treat cattle or cats or elk. Matt was entranced with horse veterinary work; he found the equine combination of animal and athlete irresistible from a clinical standpoint. Soon into the semester, he decided to change his focus and specialize in equine veterinary coursework.

There was only one minor hitch. Matt had absolutely no experience with horses. He didn't even know how to halter one or lead it properly. Their large physiques and rapid movements always surprised him. Nearly all the other vet students in the equine program had ridden horses before, often growing up in equestrian families. Matt was unfazed: "Well, there were a couple of advantages to my situation. First, I was always excited and enthused about even minor horse information. A professor would say something obvious like, 'Horses can only breathe through their nose' — and I'd go, 'No way! That's *so* cool!'"

Matt mastered horse handling in a remarkably short period, amid a group of very tough critics (professors, fellow students, annoyed equine patients). By the time he graduated, Matt was skillful as well as compassionate with

horses. He quickly won the trust of the ex-racehorses at our ranch —
Storm's "French" attitude aside, they all sensed his kindness and determi-
nation to help them.

"There it is!" Matt's voice was muffled by his proximity to the ground.
Finally, a glimpse of something metallic — there was indeed a foreign
object in Babu's throat. Matt gave a triumphant grunt, then put aside the
scope with a sigh. It was too dark to continue, but he now had a specific
location for the surgeon.

"I'll call Dr. Dutton's office tomorrow. And we can send over the
ultrasound record, too. He should be able to schedule you for Monday."
Matt then departed, in search of wool gloves and a long-overdue dinner.
More puzzling news soon came from Damon, back at the Austin Equine
office. One of the radiographs also showed a small, metal object in Babu's
tongue.

Worried that Babu was slowly swallowing decaying metal from his
tongue, I was relieved when Monday arrived. Loading Babu up in our
trailer, I drove to the surgeon's office through state highways and speed-
ing 18-wheeler traffic. Julia, Tawakoni's new owner, had donated the elderly but sturdy trailer to us. While its exterior was ugly, with peeling gray
paint and surface rust, the interior was roomy and comfortable for horses.

My hands clenched tightly on the wheel as our weary truck wheezed
along — this was only my third experience hauling a horse. I was afraid
to pull trailers, especially ones with bumper hitches, as this one had. Tory
had regaled her students with lurid tales of bumper pull hitches breaking,
trailers flying uncontrollably down highways, their equine passengers
trapped and doomed.

Tom took a day off from work to accompany me, coaching me from
the passenger seat and making sarcastic comments about any driver who
tailgated us. His wit lightened my mood, calming me as I steered along the
crowded, winding roads.

We arrived at Dr. Dutton's clinic two hours later. A dapper man with
a neatly trimmed black mustache, Dr. Dutton was a very successful equine

surgeon. Damon had once worked for him, fresh out of vet school. While Tom checked in at the office, I stayed behind to unload Babu and get him settled in the clinic barn.

A gleaming, aluminum trailer was parked nearby. The bay gelding being led out matched the trailer's sleek grandeur — a show horse, he moved with graceful precision. A well-dressed couple hovered anxiously, monitoring the bay's every move. The woman glanced briefly at Babu's Reagan-era trailer, shaking her head.

After checking on Babu through a side window, I struggled mightily to pull down the trailer ramp, which seemed to weigh a ton. One of the vet techs offered to help, his voice familiar. Panting slightly from exertion, I looked up as a stocky, smock-clad man approached, his freckled face and crooked grin also familiar.

It was Doug, a former riding instructor from my DC polo barn days — he had gone away to school years ago. I stood shocked into silence, suddenly very self-conscious of my rusty trailer, hay-speckled hair, and duct-taped truck bed. My brain feebly attempted to process the long-shot odds that would bring Doug, not only to Texas, but to this vet clinic — and on the one day that I would be there, too.

Wincing internally at my disheveled appearance, I braced for his moment of recognition, the forced jolly greeting, and the recitation of his latest polo tales. But Doug didn't seem to remember me, barely giving me a second glance. Politely, he pulled down the ramp — "Well now, that's a heavy one. Kind of an antique, isn't it?" — pity and amusement in his eyes. Pretty much the same expression I remembered from the polo lesson days. Flustered, I slouched over Babu, averted my face, and (of course) dropped his lead rope into a manure pile.

Babu went into surgery that afternoon. Dr. Dutton quickly discovered the true cause of his distress. His clinic was equipped with the latest in diagnostic tools, including digital radiography, an X-ray technology that uses computers instead of film. With a laptop hooked to the radiograph equipment, Dr. Dutton could see instant images each time he took an X-ray. Digital radiographs are much crisper, and computer screens contain no ghostly artifacts.

Babu had an abandoned surgical needle in his throat, from the previous flapper surgery — along with a piece of wire in his tongue. Dr. Dutton called me from the operating room, relaying this information in a matter-of-fact tone.

"He has a *what*?" I stared at my cell phone, certain that a bad connection must have caused me to hear incorrectly.

"A surgical needle."

"Was that done for a reason? I mean, is it a common..."

"I make it a practice to never leave needles behind. Personally, anyway." Dr. Dutton's dry tone made me smile, for the first time in several days. He then explained that the other problem, the wire, was simple to remove.

"And the wire and the needle are unrelated?" I was confused.

"Just one of those weird coincidences," replied Dr. Dutton. "Probably just got some wire in his hay. Sometimes the baler machine hiccups and packs some wire into the hay. The surgery won't take long, simple procedure."

"I usually don't feed wire with hay," I stammered, worried that Dr. Dutton would think I made a habit of adding metal supplements to Babu's diet.

"Oh, I'm sure you were careful with that. Horses sometimes chew strange things. You'd be amazed at what we've seen here in surgeries."

Remembering Dr. Wagner's wood fence story, I refrained from asking Dr. Dutton to elaborate. A surgeon's idea of "amazing" would no doubt be grisly.

During the surgery, Dr. Dutton deftly removed the wire, but he left in the needle; this was the safer approach, since the needle was now walled off by scar tissue and thus "harmless." Dr. Dutton said, "Now if it had been in danger of traveling, then that would have been a different deal. The spot between the trachea and esophagus is very dangerous surgically. Not sure I could have done anything then. Maybe, but not likely."

Dr. Dutton sounded wistful, the thought of uncharted surgical territory a source of inspiration, rather than fear.

A FEW DAYS LATER, I pulled back into the clinic parking lot, ready to take Babu home. I was alone this time — Tom couldn't take another day off from work. Without his soothing presence, my weak trailer-driving skills deteriorated. As I maneuvered down Dr. Dutton's narrow driveway, I turned too sharply into a parking space, causing a painful, rusty screeching from the trailer hitch.

A cluster of sleek dressage riders looked up, grimacing at both the sound and the sight of our battered two-horse rig. My face red, I headed for the reception desk to check out Babu. A junior vet trotted off to bring Babu from the postsurgery barn.

Doug also appeared to lend a hand with the ramp again. As I bustled around the trailer, Doug asked me if I was "one of those rescue ladies." He commented on Babu's thinness, unaware that he had recently been on a "wire in tongue" diet. Then he launched into a lecture on proper equine care and nutrition — in case I "didn't know about these things." My face must have reflected the Rodney Dangerfield "can't get no respect" patter in my brain; Doug stopped his presentation, looking at me quizzically.

I was relieved when I finally got Babu home safely. Dr. Dutton's postsurgery instructions were simple. Give him some anti-inflammatory pills once a day, feed him watered-down grain (to reduce chewing), and flush the surgery site twice a day. For the last item, Damon presented me with a giant syringe device, a bulky cylinder of metal and plastic. His directions seemed easy enough. "Just fill this with dilute solution, then insert into Babu's mouth. Aim for the surgery site and flush with the water."

Babu had other ideas. Even after I sedated him, he tossed his head impatiently each time I tried to insert the hefty syringe. Tom came to my aid with a flashlight — as I held Babu's jaws open, we peered into his mouth with the light. But we still couldn't see the surgery site — Babu's grinding teeth and undulating tongue created too much hazard. After getting my fingers sideswiped by equine molars, raising welts, I settled for aiming the water in the general direction of his back teeth. It was Babu's only display of temperament throughout the entire veterinary ordeal.

Babu recovered steadily, and soon I was riding him, enjoying his personality under saddle. I could see a change from his pre- and postsurgery saddle sessions. Babu's self-esteem was somehow boosted by his harrowing vet experience. He no longer worried about going fast, and he relaxed into slower paces readily, dropping his elegant head and sighing with contentment.

However, unlike Babu's, my self-image had deteriorated. My encounter with Doug had reminded me of how little progress I'd made in my big goals to become an expert trainer and rider. I had developed an interesting skill set, like how to feed fifteen horses from my truck and the proper technique for tracheotomy assisting — but these were the badges of an equine social worker, not a true professional equestrian. As I knew too well from Doug's amused eyes, anyone can do horse rescue work — even adult beginners.

Another familiar anxiety dominated my thoughts. Babu's surgery bill was over $1,000, a serious hit to our bank account. But that wasn't the only financial blow — our anonymous donor's two-year commitment was nearly up. As 2005 drew to a close, I had to somehow replace his generous (and much-needed) $25,000 annual contribution.

True to my nature, I brooded on both these topics endlessly, as well as on the dilemma of how to find Babu a good home. He still was prone to aspirating his feed, and he had a walled-off needle permanently embedded in his neck. I didn't envision a surplus of adopters eager to take Babu home.

I was soon proved wrong. Amy, a young dressage instructor with a new lesson barn, came to visit the ranch a few weeks later. She was looking for two horses, one to be a dressage prospect, the other to be a lesson horse for her beginner students. As I showed her around the ranch, she talked with me about her facility in the Texas Hill Country.

Amy brought her own trainer, a dressage judge named Debra. She lent an air of equestrian opera to our ranch, regaling us with stories of ex-husbands, dressage wins, and favorite judging moments during competitions. Her diva delivery was greatly softened by her rollicking humor — Amy and I laughed nonstop throughout the visit.

Debra homed in on Babu almost immediately. "Who is the dark bay? He's a classy mover." As I explained his oddities, Debra brushed aside my comments. "Who cares about a needle in the neck? He's lovely. And he wouldn't have to work hard at all with Amy. She's very considerate of her lesson horses."

Surprised, I stared at Debra — who would have thought a dressage queen would be so matter-of-fact about permanent neck shrapnel? She was quite a contrast to the show competitors I had encountered with Sugarfoot.

"And look at his face — what a kind eye. Amy, you have to ride Needle in the Neck," ordered Debra.

"Well, don't call him that. Poor guy, that's all he needs — to be taunted," Amy teased, prompting a flurry of witticisms from Debra.

Amy carefully looked at each horse and decided to ride a few — including Babu. In the end, she was the most impressed with Babu; she liked his pretty, flowing gaits, quiet manners, and shy personality. Debra coached her from the sidelines, calling out, "How does he feel? He looks great, very nice mover. Needle in the Neck is a winner, you *must* adopt this one." I was liking Debra more and more.

Although Babu had no experience with children or dressage, Amy agreed with Debra. She adopted him, delighted with his low adoption fee. "He just needs to have his confidence built up," she said, petting his head.

So did I. My original goal to be an expert trainer, a real professional like Amy or Debra — not just a disheveled "rescue lady" — still seemed far away, especially after seeing myself through Doug's amused eyes. Maybe it was time to get some instruction, some formal lessons again — and not just from DVDs.

PART VI

The Homestretch

In the beginner's mind there are many possibilities,
but in the expert's there are few.

SHUNRYU SUZUKI,
Zen teacher

CHAPTER THIRTEEN

Lightening Ball, aka "LB"

H E'S A BAD ACTOR," Priscilla said vehemently. Her voice sounded tense, even over two cell phones. "I talked to his old trainer, and he said the horse was a kicker, spooked all the time. A really *bad* actor!"

Lightening Ball (aka "LB") needed to stay in Priscilla's barn at the racetrack for two days. The racetrack planned to give LB a "retirement ceremony" during Texas Champions Night (an evening of high-stakes racing). Recently donated to LOPE, LB was an aging star in Texas racing. He had won over $300,000 in his career, and he was just now retiring at age nine. The track staff had "sort of" talked Priscilla into lending a stall in her barn. Clearly she was close to backing out of the deal.

I summoned up all my persuasive skills, explaining to Priscilla how quiet LB had been at our farm for the past few weeks. She unenthusiastically agreed to keep him at her barn and, after a couple more muttered "bad actor" comments, clicked off the phone.

My goal of finding an instructor would have to wait until after LB's retirement ceremony. It was a big honor that LB's owners had donated him to LOPE. Until the event was safely behind us, I didn't feel justified taking time for lessons or any other nonfundraising activities.

I walked out to LB's pasture. Like all big-money winners, he had a commanding presence, a real poise about him, even while just standing in the pasture. Most successful racehorses are dominant and supercompetitive by nature. As Seabiscuit so joyfully demonstrated, they revel not only in winning but also in beating the other horses.

LB was dark chestnut, a pretty shade of brown, with a long tail and a thick mane. An irregularly shaped white stripe trickled down his face. His build was impressive — stout body, powerful hindquarters, and sloping shoulders that looked all business.

His face was his most striking feature, with intelligent, wary eyes looking intently at you. LB's mouth was expressive, usually set in a hard, tight line that curved slightly at the end — as if he expected little from you but still hoped to be pleasantly surprised. His head was masculine and well proportioned, with a strong jaw and surprisingly refined muzzle. LB could produce the best look of disgust of any horse on the ranch. His upper lip would curl, stopping just before his teeth were exposed. Then he would tighten his nose muscles into an eloquent sneer.

During my research on his ancestry, I came across a black-and-white photo of a horse that stopped me in my tracks. It was a Thoroughbred named T. V. Lark, an exuberant turf horse during the 1960s and LB's great-grandfather. T. V. Lark's head matched LB's almost perfectly, another compelling example of how some stallions "stamp" their progeny, often for generations.

LB carefully sized up everyone who approached him. He had recently been running in lower-level races when his original owner bought him back, specifically to retire him. Horses in that type of race circuit are often passed around, sometimes ending up with rough-edged trainers. Priscilla's tense voice replayed in my mind. I had a hunch that LB had been mishandled in the last years of his career. No doubt he had reacted strongly to such treatment, eventually earning a reputation as a mean horse at the track.

The equine mind can be a paradox. Like any other animal, horses live in the now — what matters most is the present moment. But horses also have long memories, often remembering previous owners, past negative experiences, and childhood equine playmates. And they hold grudges.

ALI WAS A POLO PLAYER at the polo club. Born in the Middle East, he had emigrated to the United States decades ago. A trim man in his fifties, Ali carried himself elegantly and liked to stride around in his fashionable polo gear, shouting at his groom to bring him a horse for the next chukker.

Ali was hard on his horses, yanking their mouths to slow them down, spurring their flanks during games, and treating them like substandard equipment. Ali had a temper and blamed his horses when he missed the ball, whipping them in disgust. His horses had the look of POWs, huddling next to each other at his trailer, trading furtive communication with their ears and eyes, their faces full of fatigue. Ali usually kept his horses for years, selling them only after he had ruined their legs and spirit with his harsh riding.

At the start of one spring polo season, Ali was spotted watching a practice. His leg was encased in heavy plaster from ankle to midthigh. Balancing on crutches, Ali could only hobble in painfully small steps. Ali dismissed questions with an airy, "Oh, just had a horse accident. Nothing to fuss over." Soon, players and students were whispering behind trailers, and the groom gossip network flared into action, with Ali's groom spilling the story to Chad's groom, who passed the word to us students.

Before spring polo begins, players and pros must get their horses in shape. Most polo horses are turned out to pasture for the winter, giving them a long vacation after each polo season. The horses come back to work full of energy and sometimes rebellion — most buck-offs at our barn occurred in April, before the first official May polo practice.

Ali rarely conditioned his horses properly, instead relying on his whip to cow his horses into performing. A few weeks earlier, his groom had saddled one of Ali's favorite horses, straight from his winter pasture break. Ali took the reins and began to mount, putting his foot into the stirrup. But his other foot slipped in the soft April ground. As he hopped, trying to catch his balance, his horse saw an opportunity. Years of poor treatment had made him malicious under his docile exterior.

The horse bolted, a mad rush for freedom and revenge. Ali's right foot left the ground, his left foot still in the stirrup. His boot became caught in the stirrup's iron, his hands lost their grip on the reins — and the horse dragged him at high speed across the pasture. Ali's leg broke, a spiral fracture that spun everywhere and took months to heal. He counted himself lucky to have survived.

But the horse was even luckier, the grooms whispered behind the polo trailers. The horse's desperate plan had succeeded — he was for sale, years ahead of Ali's usual schedule.

LB MIGHT BE DIFFICULT, but like Ali's horses, he also had a look of injustice in his eyes. So far, he'd been a gentleman with me, and I felt compelled to give him the benefit of the doubt. I liked him and his tough-but-smart De Niro personality. And so did Bob, LB's original race owner.

Lightening Ball was the third purchase of an unlikely racing partnership. Bob and Greg were both Shell Oil engineers — their friendship extended into a shared dream of racehorse ownership. After years of pep talking each other, they finally took the plunge and bought a racehorse. Their first two horses weren't particularly spectacular on the track, but Lightening Ball more than made up for their poor performance.

Within a couple of years, he was bankrolling Bob and Greg's entire racing operation. Lightening Ball won over $180,000 by age four, a tidy sum that underwrote Bob and Greg's stable of twelve racehorses. Even by engineering standards, LB was an excellent return on his purchase price of $10,500 as an unraced two-year-old.

Lightening Ball was an exciting runner: he liked to come from behind, sometimes from way behind. Bob especially would feel the suspense, commenting in one newspaper article, "So when the race starts, your heart is in the right place, but then all of a sudden it moves to your mouth because

you're trying to figure out if this is going to be the day he kicks it into gear
or just lopes around the track."

Rangy and long-legged, Lightening Ball covered tremendous ground
with each stride.. His lanky physique belied his name — not much was
"ball-like" about Lightening Ball. He was bred at a stallion station of a
Texas breeder, a kind man who allowed his young granddaughter to name
the farm foals. She thought of the name Lightening Ball, including the mis-
spelling. The offbeat moniker was duly entered on LB's official Thoroughbred papers. Once registered with the Jockey Club, it can be difficult,
if not impossible, to change a racehorse's name.

With such a promising start to his career, Lightening Ball seemed des-
tined for great things in spite of his odd name. Bob and Greg made sure
he had an excellent race trainer and the best of care, including periodic
breaks from racing. Bob and his wife, Pat, often visited Lightening Ball
during his farm vacations. Pat especially fussed over him, giving him lots
of pats and handfuls of horse cookies. "He just seemed like such a great
personality," Pat fondly told me. "I could tell he liked the attention. And
of course the horse cookies, too."

Like all athletes, even equine superstars fade eventually. Lightening
Ball's earning record tells a familiar, roller-coaster story (the result of
being passed from trainer to trainer). After winning close to $200,000 by
age four, his wins dropped sharply for the next two years, down to $17,000,
then back up to $19,000. Then in his fifth year of racing, he had a bigger
jump, to $30,000, followed by an increase to $38,000 as an eight-year-old.
But in his last year of racing, he earned only $2,000. That was in claiming
races, the lowest rung of the racing ladder.

In a claiming race, every horse is for sale with the same set price tag.
All the racehorses entered can be bought or "claimed" from the race for
that price. But there is a catch. Whoever wants to claim a horse must put
in the request before the race — not after. Once the race is over, if the
horse has been "claimed," the horse officially belongs to the new owner
— no matter how well or poorly the horse performed.

The original owner retains any winnings that the horse earned in the race. And the new owner takes possession of the horse for the claiming price — even if the horse became injured during the race. Roughly half of all North American horse races fall into the claiming category. Many of the horses at our ranch, like Zuper and Tulsa, had been claiming horses at one time.

Claimers allow working-class racehorses to compete equally. If all races were open to any entrants, the same horses would win over and over again. Stakes horses, the elite Thoroughbreds of racing, would use the cheaper races for workouts and easy purse money. But claiming races motivate trainers to enter only those horses they are willing to lose for the set price.

There are a wide variety of claiming races, with multiple classes based on the price of the horses entered. The optional claimer is the top level, with horses running for high prices, such as $75,000. Most claiming races are at the mid- or lower levels, with prices ranging anywhere from $2,000 (at the seamier tracks) to $60,000 (at major tracks such as Santa Anita). The lowest-level claiming races often have horses at the end of their careers due to age, injuries, or both. Too often, race trainers will enter their declining racehorses in cheap claimers, hoping someone will claim them — and take them off their feed bill.

Even after he no longer owned him, Bob had followed Lightening Ball's career. When he saw Lightening Ball running in seedy claimers — he was being entered in $5,000 claiming races in West Virginia, the equivalent of a famous shortstop ending his career with a class A minor league team — something stirred. Bob wouldn't have survived in the racing business if not for Lightening Ball, and it just didn't seem a fitting end to the horse's grand career. Impulsively, he claimed Lightening Ball, paid the $5,000, then shipped him to Texas.

Some of Bob's racing cronies thought he was crazy; they advised him to sell Lightening Ball off immediately. Racehorse owners aren't supposed to bond with their horses — it's a business. Instead, Bob decided to retire him, and he eventually contacted LOPE.

LB'S RETIREMENT CEREMONY would be held at Sam Houston Race Park. He had run his best races there, including a big $100,000 win in 1997. Each year, the track held a Texas Champions race event, a night of competition for Texas-bred Thoroughbreds only. LB would lead the post-parade to one of the races, an honor given only to special racehorses. LOPE would also hold a silent auction fundraiser later that night — space was set aside for our tables at the most heavily trafficked track entrance.

The Houston racetrack was eager to help. Sam Houston had always displayed a strong commitment to ex-racehorses. Long before LOPE came on the scene, the track had its own adoption program. Run by racing office employees in their spare time, it found homes for dozens of racehorses. Sam Houston was the first Texas track to endorse LOPE — a stamp of approval that went far with race trainers.

The track has a reputation for intervention. One day, a race owner named Jack called me to list a horse. "I got a nice, older gelding that needs a home," he drawled. "He's a sorrel, real good-looking. But now, I don't want him to end up racing again. I had a problem with that one time, with Sam Houston. With their adoption deal there."

"What happened?" I was surprised — the track had prided itself on carefully following up on the horses.

"Well, I had a good little mare — but she got tired of racing and slowed down. So I put her in their program. The guy in the office there, he told me how she found a nice home. But two months later, I was getting a horse ready for the fifth race, and I heard my mare's name being announced for the next race! I was hopping mad, and I called up the head honcho right then and chewed him out good."

"You mean Dave?"

"That's the one. He was embarrassed, let me tell you. Something had gone wrong in the adoption. Guess someone lied to them about not ever racing the horse again. But he made it all right in the end, made it up to me and the mare. Dave took a personal interest in the situation and talked to the trainer who had my mare. That jackass — pardon my French, ma'am — that trainer, he told Dave he owned the mare and wouldn't give her back."

I suppressed a laugh, holding my head away from the phone. Only a Texas man would say something like "Pardon my French, ma'am" in the twenty-first century. Jack continued, his East Texas twang and my cell phone reception forcing me to listen attentively.

"Dave, he told me not to worry about it — he'd make sure my mare never raced again in Texas. And that's just what he did, too. That ass—, I mean trainer, he never run her again in this state." Jack chuckled.

Film noir scenes rolled across my mind. "Did he suspend his license?"

"Even better. Ol' Dave, he's good friends with the track veterinarian. You know how the vet has to approve the racehorses before every race, right? To make sure a horse isn't running drugged or hurt — it's the state law."

"Sure."

"Well, every time my mare came up to run, the track vet found a reason to scratch her from the race. And I mean *every* time. A vet can always find something wrong with a racehorse. Trainer couldn't run her anywhere — so he finally gave the mare back. He knew he was licked. To this day, Dave and the vet still deny it — but I know they saved my mare from a bad deal."

Dave was a dapper corporate executive — with his pinstriped suits and ever-pinging Blackberry, he could have passed for an investment banker. But under his Armani tie beat the heart of a cowboy sheriff, ready to enforce Texas-style justice when necessary.

Another official at a different racetrack liked to walk the backside shedrows, personally scrutinizing the stalls. If any horse looked thin or poorly cared for, he was quick to confront the race trainer, making sure that the horse was well treated from then on. Or else that horse just might be scratched from future races, too.

EQUINE EXPRESS, a professional horse transport company, sponsored LB's trailer trip to the Texas Champions event. By the time their rig arrived in our driveway, I'd already heard some rumors about LB's trailering issues. "He can be difficult about stepping up the ramp," reported one outrider. "I heard he likes to kick the walls for the entire trip. No one wants to haul that horse."

I consulted with Damon. Right before LB's scheduled trip, I injected LB with Ace — to keep him calmer and hopefully easier to load. He took the shot in stride, his eyes suspicious but his body cooperative, as I slowly inserted the needle into his neck.

About twenty minutes later, a six-horse trailer chugged through our gate, right on schedule. The driver was Rick, a burly, jovial type originally from Massachusetts. Bodybuilder muscles flexed under his shirt as he prepped the trailer ramp, laying down thick, rug-like footing.

"Is that him?" He pointed to LB, who was sleepily contemplating his knees. "I'll be sure to take lots of time with him, in case he's nervous. He looks like a *good boy!*" Rick's deep voice boomed. "What a big, handsome fellow, too. These older racehorses, they're always such characters."

LB relaxed visibly in the presence of Rick, who was a comforting combination of den mother and Rocky Balboa. Within a few minutes, Rick had coaxed LB into the trailer with a minimum of melodrama and no kicking. "I'll call you from the road, to check in," Rick shouted over the rumbling diesel engine.

When the truck was halfway out our gate, LB's back hooves began pounding at the trailer walls. Unperturbed, Rick pulled out onto Highway 21, his truck heading eastward toward Houston. True to his word, Rick left me multiple messages, his Boston accent a refreshing contrast to the Texas drawls normally populating my voice mail. "LB is doing *great*, he stopped kicking. I pulled over and refilled his water. He's being a real trooper." Then a second message. "I just unloaded him at the track. No problem. I have to tell you, he's a *good boy*."

A surprised Priscilla called to report on LB later that evening: "I was expecting him to be tough, but he has been good so far. Now, I didn't feed him as much as I would if he were running — why ask for trouble, right?"

I drove to Houston the next day, meeting Priscilla in person for the first time. Like Rick, she exuded a steely maternal air. Her shedrow was meticulous, with color-coordinated halters and hay nets hanging from each stall door. A row of beautifully groomed equine heads looked over the doors, calmly awaiting their afternoon hay snack.

Attired in sensible sweatpants, Priscilla peered at me under a fringe of brown bangs and pink bandana. She wasted no time, bustling me over to LB's stall. "I brushed out his mane and tail. He likes to swish his tail in the shavings. He's been quiet today, too. Maybe the other trainers are wrong about him. I don't know, though. He must have done some bad stuff in his day." Priscilla was wary but warmed at the sight of LB stretching his head at her, begging for a peppermint treat. Like any good race trainer, she had pockets full of the round candies, a favorite with Thoroughbreds.

"I think he likes you, Priscilla," I said hopefully.

"He's a good boy," she said, a smile softening her eyes as she unwrapped the treat for LB.

THE RETIREMENT CELEBRATION was the following evening. By then, LB's continued good manners had made a convert of Priscilla — she was now a fan, insisting on grooming him herself for the big event. Pushing aside the red wraps and saddle blanket I brought, she rummaged in her tack room.

"I want him to look good out there," she said, bringing out snowy white polo wraps and a gleaming leather halter. "The white is perfect for his color. And I want to brush out his tail again — look at all those shavings in it."

I squinted at two cedar specks nestled deeply in LB's tail. Priscilla bustled around LB with multiple brushes and a curry comb. "I like my horses to look their best on the track," she declared, pleased with her handiwork. LB glistened like a show horse, Priscilla's white polo wraps accentuating his long legs and seal brown coat.

Although she didn't notice, I saw a big difference between the farm and racetrack LB. He strutted in Priscilla's stall, pausing occasionally to throw baleful glances at the young gelding across the aisle, kicking impatiently at the wall and even pinning his ears at me (until he saw the peppermints in my hand).

During the long walk from her barn to the racing stands, LB seemed to swell two feet in height, the familiar bells and clank of the starting gate exciting him. I led him, following a line of other horses, keeping close to the rail separating the audience from the track. Racetrack fans, rows of benches, and manicured bushes filled the public area. A motley country rock band wailed from a raised platform, their music not improving with proximity.

At the saddling paddock, where the racehorses are tacked up in front of spectators, one of the track officials met us. Eric, a formidable presence at six foot two, was the racing secretary, a position of large responsibility and little reward. A racing secretary's duties include organizing the individual races, keeping an accurate record of all race results, safekeeping racehorse ownership papers, and acting as a liaison with state regulators.

"I was worried he'd seem too laid-back after his time off," Eric said. "But he's really on his toes. Looks like a racehorse, that's for sure." He beamed with approval as a loud *crack* snapped behind me. "What was that?" I asked as LB snorted, pulling hard on the lead rope. "He kicked the paddock wall. Guess he's letting these other horses know who the boss is." Eric smiled and adjusted his glasses for a better look. "He's quite an animal."

LB glowered at the other horses as they were saddled for the race. He pawed impatiently, annoyed that his saddle and staff of grooms hadn't appeared yet. "Looks like he thinks he can win this race," I offered nervously.

Eric glanced at the race program and chuckled. "Well, he probably could beat this group. Even at age nine."

The prerace ritual for the track never varied. As the announcer blared, "Horses to the saddling paddock," several racehorses were led from the shedrows to a line of stalls near the track building. A wall kept the public from touching the horses, but anyone could watch the horses as their trainers groomed and saddled them for the race. Some horses were calm, standing patiently while the tiny racing saddles were cinched to their backs. Others, like LB, exuded irritated machismo, aiming their teeth and hindquarters at their handlers. Such misbehavior was tolerated, even encouraged, as a sign of a fierce competitor.

The trainers led the saddled horses around a small, circular walkway in front of the stalls. The jockeys joined them now, their bright silk jackets matching the saddle pad colors. Then as "Riders up!" bellowed through the loudspeakers, the jockeys were hoisted up onto the saddles, their horses often sidestepping in excitement. Still escorted by the race trainers, the jockeys steered their mounts up a side pathway toward the track. Before they reached the broad rail and thick footing of the racetrack, a group of pony riders met them, each outrider pairing with a racehorse, leading the way to the starting gate.

At the sound of "Riders up!" LB pranced in frustration, straining at the lead rope. My arm ached, LB leaped sideways, and then Laurie, Storm's vet, appeared, with a big grin on her face and a syringe of Ace sedation — just in case. Damon had originally planned to be here for the retirement ceremony but had a last-minute conflict. Certain that a vet's presence could prove key, in case of wild behavior on LB's part, I had asked Laurie to come in Damon's place.

Eric was paged back to the winner's circle, leaving me and Laurie to navigate LB to his pony horse. Our assigned outrider, a trim but tough-looking blonde, chastised us. "You can't put the chain shank like that," she said, irritation in her voice. "He could pull the wrong way and drag me right off my horse." With the help of another outrider, we hurriedly corrected the chain portion of the leadline, re-draping it through LB's halter. He bore our anxious chain flapping with annoyance, his eyes fixed on the track.

LB's pony rider handled him capably — he walked regally beside her thick paint gelding during the post-parade. Afterward, as I took his lead rope from her, she leaned down and gave LB a pat. "He was a real good boy out there," she said, almost smiling. "Surprised me."

All Lightening Ball had to do for the rest of the evening was eat hay in his "exhibit" stall. A portable pen, with high walls and a sturdy gate, was set up near the track entrance. As people streamed back and forth between the saddling paddock, winner's circle, and betting windows, they could admire Lightening Ball in all his racehorse majesty.

We hadn't taken the children into account.

Dozens of children cavorted around the track building, shrieking and clutching enormous cups of soda. None seemed to have parents — at least not ones who would publicly claim them. Fearless and spry, a horde of ten-year-olds spotted LB in his exhibit area.

"Horse! *Horsie!*" A cry to battle — the children descended on LB's stall, trying to climb on, up, or under it. "Throw your Coke at him," one boy dared his sister, a tall girl with feral eyes. LB leapt in dismay, backing into the farthest corner. "No, no! Get away from the stall!" I yelled. Laurie, Tom, and I hurriedly built a barrier of folding chairs around the pen, then we stood guard against the next wave of suicidal fifth-graders.

Adult racing fans mobbed our silent auction table, encouraged by frequent announcements over the track PA system — "Hurry, the LOPE auction closes in twenty minutes. Go get a bargain for a great cause!" The table was laden with donations from racing and horse people, including stallion seasons, dressage lessons, and artwork. Our volunteers hustled around the display, answering questions, not resting until every item had multiple bids. Including Lightening Ball.

As part of the retirement event, the track and I had come up with the idea of auctioning LB, too. Bidders would be approved adopters only, their

applications reviewed and finalized well before the auction night. Several
prospective bidders had contacted me beforehand, sending in detailed references.

Brad had recently lost his favorite foxhunter, Sir William, to colic.
Heartbroken, he was ready to start looking for a new mount. LB bore a
striking resemblance to Sir William, especially in his height and coloring.
Armed with impeccable references, Brad was quickly approved to bid on
LB. He seemed like an ideal home; a former steeplechase rider in college,
Brad was well-versed in retraining racehorses. During the auction, he
came up to introduce himself in person, his eyes full of emotion. Brad
watched LB pace restlessly in his exhibit stall, then shook his head. "What
a magnificent athlete. So much like Sir William. I hope I win."

When it was over, our auction had earned over $7,000, a huge wind-
fall for LOPE's tiny budget. It was a promising outcome for our first large
fundraiser, boosting my confidence as well as LOPE's cash flow. The event
also raised our profile among potential donors in the horse industry.
Within a few months, in spring 2006, we received an unsolicited grant
from a Houston equine research foundation. The $14,000 contribution
helped tremendously with our ranch and horse care needs — and completely bridged our income gap for the year.

By the racetrack's standards, the retirement ceremony was a smashing
success. The race crowd enjoyed LB's "live" exhibit, adults and children
alike swarming near his stall throughout the evening. Priscilla was proud
of LB and came by several times to comment on his glamorous looks and
"up" demeanor. "He still looks like a champion," she said.

I smiled weakly. What looked majestic to Priscilla and Eric seemed terrifying to me. LB was reverting back to his racing self in more ways than
one. He circled rapidly in the pen, grinding his teeth. His still-powerful
muscles were tightly flexed — tension seemed to pop from his pores.
Laurie's gentle Ace cocktail was steadily wearing off. I watched the race
results anxiously, eager to get back to Priscilla's shedrow before LB went
into his full champion mode of kicking and biting.

Finally, the last race was starting — we could leave. Hastily, I haltered LB and led him back toward the safety of the pony horses and track rail. But the outriders were gone, escorting the last race's entries to the starting gate. I followed the tired horses from the previous race as they headed back to their barns, keeping a safe distance between them and LB's hostile strides.

I did my best to fake a professional, in-command demeanor, even with my arm yanked skyward and a thousand pounds of turbo-charged LB shoving into my shoulder with every step. Laurie again walked beside me, a second syringe full of sedatives in hand, whispering, "Just say the word, Lynn. I'll inject him the second you can't control him."

We inched our way along the rail, as track revelers shouted, urging on their favorites in the final race galloping behind us. My arm muscles twitched painfully. I stared grimly at the shedrow roofs off in the distance, our home base and safe zone. "Fifty more steps, maybe fifty-five, and you'll be past the track," coached Laurie, her thumb still poised on the syringe. "You're doing *great*!" Her voice stayed at a whisper — even Laurie's exuberance was tempered by LB's aura of menace.

The bandstand was the last structure on the track deck. The wretched country band was still there, playing a vaguely bluegrass dirge. As we drew alongside, the song paused for a moment. Out of the corner of my eye, I saw the drummer raise his arms, sticks high. Suddenly, the song flared into a crescendo of bass, drum, and screaming vocals. It was a horrible cacophony, White Snake meets the Sex Pistols with a Southern twang.

LB and I were less than ten feet from the bandstand. He half-reared, his ears and spirit affronted by the din. An entire evening of frustrated confusion erupted in LB's body, and his front legs lifted again, his lips curling as he swelled his body into an offense-ready pose.

The rail was full of people, laughing and dancing. As we lurched closer, silence fell — I glanced over and saw every set of eyes averted, not wanting to stare at the nice lady about to get run over by the angry racehorse.

I exhaled slowly. Ignoring the burning sensation in my wrist, I tightened my grip on LB's lead. "Easy, LB," I breathed. He glared down at me. "I'm sorry about the band. You're right — they're terrible. Can't blame you for being mad. Let's get back to the barn, okay?"

LB's ears twitched, his steps slowed. I slowed my pace, too, matching his strides. LB snorted and sighed, his neck muscles relaxing. My arm sank down a couple of inches, the tendons no longer strained to their limits. "Ten more steps and you're on the backside," Laurie said, her voice coming from the other side of LB's neck. I saw her hand drop, her thumb off the syringe for the first time in fifty steps.

SOON LB WAS BACK AT OUR FARM, with happier eyes and a softening face. Brad had indeed placed the winning bid, but then decided against LB. Instead, he bought an expensive jumper at a commercial barn, changing his mind a week after the auction. LB would now need to be ridden, assessed, and adopted out — just like the other horses. But we had never had a stakes winner before, other than Zuper, and his injury kept him saddle free.

Priscilla's "bad actor" comment echoed in my head as I faced LB one day. Saddle over my arm, I was suddenly sobered by the realization that I had never ridden a "real" racehorse, a truly big winner, let alone one whose last ride was a wild racetrack gallop months ago.

"That horse will kill you," murmured a voice from my past.

Most horse trainers have a negative view of older racehorses. Young, slow, and lightly raced Thoroughbreds are the ideal for sport-horse prospects. "The older ones, they never learn anything else," one jumper trainer told me. "All they know is run, run, run. Can't teach an old dog new tricks — or an old racehorse to stop."

In addition to his age, LB had serious baggage according to his track reputation. While I was at Sam Houston, a jockey and yet another race trainer confirmed the rumors about LB. He kicked, spooked, and bucked during his workouts and prerace warm-ups. "I heard he's a rogue, a tough horse," said the jockey, putting aside his profession's normal daredevil ethos. "I wouldn't want to ride him."

"He's, well, quite an athlete," said the race trainer. "But if you yell at him to knock it off, most of the time he stops. Unless he's biting you, then yelling doesn't work at all. And he's a real dragon in the trailer." He wanted to tell me more, but I cut him off. LB already had the worst history of any racehorse I had ever encountered. I didn't want to hear more.

Rick's hearty "He's a *good* boy" rang in my ears, dueling with phrases like "real dragon" and "rogue." Priscilla's voice argued with itself, her glowing compliments for LB fresh in my memory. Her own "good boy" blended with the blonde outrider's same praise, two tough female faces softening into pleased surprise.

LB and I stared at each other in the round pen. He was back in farm mode, more relaxed, less high-strung than at the track. His expression was still slightly suspicious, but he pricked his ears when I said his name, and he stood quietly as I mounted him. But there was tension in his body, as if he was just waiting for me to make a wrong move.

I recognized that tension right away — because it mirrored my own. Both our faces had the same wariness of each other's intentions, a low-grade De Niro and Pesci duel.

Just before LB's retirement ceremony, during our long walk from Priscilla's stall to the saddling paddock, it finally dawned on me that what I was doing could be dangerous. Still ignorant of LB's full track reputation, I was blithely leading him through a racing routine full of provocative memories. It was a routine I knew little about, other than from a quick coaching session by Priscilla. As we walked, I began hiccupping with sudden anxiety, and I turned to look at LB, wondering if he would suddenly snap, maybe bolt for the track spectator section, biting anyone in his path. LB looked back at me, his mouth turned upward, a questioning stare that seem to say, "Lady, I don't know what you are doing, but I'm going to give you the benefit of the doubt here." My hiccups stopped and I breathed again, walking forward steadily, leading LB toward the grandstand and saddling paddock. It had been a quiet, but important, moment.

Up on his back now, I sat in silence. For a long moment, LB and I were motionless, the saddle bridging our thoughts. Then suddenly we both exhaled together, a mutual trust agreed upon, an invisible threshold crossed. Once again, I decided to believe LB's eyes instead of his reputation. A wise choice that made for a great ride, as LB began to stride majestically around the pen, arching his neck, relaxing his back, relearning how to go slow — and teaching me again the relationship between expectation and outcome.

CHAPTER FOURTEEN

The Prom Queen

GET ON HIM!" Ray Hunt's voice blared across the arena. "Oh my, look at that. The boy don't know what to do. What is he waiting for? The horse is ready, the boy isn't!" The rest of us in the Colt Starting class ducked our heads, relieved we weren't "the boy." A red-faced cowboy in his thirties tried to mount his little brown colt, the horse nervously side-stepping.

Finally, in spring 2006, I had followed through on my plan to get some lessons. LOPE was hosting a full clinic with Ray Hunt, a three-day immersion of colt-starting and horsemanship techniques. In exchange for planning and marketing the clinic, I was riding in all the classes for free.

The Colt Starting class was full of Western saddles, professional horse trainers, Quarter Horse colts, and cowboy hats. I was the only amateur, an English rider looking out of place with my helmet and Thoroughbred mount (at least his name was Tex). Tex, a three-year-old, had been ridden already at the track — but only for a sixty-day crash course.

One of the godfathers of natural horsemanship, Ray was then in his seventies and couldn't ride much anymore due to health issues. His eyes were sharp — as were his comments — but he radiated compassion for the horses (if not the riders). I liked him — he was the epitome of a horseman. And Ray was my hero — it had been his tapes that had helped me with riding horses like Nacho and PJ at the ranch

During my lesson quest, I had looked up Ray's teaching schedule on his website. Ray gave clinics all over the world, often traveling for ten months out of the year. Although none of the dates were in Texas, something else caught my eye: one sentence read, "All clinic hosts please contact Julie for information on Ray's available dates." On a long shot, I emailed Julie, assuming I'd never hear back. But within a couple weeks, we were approved to hold a Ray Hunt clinic.

As our clinic date approached, I busied myself with logistical details. The clinic would be divided into two classes, Colt Starting in the mornings and Horsemanship in the afternoon. Up to thirty riders (and horses) could attend, far too many to hold the event at our arena-less ranch. Through Storm and LB's old friend, Laurie the vet, I found a fairground at a nearby town, complete with multiple riding rings, stalls for horses, and lots of parking. Our clinic would be in a covered arena, with bleachers, concession stand, and restrooms all nearby. Plus, the county Horse Committee, headed by Mark and his wife, Sharon, volunteered to help with clinic chores like checking in attendees and supervising the arena.

An adventurous couple, Mark and Sharon gravitated toward high-speed hobbies like Porsche racing and cutting horse competitions. Courteous and hardworking, they often volunteered their time to run local horse shows and events. At our first meeting, they eyed my lumbering truck and lack of cowboy boots skeptically, a bit uncertain of my credentials to host an elite Ray Hunt clinic.

SOON ALL TYPES OF RIDERS were calling and emailing, interested in the clinic: cowgirls with reining horses, ranch hands with yearlings, equestrians from every discipline. Then Cal's familiar voice hit my message inbox.

Cal was another reminder of my adult beginner status with professional trainers. During my first months in Texas, when I was searching for horse-related work, Cal's name came up as a possible employer. Tory had once recommended him as a polo pony trainer and all-around pro, calling him "the real deal."

I had set up a meeting with Cal, hoping to parlay our session into a job interview. His polo barn was big, new, and spotless. Inside, high ceilings created multiple cross breezes, a real feat in August. Polo ponies peeked from the stalls, some saddled, some tied, some dozing.

The sleeping horses awoke with a start as a loud clatter of hooves, barking, and gruff Spanish cascaded into the barn. Cal appeared on horse-back, talking over his shoulder to a groom. Several dogs milled around the horse, oblivious to hoof danger. Spotting me, Cal dismounted, his features tightening into unenthused resignation. He pulled off his cow-boy hat, revealing close-cropped blondish hair and a broad forehead. Cal's eyes were deep-set and icy, his cheekbones weathered. Images of Steve McQueen playing a cowboy desperado flitted across my mind as Cal stamped his boots, brushing the mud off his spurs.

We talked for about an hour, my side of the conversation full of eager statements like, "I'd love to have a job exercising horses. Your barn is gor-geous! I really like your mare, she's so well-trained." Cal responded with monosyllabic grunts and the occasional sentence, his eyes often drifting to the horses or grooms.

Needless to say, no job offer was extended.

Now, three years later, Cal had left me a message. "Cal Murphy here. Sign me up for the Ray Hunt Colt Starting clinic. Call me to confirm."

Cal epitomized the term "hand," the ultimate compliment among old-school Western trainers. I heard the title often, especially from Cory. Many "hands" populated his ranch, working cowboys who had mastered the skill of horsemanship. "Lynn, meet Lonnie/Hank/Jeff. He's a real hand with colts." A brawny fellow would always grin back at me, his leather chaps faded from many rides, the lead rope of a nervous horse tucked under his elbow.

Ray Hunt's videos were full of apprentice hands, quiet men who moved with calm purpose around the horses. They wore fringed chaps, long-sleeved plaid shirts, and spurs. In cold weather, this rugged ensemble was enhanced by wool vests and bright scarves. Long mustaches and suitably weathered cowboy hats completed the look.

I envied their cowboy cool and longed to be a hand myself, to have someone introduce me with, "Meet Lynn, she's quite a hand." But the hands were implausible role models for me. Most had followed horse careers since childhood, usually in Western disciplines like roping, cutting, or reining. Few were female. And none shopped at the Gap for their ranch jeans, an unfortunate devotion to boxy Wranglers dominating the hand style ethos.

WITH THE CLINIC REGISTRATIONS FLOWING IN, my next task was to decide which horses to ride in the classes. Our pastures were full of possible candidates, their temperaments ranging from spooky to quiet. I settled on Tex, the gentle young horse with minimal saddle training, for the Colt Starting class. Sally, a petite but confident filly, seemed like an ideal choice for the Horsemanship class.

This time, I was determined that the LOPE horses would arrive in style. Our elderly trailer, the one that transported Babu to Dr. Dutton's clinic, needed repairs before it could safely haul two horses. Plus the look on Doug's face as he had pulled down its massive ramp lingered painfully in my mind. I wanted to look more professional for the Ray Hunt event.

The clinic location, at the fairgrounds, was too close to call in Equine Express, and most of my equestrian friends were already using their trailers on our clinic dates, which fell on a popular weekend for spring horse shows. Just as I was running out of ideas, Krista emailed me. A fresh-faced junior high teacher, Krista had considered adopting Nacho several months earlier. New to horses, she was a jaunty combination of fearless enthusiasm packaged in "Hello Kitty" style. Krista sported bright pink cowboy boots, hip-hugger jeans, a diamond nose stud, and fluorescent-colored barrettes in her curly red hair. She giggled easily yet handled horses with confident aplomb — a true natural. Her cheerful, adventurous attitude was contagious — my own giggling ratio increased markedly in her presence.

Krista had just bought her own truck and horse trailer. She was eager to practice. "I love hauling horses! It's so much fun," she said. "If I can help LOPE with transporting, please let me know."

Krista's enthused approach contrasted with my own anxious trailering style. Recalling my death grip on the steering wheel as I drove Babu, I marveled that anyone would seek out opportunities to haul horses across Texas highways. I quickly accepted Krista's offer, happy to have a ride for Tex and Sally.

However, I didn't expect the ride to be quite so, well . . . pimped.

The day before the clinic, Krista pulled into our driveway. Her truck was a dually, a massive vehicle made all the more noticeable by its deep, jungle green color. It was an unusual look for a Texas truck — most ranch vehicles are a sensible white or silver, to deflect the heat. But for all its impracticality, the bold green definitely suited Krista's fashion palette.

Then, as she pulled around and it was no longer obscured by the big truck, I saw her trailer. A sturdy stock model, it was roomy and inviting for horses. Probably the trailer had once been factory-issued brown or gray, but no more. Krista had decided a new paint job was in order, and after its custom color job, the trailer was now purple. Not a subdued plum or dusty mauve — but a bright, grape-hued, in-your-face, Britney Spears purple. Together, the purple trailer and the green truck made a splashy MTV-ready rig.

A large horse peered through the slats. "That's Dustin," Krista said. "He's my dream horse. I thought I'd ride him around the fairgrounds after we drop off your horses." Krista led Dustin out of the trailer. "He likes to travel near the trailer gate, so he needs to be loaded last."

Dustin was a Warmblood cross, a tall, thick horse built like a medieval charger. His mane and tail were silver, a dashing contrast to his black coat. His hooves gleamed suspiciously in the grass — I reflexively looked for a cut or abrasion.

"Oh, well, Dustin got a makeover. He's kind of embarrassed about it."
Krista led him out of the tall weeds. I laughed — the gleam on his hooves
was glitter. Pink glitter, in fact. And his tail was elaborately plaited, in the
same French-braid style that was all the rage in my fifth-grade homeroom
class.

Sally and Tex stared at Dustin's rose-colored, glimmering feet as they
walked into the trailer. When Sally balked (purple apparently isn't her
color), Krista briskly shooed her up the ramp, her pink boots leading the
way. Tex ambled in behind Sally, followed by Dustin.

As I drove ahead along the highway, with Krista following behind, I
worried about our reception. Krista's rig didn't say "rescue lady" or "adult
beginner" — instead it screamed "preteen cowgirl on too much sugar."

I wasn't quite sure which was worse for a Ray Hunt clinic.

RAY GREW UP IN IDAHO IN THE FORTIES, one of nine children born into
a no-nonsense ranching family. As he often said at clinics, "Back then, we
had jobs for the horses. We rode them to school, to check fences, even to
the mailbox and back." Ray soon became known as a bronc rider and all-
around cattle hand, his riding skills nearly eclipsed by his roping talent. A
physically imposing, tough man, Ray eventually realized that brawn alone
wasn't effective with horses. He embarked on a quest to find a better way,
a journey that ended with an unlikely mentor.

"I ruined a lot of horses before I found Mr. Tom Dorrance. I'm still a
student, but the horses tell me I'm on the right track, thanks to him. He's
the only man I met who was as good as the horse. Most people can't even
hold a candle to the horse."

Tom Dorrance was a slim man, mild-mannered and quiet — on the
surface, he had little in common with Ray. But Tom had a way with horses,
a gentle approach with results so compelling that even Ray was impressed.
His philosophy was based on understanding the horse's point of view, on
working with the horse to achieve a voluntary (rather than forced) partnership. Ray studied with him for years, hoping to emulate Tom's serene
technique and put aside his own rougher edges.

It didn't quite work out that way. Decades later, Ray's clinics were full of meditative slogans such as "You gotta fix it up and let the horse find it" and "Let your idea become the horse's." He delivered these mottoes gruffly, his fierce expression daring any rider to mistake him for a New Age, touchy-feely kind of guy.

If a horse bucked off a rider, Ray guffawed — then admonished the crowd to not feel sorry for the unseated cowboy. "That's just part of the deal, folks. That boy, he can take that. If he couldn't, well, he shouldn't be here in the first place. You gotta take the bitter with the sweet."

Ray's mix of philosophic koan and machismo grit was fascinating — and a little intimidating. Whimsical purple trailers and glittered hooves seemed much too frivolous for his clinics, if not downright provocative.

KRISTA AND I BECAME SEPARATED on the longish drive. I arrived first at the fairgrounds and was immediately besieged by several clinic riders.

"I'd like to sleep in my truck in the parking lot. Is the public restroom kept unlocked?"

"There aren't any hoses in the barn, and we need to rinse our horses."

"Will you watch my trailer for me while I get some food? It's locked up. I just want someone to keep an eye on it."

"Can I park my trailer right in front of my horse's stall? She won't sleep if she can't see me."

"Lynn, where do you want Tex and Sally?"

It was Krista, smiling from her truck window.

"I got lost. And then they kept telling me to go to the wrong barn here."

We quickly settled Sally and Tex into stalls at the back of the barn. Wide-eyed, they snorted gently at each other, then attacked their hay, relaxing into their usual postdinner stupor.

"See you on Monday, after the clinic!" Krista scrambled back into her green truck and headed for the exit. The grape trailer swayed behind, its extravagant color leaving behind a wake of turned heads.

The stares, it turned out, were envious. Mark approached me later, as

I was gulping down a dinner of Power Bars and Coke, and asked, "Hey, did your horses get to the barn?"

I nodded, excessive carbonation and protein preventing further communication.

"We saw your friend's truck and trailer, and just assumed she was a barrel racer. So Sharon kept directing her to the barrel-racing arena around back."

Bracing myself for a Doug-like look of pity, I glanced at Mark. He was smiling with approval — LOPE and I had passed some kind of test.

"We couldn't believe she was with LOPE. She really looks like a barrel racer, with those pink boots. Are you sure she doesn't run the pattern at all?"

Later, when I relayed this information to Krista, she beamed. "You know, I've been thinking about trying that! Do you think Dustin would like barrels?"

AS THE PARKING LOT FILLED UP the next morning, I realized it was time to get ready for Colt Starting 101. Uncertain if I was supposed to bring my saddle as well as Tex to the arena, I looked for Carolyn Hunt, Ray's wife and all-around clinic administrator.

The rumor was that Carolyn originally met Ray at one of his clinics. An elegant brunette, she rode with refinement and skill, catching Ray's eye immediately. Carolyn was raised in the tradition of old-school great ladies — she could rope cattle, ride colts, herd clinic students, and keep Ray on schedule (no mean feat), all with graceful serenity and smudge-free makeup.

I spotted her near the stands, standing at a long table. Carolyn was registering auditors, collecting payments, and graciously answering the same three questions over and over: "What time does the first class begin?" "How much is the audit fee?" "Can I take photos of Ray during the clinic?"

At least I had a different question. "Will we be saddling the colts this first morning of the clinic?"

She smiled. "Oh, you'll actually be riding the colts this morning. Not just saddling them." She paused, perhaps expecting a sign of dismay from me.

"Great!" I said cheerfully, now very relieved that I had selected Tex for the class. As the bleachers filled with chattering spectators, Carolyn tested the microphone system, and Ray's horses loped in the ring, saddled but bridle free. It had all the makings of a three-ring circus. A spookier horse, like PJ, would have keeled over by now, his mind blown like a cheap car stereo speaker.

I grabbed my tack from the barn, then dashed back to the Colt Starting class, plopping everything on the arena fence. The other colt starters were doing the same, hoisting heavy cowboy gear up on the railing. My English saddle looked ridiculously dainty next to the bulky Western saddles, and my helmet was the lone example of protective headgear. "I don't need no brain bucket" is a common credo among cowpokes.

The colts milled around the arena, looking confused. Ray's assistant, Harley, rode up on a tremendously stocky mare. Harley herded the colts, waving his flag at any stragglers. A feisty palomino stud colt darted away, only to quickly reverse direction as Harley's big mare bore down on him, cutting off his escape route.

Tex was the tallest horse in the herd, his Thoroughbred legs elevating him several inches above the stocky Quarter Horse youngsters. Despite his height, he was the meekest of the group, obeying Harley's flag readily and avoiding the "bad kid" alpha colts led by the palomino.

Like Tex, some of the colts had been ridden before, but most were unbroken without any saddle experience. A few weren't even halter trained. One dun had already reared and flipped over while being led from his trailer, terrified at the unfamiliar pressure of a halter and rope. Another buckskin had refused to be caught, whirling away whenever anyone approached with a halter in hand.

The Colt Starting students matched their rugged mounts. Two young ranch hands, Donny and Jake, brought colts from their cattle outfit's herd, their jeans still dusty from yesterday's calf chores. Jose had driven twelve hours from Mexico to attend the clinic, his vaquero roots evident in his clinking spurs and thick lariat. Mike hailed from East Texas, where he trained cutting horses and roping mounts. Stephanie was the only other woman, her tan cowboy hat and buckskin chaps matching Jake and Donny's ensemble. Other cowboys of varying ages rounded out the class, all nearly identical in accent, wardrobe, and spitting prowess.

The only person missing was Cal. As we waited for the class to begin, I looked around for him. A beat-up trailer pulled up in the parking lot, accompanied by barking dogs. It was Cal, looking flustered and hurried. Within minutes, he had made his way to the arena, with a gray mare and an armload of saddle.

Ray Hunt appeared in the middle of the bleachers, his microphone-enhanced voice booming out to us, a toothpick clamped in his mouth. The class looked up in unison, an eclectic assortment of professional ranch hand, cutting horse expert, polo professional, Mexican caballero and Annie Oakley–style cowgirl. And me.

Ray quickly dispensed with the formalities. "Go ahead, saddle your colts. And then let them loose in the arena." Some of the young horses didn't cooperate — like the little brown gelding. He'd never been saddled before and danced away whenever his cowboy owner approached.

No matter how seasoned or experienced, any ranch hand in the class was addressed as "boy" or "son" by Ray. Of a lean cowpoke approaching middle age, Ray said, "That boy, he needs to do something with that horse's feet." The sidestepping brown colt's owner sweated under Ray's barrage of fatherly insults. "The horse knows more than the boy, that's for sure," Ray chuckled. Every time a cowboy handled his horse well, "You're doing just fine, son," echoed in the arena.

Stephanie and I fared no better. "Where are my girls?" Ray barked whenever we drifted out of sight, hoping to avoid scrutiny in the darker corners of the arena.

Donny's buckskin blew big snorts through his nostrils but stood still for saddling, surprising Donny — but not Ray. "That little guy, his big concern is being caught. Once he's haltered and with you, well, he's pretty open to things. You be sure and keep him that way, son." Donny nodded, his eyes fixed on the buckskin as he tightened the cinch slowly.

Cal wasn't so lucky. His mare didn't settle for just sidestepping away from the saddle. Instead, she walked backward rapidly, forcing Cal to hop alongside her, juggling his heavy saddle on one arm. A barrage of "boy" and "son" rained down on Cal, his head lowered, until at last he saddled the mare. He blew a sigh of relief, taking off his cowboy hat and wiping his sweaty forehead.

In Ray's version of colt starting, we rode our saddled horses — but with only a rope halter and lead rope for a bridle. We had to flip the lead rope over the horse's head to change direction. All of us rode together in a small round pen, the big-eyed colts scooting away as Harley snapped his flag at them. It was quite a scene, and I was glad for Tex's placid nature.

Tex's registered name was Uncle Tex. At the track, he was so slow in his workouts that he never was entered in a race. In temperament, he could have been a brother to Sugarfoot or Spider — kind, docile, and easy to ride. Although his saddle training was slight, just a couple of months, he was the calmest horse in his race trainer's barn.

Tex towered over the other horses in the pen, their backs level with my knees. Perched in my English saddle, I flung Tex's lead rope over his nose, balancing uncertainly in the narrow stirrup irons. My feet bumped into Western saddles every few steps, as cowboys swirled around us, urging their colts forward.

"Watch where you're riding," Ray bellowed. "You get up too close to a big horse like that Thoroughbred, he can kick you from a mile away." At the word "Thoroughbred," a nearby spectator gasped. The cowboys glanced at Tex, taking Ray's advice to heart, steering their mounts away rapidly. I felt a shift in the ring — I was now being eyed with respect, rather than amusement, the Thoroughbred reputation for danger lending me a daredevil aura.

We heard many commands from Ray that morning, such as "Think!"

and "Make the right thing easy and the wrong thing hard." My favorite was "What happened before what you wanted to have happen, happened." These cryptic, Zen-like instructions confused me, but I tried earnestly to understand them, good grasshopper that I was.

The colts already seemed to understand Ray's technique. As the class drew to a close, all the horses had visibly relaxed, each showing marked improvement. The dun no longer fought the lead rope. The buckskin allowed Donny to catch him, even sniffing the young cowboy's hand. And the brown colt stood for the saddle, no longer shying from "the boy." One bay filly kept an ear cocked for Ray's voice, turning her head toward him each time he addressed the crowd.

Ray liked to conclude his classes with a Q&A session, his mysterious answers often drifting into lengthy monologues. A practical question such as "What's the best way to ride a bucking colt?" could prompt a soliloquy along the lines of "In the midst of difficulties, there's lots of opportunities. It's best to stay on the edge of trouble, not in the middle of it."

Sensing confusion from the crowd, Ray would continue on, sometimes tapping his knee for emphasis. "See, you got to adjust to fit the situation. It's the little things that make a big difference. Recognize the smallest change, the slightest try. And remember — I might not know where I'm going, but I'm not lost. Just another student of the horse."

With an enigmatic smile, Ray then would sum up with some of his most favorite mottoes. "Observe, remember, and compare. And if things don't go the way you expected, just whistle, grin, and ride."

AFTER THE CLASS ENDED, a spectator approached me. "You're Lynn, aren't you?" I nodded, surprised. "We've emailed a few times. I'm Darla — I was interested in maybe adopting a horse someday." Darla had the attire of a prosperous ranch lady — prairie skirt, concho jewelry, and tooled leather belt.

I pounced at the opportunity. "You might want to consider Tex," I said, imagining him as a pampered trail horse. "As you can see, he's very sweet. And he's only three."

"Oh, no, not me. I couldn't take on such a young Thoroughbred. Too scary."

I pressed Tex's case. "Tex is truly gentle. Did you see him in the Colt Starting class just now? He took great care of me in there — he was so quiet."

Darla pulled out a cigarette case studded with turquoise decoration. Lighting an American Spirit, she inhaled with a smile. "You make him quiet, Lynn. Come on, you're a hand."

There it was, the elusive compliment — someone actually thought I was a hand. I glowed during my hurried lunch, brushing aside a twinge of guilt at taking credit for Tex's inherently calm nature.

In the parking lot, I spotted Ray sitting on his truck's tailgate. Cal sat next to him, his face lit with enthusiasm, Steve McQueen no more. "I saw you at a clinic almost ten years ago," he gushed. "Never forgot it. I'm fifty-two years old now, still love my work with the horses." Then I heard something so odd, so impossible that I halted on the spot, staring — the sound of Cal giggling.

MY GLOW FROM DARLA'S COMPLIMENT didn't last long. Although Tex saved me in Colt Starting class, I was in for a different experience in the afternoon Horsemanship class. According to the class description, the Horsemanship goal is harmony between horse and rider: "Mentally the horse and rider need to be attuned. The rider needs to learn to prepare the horse to react in a way that is natural and understandable to the horse."

The Horsemanship riders were much different from those in Colt Starting. Dressage divas and trail riders were mixed in with the cowboys. All of the horses had years of saddle training, some even with show experience. Beefy Warmbloods jogged alongside colorful Appaloosas, with high-stepping Arabians blending into the usual Quarter Horse cadre.

Sally, an adorable filly, was my mount. A petite bay barely 15 hands tall, she had only raced twice. Her trainer told me that she finished last in her first race. In her second, one of the other horses stumbled a little and she was able to pass him. "She came back to the barn, prancing and proud, like she'd won the Kentucky Derby," her trainer told me with a sigh. "I said to her, little girl, you need to pass *all* the horses before you get to prance like that."

Sally's breeder was a Mississippi businessman. Earl called me several times, his Southern accent expanding his sentences (and our conversations). "I named her after my granddaughter, Sally," he said. "That filly, she liked to give kisses when she was a baby. You put your face close and she'd nuzzle your cheek. I don't want to sell her — around here, Thoroughbreds don't do so well."

A classic track washout, Sally was sweet but willful. Short, round, and brown, she had a pretty face and a sleek coat. Her trainer had stopped her racing career before Sally discovered her degree of failure at it. She walked with self-centered poise, flirting shamelessly with all the geldings at the ranch.

Although Sally was mellow during our few rides together, I hadn't had much time to practice with her before the clinic. Not sure how to prepare for a class on horse-human harmony, I settled for occasional trotting sessions squeezed in between ranch chores. A mistake I came to regret deeply.

As soon as we stepped into the clinic arena, Sally was tense and annoyed. Her feminine looks and haughty air had earned her the nickname "Prom Queen" at our ranch. Right now, the Prom Queen wasn't happy at all. She didn't like the arena sand, the other horses, or the crowd.

Ray called out instructions from his usual spot in the bleachers. "How slow can your horse walk? Now, how fast? Pick up a soft feel in those reins. The horse tells me where his rider's at." Like an equine square dance, my fellow classmates rode easily to Ray's commands, guiding their horses into increasingly elaborate maneuvers.

Sally didn't like square dancing either. As Ray barked out more directions — "turn left, walk ten steps, trot" — she pinned her ears and lunged wildly out of line, tensing her back and threatening to buck.

A familiar feeling of shame and inadequacy washed over me. Clearly, I didn't belong here with my clumsy novice skills. I could see Ray looking at me, his mouth tightening at my poor horsemanship, a sharp comment about to be flicked my way. Desperately, I tried to "think" or "fix it up," but Sally wasn't interested in my weak Zen attempts.

I knew where Sally and I were headed — and it wasn't good.

BESIDES MY MANY HOURS OF VIDEO STUDY, I had once seen Ray in person. The previous year, Ray had held a big two-day clinic exhibition in Fort Worth. Cory had alerted me to the event, urging me to attend in his laconic way.

"You should try to go." Silence. "Lynn."

Not sure what to expect, I tackled the three-hour-plus drive. My battered truck sputtered along, the fitful AC finally dying an hour into the trip. I arrived just in time for the Horsemanship class, my T-shirt sweat soaked and my eyes burning from two hundred miles of sunny plains.

The covered arena was big, with concert-style seating and vendor booths spread out in the hallways. About forty riders clustered along its perimeter, their abilities ranging from expert to self-delusional. In the center, Ray sat astride a big sorrel mare, his voice pitched through a headset microphone.

Ray cut a formidable figure on horseback. His physique was imposing, his posture ramrod straight — he loomed over the arena, his height exaggerated by a black cowboy hat. His voice blared across the arena. Occasionally, I could hear a faint wheeze between his words, a labored sound that steadily increased in frequency. A lifetime smoker, Ray had developed severe emphysema — he now had only one lung.

He put it to work in that arena right away. "You look like a bunch of *maggots* wiggling around there. What a mess." Ray shook his head, his mare casting a contemptuous glare at the other horses. The more skillful riders looked relaxed, some even smiling at Ray's insult. Other riders tensed, their necks disappearing into their shoulders.

Ray directed them into a now-familiar equine dance, having the riders weave in and out, reverse direction, then halt and back up for several steps. As the equestrian choreography grew more complex, some riders began to fade, their horses barely going through the motions. A few were heading for trouble.

One pretty blonde woman, dressed in ultra cowgirl chic, was struggling with her paint gelding. A handsome horse, he radiated dismay, flipping his head and pulling the reins from the rider's hands. Every few steps, she regathered her rope reins — only to have the gelding yank them away again.

She scolded her horse, kicking him forward, tossing her own head in annoyance, her curly hair flying from beneath her pastel cowboy hat. Another rider deftly steered his roan away as her paint skittered by, nearly clipping him. He'd seen the possible collision coming for several strides.

Ray had seen it, too, his eyes narrowing. He continued to address the group, still watching the paint. The gelding's head was now flinging almost constantly, his eyes wild and rolling. The blonde had lost the hat and hair swung in her eyes, her face pale but her chin high.

Ray's voice boomed. "Now there's a horse that's troubled in his mind. He needs some help with his feet." His advice wasn't helpful for the cowgirl. She looked up, her confusion flaring into irritation. The paint took advantage of her distraction, ripping the reins from her fingers again.

"Now, don't let him do that. You're teaching him the wrong thing."

I could see the blonde's thoughts on her face. Tightening her lips, she looked over at Ray, her expression saying, "Well, if I could stop him, I would have already."

Ray's tone was gruff, and it didn't sound any kinder projected through the enormous arena speakers. He continued to coach her, growling directions such as "You got to do what it takes, but no more and no less, to get the job done."

Her back tensed even more, pride and shame battling in her rigid frame. The paint hopped violently, his ears flat.

"See, he's just trying to tell you something, . . ." Ray began, shaking his head.

The cowgirl suddenly slumped, her head down. She was crying, her ruffled ego melting into tears.

"Why... well, don't do *that*." Ray sighed, his tone rasping into bewilderment, then dismay. From Ray's resigned expression, I could tell this wasn't the first time someone had cried in his clinics.

NOW, AS I SAT ON SALLY, I hoped I wouldn't be next. I could feel people staring as she got more serious about her bucking threats. Sally wound up for a big pitch, jolting my back and then my memory, as the morning class lesson resurfaced in my mind.

In Colt Starting, several of the pro riders had come under fire from Ray. The dashing Mexican caballero, confident in his talents, twirled a rope around his colt's feet, annoying the horse. An older ranch manager, with decades of training experience, became impatient while trying to bridle his edgy, tall filly. And a teenage cowboy, full of classic, brooding machismo, sulked as his colt danced around him, refusing to stand for the bridle.

They all were having trouble of some kind with their horses, trouble that was actually their responsibility to fix, according to Ray. The horses are never wrong, just the people. Ray was an enigmatic teacher, and his horsemanship philosophy had many layers. He had taken the spiritual approach of Tom Dorrance — that you must be there for the horse, not yourself — and translated it into a grittier ethos. For Ray, "rising up" for the horse might mean that you had to be a brave, scrappy rider one day — and the next day, you might have to be soft and gentle. It was up to you, as the rider, to interpret what the horse required and then deliver it.

Ray also embodied a powerful mix of yin and yang — just when you'd be ready to dismiss him as a macho throwback, he'd stun you with his sensitivity to a frightened horse. And just when you thought that all you needed to do was love the horse, he'd berate you for not respecting the horse's strength and its need for true leadership.

In the morning class, Ray's brand of Western yang was in full force. He didn't dispense his advice kindly to the struggling colt starters — first, a brusque comment, then a barked order, and finally a bellowed command across the arena. "Fix it. No, you're too late again. Fix it! The horse has a right to his opinion. You're the one that's got to adjust to him. Don't let the human ego get in the way.

"Discipline is one thing that any horse needs. But punishment isn't — that's when you correct after the thing happened. I won't stand for that here."

Ray's face tightened into a sarcastic smile.

"You know what I hate? How any idiot can hang out a shingle and say he's a horse trainer. Hell, you gotta get a license to train a dog, but not for horses. A real shame!"

Ray's voice got deeper, his lips moving rapidly around the toothpick dangling from his mouth. "Folks always got to drag the horse down to their level, instead of working where the horse is at. They won't fit the horse. The horse is always right. It's the human that needs to change. Smart horse, dumb human."

Like the blonde in Fort Worth, the cowboys' backs stiffened with stubborn embarrassment, an affronted silence radiating eloquently from their clamped jaws. They knew what they were doing, no one tells them what to do, not even for their own good. Not one would look Ray in the eye, let alone ask him to explain his crusty Yoda directives. Their horses remained unruly, their tense bodies and tossing heads mirroring the cowboy angst in the arena.

A four-word mantra hummed in my mind. "Observe, remember, and compare." I felt Sally's back muscles clench tightly, matching my own rigid shoulders. Something needed to change — but what?

Unexpectedly, insight dawned. I pulled Sally over to Ray and tossed my human pride down. "I need some help, please."

Ray smiled, a real grin without any pointed edges, and replied, "Well, yes, I know you do." And so my lesson both began and ended — in classic Zen fashion.

CHAPTER FIFTEEN

Down to the Wire

A FEW WEEKS LATER, at the Equine Expo in Fort Worth, my last-minute cadre of volunteers was bustling — Vicki was brushing Sally's bay coat to gleaming perfection, and Donna was trimming her mane deftly, as I hustled into my silks, helmet, and boots. Sally looked adorable in her racing gear — with the little race saddle (all of five pounds), the festive saddle pad, and bright-colored blinkers.

The Expo was a weekend full of Texas horse exhibits and professional equestrian acts. LOPE had been invited to set up a booth display and also to perform a demonstration in the arena. I had agreed to both, seeing the event as a rare opportunity to educate a large audience about the true (non–pit bull) nature of Thoroughbreds.

Equine Express had offered a large discount to ship two LOPE horses, relieving me of the chore of begging volunteer transport. The only task that had remained was to figure out the LOPE arena presentation. As the Expo date was rapidly approaching, my usual strategy of procrastination wasn't an option.

I perused the Expo website for ideas. The presenters were all described in breathless prose. There was Allen, a local trainer who taught horses tricks, such as rolling beach balls and sitting on barrels. His blurb gushed,

"With a little imagination and a willing horse you can have a circus in your own backyard!" Another demonstration focused on "cow horse versatility training." Lipizzaners were featured for the Saturday afternoon slot, followed by a dressage exhibition. The Expo was also hosting something called the "Superbowl of Texas Equine Drill Teams," a title that conjured up images of horses and twirling batons.

There were over twenty-five arena acts — description after description filled the schedule page, each an extravagance of exclamation points — until there it was: my demonstration. As yet it was nothing more than a blurb on the website schedule: "How to Adopt & Retrain a Thoroughbred Ex-Racehorse. Come see an ex-racehorse-training demonstration. And you might want to adopt one of the horses that will be at the Expo!"

Uh oh. How, exactly, was I going to fulfill that promise? I had never given a racehorse-training demonstration before. Or been in front of a big audience.

I continued to read the exhibitor list, my stomach tightening at the expert credentials. A familiar name caught my eye. "Aaron England presents the exciting world of Cattle Cutting using a mechanical cow! And the plot thickens — there will be Man Vs. Woman in BRIDLELESS Cutting & Maneuvering. Riva and Aaron will show you their incredible skill. Help us choose the winner!"

I'd first met Aaron through his wife, Riva, last year. A slender blonde, Riva was a skilled rider and trainer in her own right. While Aaron was drawn to the Western disciplines, Riva focused on English riding, especially eventing and dressage. A champion cutting horse competitor, Aaron was also well versed in natural horsemanship. His colt-starting techniques were already available on DVD and he was steadily attracting notice as a training expert.

Riva had bought Tree Shaker (aka "Shaker"), a handsome gray gelding, through our website. She kept in touch, inviting me to an open house at their sprawling ranch. There I watched Aaron ride unbroken colts bareback and admired Riva's unflustered handling of green horses, including Shaker, a high-energy youngster of impressive height.

Soon after that visit, Riva and Aaron even hosted a benefit clinic for LOPE, donating the proceeds to our adoption ranch. It was a relief to see their names on the Expo website. At least I would know two of the professional trainers there. As I looked up their scheduled demonstration time, an idea hit me.

According to the website, my demonstration would be short — fifteen minutes. That would be just enough time to do a racehorse "before" and "after" act. I could ride Tex in racing tack and talk about how racehorses have unfair reputations for being difficult. Then Riva could perform a dressage demonstration with Tree Shaker. Two days and three emails later, Riva was on board, graciously accepting the starring role in the LOPE arena act.

I was pleased at my plan — all I had to do was sit on Tex and look like an overgrown jockey. Riva's professional dressage act would then wow the crowd. No pressure on me at all — especially with Tex as my mount.

ROARING INTO LOGISTICAL ACTION, I gathered the necessary props for the show. Glen, a race trainer at Retama track, agreed to lend us a racing costume. Called "silks," the official jockey uniform consists of a light-weight jacket worn over a cotton shirt and breeches. Emblazoned with the racing stable's colors, the jacket is designed for quick changes between races, with a Velcro strip instead of buttons or a zipper. My borrowed silks were red, with aqua blue trim on the cuffs and collar.

A couple of days later, I visited Retama track in search of racing tack. Tulsa's old trainer, Keith, was happy to loan me an exercise saddle and bridle. "This one's nice and flashy," he said, pulling out a white saddle with a blue Texas star emblazoned on its flaps. Decorative red stitching completed the patriotic motif. Weighing just a few pounds, it seemed more suitable for riding ponies than racehorses.

Keith rummaged in his shedrow tack room, scattering a litter of black kittens. "Here's some blinkers. They'll look good with that saddle color." The blinkers were a form of equine hood, made of white, stretchy fabric, with red half-cups of plastic resting along the eyeholes. A buckle under the horse's jaw kept the hood snugly in place.

"Most of my horses don't run with blinkers, but sometimes the young ones need them. They get distracted in races, keep looking all around at everything except the finish line," Keith said.

A white bridle followed the blinkers, along with a neck strap. The reins were thick and heavy, weighing almost as much as the saddle. I hefted them, their canvas material catching traction in my palms.

"So, you want an exercise rider job?" Keith asked, only half-joking. Like many race trainers, he was always on the lookout for morning riders. "I'm having the worst time with 'em now. Show up late or not at all. And none of them ride right anyway." He eyed me appraisingly. "You're kind of tall, but you could do it. Come on, give it a try sometime."

I demurred reluctantly. Galloping a racehorse down the track was a long-standing (and unwise) fantasy of mine. Keith's offer, even in jest, was dangerous encouragement. Still, I couldn't wait to try out the exercise saddle, imagining myself gliding around our pastures, my silks flapping in the wind.

As soon as I got back to the ranch, I put Keith's racing gear on Tex. The saddle looked especially tiny on his wide back. Tex peered through the blinkers at me, baffled but cooperative. He looked like a costumed puppy, masquerading as a fiery racehorse for Halloween.

I decided to pretend to be a jockey. Excited, I put my foot in the stirrup. Or tried to. The stirrups would drop down only to Tex's rib cage. On my polo saddle, I set my stirrup leathers much lower, so I could raise my foot easily into the stirrup. When I was in the saddle, my legs would then dangle down the horse's sides, a good position for seat balance.

But jockeys perch on the stirrups, with their knees and seat above the horse. Instead of mounting from the ground, they are hoisted up on the saddles as the racehorses are led off at the walk. The racing stirrups are designed to be toeholds, not mounting or riding aids. Of course I knew about racing tack. I had seen the racehorses galloping in morning workouts

— and I'd watched live racing. But the reality of the short stirrups was much different from cheering jockeys on from the spectator stands. I could barely reach my knee, let alone my foot, up to the stirrup iron. Tex turned his head to watch me, his dark eyes shadowed by red plastic.

After several tries, I could get the tip of my toe in. Grabbing thick handfuls of Tex's mane, I rappelled up his side, my boot slipping in the stirrup. My hamstrings burned, the saddle slipped dangerously to the left, and my hand was tangled in mane hair — but I was in the saddle.

My feet felt bizarre, tucked beneath me in leapfrog position. Tex walked off slowly, looking for food. As he stepped toward some grass, I nearly fell off. My seat wasn't anywhere near the saddle, my toes gripping the tiny stirrups. Pinwheeling for balance, I clutched the reins desperately. Tex's head popped up — and suddenly, I understood why racehorses often carry their heads high.

Fighting back panic, I remembered that I only had to ride Tex at a walk during the Expo act. And Tex was now an old hand at crowds after the Ray Hunt clinic. We practiced together for several sessions under saddle — Tex refined his sleepy expression and I learned to crouch surfer-style while riding.

However, mounting was still an ugly affair — after numerous attempts to spring into the saddle gracefully (only to slide down in a heap), I gave up. At five foot eight and 145 pounds, I doubted anyone would want to hoist me into the saddle. I would mount before entering the arena — to shield the public from my lurching sprawl into the saddle.

MY WELL-LAID PLAN WAS FOILED when Tex got adopted. Melissa, a show rider in California, called, asking about young horses: "I'm looking for a big, quiet, green gelding with not too many race miles. I don't like a horse that is spooky. It's a difficult character flaw to overcome. A young horse with a willing, kind mind is what I hope to find."

Tex perfectly matched Melissa's description, and to my dismay, she was too good a home to pass up. In a whirlwind of adoption paperwork and cross-country transport arrangements, Melissa adopted Tex within days. She sent a commercial truck and trailer to pick him up, the giant chrome rig arriving the week before the Expo.

Staring out at the LOPE pastures, I weighed my options for Tex's replacement. Danzen was an eye-catching gray gelding with a kind temperament. He and Shaker would make a striking pair. But Danzen was a recent arrival — an arena demonstration might be too much pressure for him.

Might Tonight was a leggy bay mare with a cute face — and a sore back. She needed more time resting in the pasture before being ridden again. Original Dancer had a showman's personality trapped in a roly-poly chestnut body. Nicknamed "The Kid," he had a Dennis the Menace zest for adventure. But he was recovering from EPM, the same neurological disorder that Lilly had when she reared and flipped over on me.

Then there was Sally. Sally and I had worked through our mutual high school girl issues at the Ray Hunt clinic. By the end of that weekend, we had bonded into a good team — and Sally enjoyed being the center of attention, showing off her pretty looks and Prom Queen hauteur under saddle.

With Tex now adopted, Sally and I practiced in Keith's racing gear. She rode like a champ, turning her head toward my knee frequently, her eyes puzzled by the strange blinker bathing cap. Still, her unruly reaction at Ray's clinic gave me pause. I'd bring both her and Danzen to the Expo, then decide which horse to ride.

OUR DEPARTURE DATE ARRIVED ALL TOO SOON. A sleek Equine Express trailer pulled into the driveway, a familiar voice shouting hello. Rick was behind the wheel, the same driver who had transported Lightening Ball to his retirement ceremony. Jumping into the ranch truck, I pulled out first, planning to arrive ahead of Rick, with plenty of time to unpack our load of hay, shavings, and brochures.

Three hours later, I lumbered into the Expo parking lot. The Will

Rogers Center is a large facility, with eighty-five acres of multiple arenas and barns. Once I was there, it was no easy feat to locate the Expo, housed in one of the many brick buildings dotting the parking lot.

The breed display area was an enormous, warehouse-type space with high ceilings. Bright plastic banners hung from the windows, horse trailers idled at every entrance, exhibitors scurried with box-laden dollies, and loud whinnies filled the air, making conversation difficult. Sturdy portable stalls created aisle after aisle of faux stables, each colorfully decorated with streamers and posters.

One was full of Friesians, huge black horses with liquid eyes and the demeanor of oversized plush toys. Another housed the Paso Fino drill team — the highlight of their act included a solo by their stallion. He and his rider would "dance" the tango as a pretty Latin dancer twirled around them, her red skirt billowing. The European dressage horses dominated two aisles, their elegantly braided necks arching for treats. Sturdy ranch horses, palominos, roans, and buckskins were sprinkled in every row, accompanied by husky cowboys or glitter-clad cowgirls.

I heard my name called over the neighs — an Expo organizer, Janet, was running the registration desk. She had spotted the LOPE logo on my T-shirt. "Lynn, good to meet you! Come to the arena by 3 PM; we're having an orientation for all the horse acts." Another voice chimed in, "Did you hear that a camera crew is here? They will film the arena demonstrations tomorrow."

As I was digesting this fearful bit of information, Rick called me. He was pulling into the parking lot with Sally and Danzen. Jogging to meet him, I passed a massive black horse with ribbons pinned in his tail, three donkeys with mischievous eyes, and a lavishly spotted Appaloosa.

The LOPE booth and stalls were next to the Paso Fino drill team's, at the far end of the warehouse. Rick walked Sally, then Danzen, through the equine melee. He hummed to himself, unworried by the traffic. Sally and Danzen followed him meekly, happy for Rick's burly leadership. Once in the stall, Sally dozed next to her water bucket, sleepy from the long trip.

Danzen settled in quickly, his attention focused on the hay bale by his door. The Paso stallion snorted lewdly at him, prompting fierce glares from the usually mild-mannered Danzen.

A few hours later, I decided to test drive Danzen in the arena. Several other acts were in the ring, also eager to practice their moves. Leading Danzen through the gates, I halted at the sight of a drill team's maneuvers. As their horses loped in a cloverleaf pattern, two other riders began working their mounts through reining moves. Their horses spun and slid, working to a boombox rendition of "Pour Some Sugar on Me."

Several donkeys were herded by, their small hooves tapping a staccato beat. Danzen was worried, his dappled gray neck tight with anxiety. He pulled at the reins, his head straight up and tense, giraffe-style. I tried to mount, but he darted sideways, unable to keep his focus.

The arena gates opened again. Heavy, thudding hoofbeats filled the ring. A giant black horse galloped down the middle, mane flying, his thick tail pluming ribbons. His rider carried a long pole — he was a jousting competitor. As he spurred his *Lord of the Rings* steed up and down the arena, Danzen quivered. More hoofbeats — another draft horse, this one white, entered the ring and began following the black charger. "Good one, Joe! Let's race now," the white knight yelled, kicking his immense horse into third gear.

Danzen's breathing rate shot up to sprinter levels. The spectacle was tipping from bizarre into scary. It was too much for Danzen and me. I headed for the exit, then paused. Another horse entered the ring, a palomino with a teenage rider carrying a flag. With barely a glance at the dueling chargers, she began cantering in circles, gently waving her banner. The palomino was nervous, but her rider was calm, and as they worked through their practice routine, the mare grew more relaxed.

Danzen flinched in place but stayed next to me, doing his best not to leap or sidestep. A hunch rose in my mind — maybe Danzen needed a confident rider to get him through this frightening experience. Unfortunately for him, I was the only one available.

Ray Hunt bellowed in my mind. "Go ahead! The horse is ready, why aren't you?" My mental accountant analyzed several spreadsheets, all pointing to the wisdom of a tactical retreat out of the arena.

Clumsily, I reached for the stirrup and mounted Danzen. We circled the ring twice, stiffly weaving around the Renaissance Fair combatants and random donkeys. Then I steered Danzen out the gates, before my inner Ray yelled at me to do something even scarier.

Back at the stall, Danzen sighed with relief, attacking his grain with gusto. Untroubled by the Expo chaos, Sally yawned. Her placid demeanor settled my debate — the Prom Queen would appear in the ring, not Danzen.

THE EXPO OPENED THE NEXT MORNING. Our booth area was disheveled, full of hastily unpacked brochures and horse photos. My volunteer team sprang into action, setting up our table, organizing the booth materials, conversing cheerfully with bystanders, and generally giving me way too much time to obsess about my upcoming demonstration.

A steady stream of people drifted by, often stopping to pet Danzen or take brochures from our table. Many skeptical questions flowed, aimed at the LOPE volunteers.

"Racehorses, huh? Aren't those Thoroughbreds too high-strung for trail riding?"

"Can you really retrain them to do anything but run? I heard they never learn to stop."

"Don't they need years to let down from the track?"

"Is this Sally horse *really* a Thoroughbred? She seems too sweet to be a racehorse."

The Expo crowd wasn't exactly packed with Thoroughbred fans. My arena demonstration might be an uphill battle, especially the part about how racehorses aren't crazy. At that thought, my anxiety erupted again, threatening to tip into complete stage fright.

To ease my nerves, I walked around the exhibit area, occasionally peeking into the arena to watch the acts. The vendor booths were color-ful, hawking services from barn building to horse embryo transfer. Music seeped in from the arena, along with muted hoofbeats and applause.

I saw snippets of several demonstrations. My favorite was the horse medium — he read horses for signs of past-life conflicts ("Who were you before this body?"), then healed them with chants and spastic hand ges-tures. "Folks, that's how you clear an entity from a horse," he'd announce with a flourish. Both the horse and the audience seemed entertained, if not enlightened.

Occasionally horses would misbehave, breaking the smooth rhythm of their well-rehearsed performances. One drill team horse began crow-hopping, a sign of exuberance that often precedes bucking. A Quarter Horse colt spooked and sidestepped, his trainer firmly loping him in cir-cles until he tired into submission. And Riva's cutting horse decided to change the program during the climax of their act.

Aaron and Riva had set up a mechanical cow, a floppy cotton creature that spun on thick cables. Aaron controlled its speed from a clicker in his sleeve, timing its moves to be erratic, like real cattle. Like Marcos, the polo horse that loved team penning, cutting horses instinctively want to chase and herd cattle. Riva's sorrel gelding, Dasher, flew up and down the arena, dueling the stuffed calf. To top the performance, Riva leaned down from the saddle and removed Dasher's bridle, guiding him with only her seat and legs, showing off his training and inherent "cow sense."

That was the idea, anyway. But the sorrel had different plans. As soon as the bridle was off, Dasher decided he'd rather just canter around — and ignore the fake cow. Without reins, Riva was missing her primary braking mechanism. All she could do was sit on Dasher as he cruised the arena, a contented look on his face.

A few people in the crowd giggled. Aaron grinned, then caught Riva's eye as she loped along, a helpless passenger to Dasher's ad-libbing. Riva threw up her hands in mock dismay, then crossed her arms across her chest, her body rocking with the saddle motion. Rolling her eyes and smiling, she exuded the aura of a long-suffering mother, waiting out her toddler's bad behavior.

"I forgot to tell you folks something," laughed Aaron. "Dasher used to race on the Quarter Horse circuit. Guess he's having some sort of a flash-back about, you know, *not* stopping." The crowd chuckled its approval at the racehorse jibe, delighted with Aaron and Riva's aplomb under fire. True professionals, they had won the audience over, converting a per-formance faux pas into a shared joke.

By contrast, I rarely was poised on horseback in front of spectators, no matter how few or friendly. My gaffes often ended with me in the air or planted in horse manure, especially during my days as a fledgling horse trainer. I hadn't ridden "professionally" since.

MUCH TOO SOON, IT WAS TIME TO GET READY for my Expo demonstra-tion. As Riva and I prepped for our show, my stomach twisted tightly. The LOPE volunteers descended on Sally, brushing, polishing, and grooming every inch of her bay coat and racing gear. I glanced at Riva — she was relaxed, fluffing Tree Shaker's mane and chatting with her team of grooms. Relieved, I reminded myself that Riva would carry the show, not me.

I pulled on my red jockey silks — the jacket fit like a long windbreaker — and my white helmet. My jeans were clean and crisp. I tucked them into my new leather half-chaps, feeling like a decent imitation jockey.

Riva appeared at my elbow, a black saddle over her arm. She was immaculately attired in full dressage regalia — white breeches, black jacket with tails, and top hat. Her starched shirt was pink, matching the velvet bow in her sun-streaked ponytail.

"Five more minutes, right? Then we'll meet up down by the tunnel." She surveyed my makeshift costume without comment, then smiled at Sally's transformation into a short, plump racehorse. "She looks cute!"

Riva turned to Tree Shaker, saddling him. He carried his gleaming dres-sage tack with panache, his bearing proud. A snowy saddle pad contrasted with his charcoal gray coat. He and Riva looked like a fashionable Olympic team, ready to win the gold and pose for *Vogue* simultaneously.

To reach the main arena, riders had to guide their horses down a long, tunnel-like corridor crowded with pillars. The ceiling was low and the lighting dim. Distorted music buzzed loudly, horses jostled backstage roadies, drill teams collided with jousters — the potential for mayhem lurked everywhere.

At a warm-up ring tucked away behind a wall, I climbed into Sally's racing saddle. Hoping no one witnessed my undignified belly flop on her back, I looked around furtively. Riva and Tree Shaker were already heading down the tunnel, Aaron leading the way. Sally snorted, her steps quick, as we followed them toward the arena gate.

Backstage was full of men with clipboards and wiring devices. The crew boss fitted Riva and me with clip-on microphones and earpieces as we waited for our cue. Thick concrete pillars were everywhere, the low light blurring their contours. Never a fan of parking garages, I fought back claustrophobia and concentrated on fitting my battery pack to my belt.

I never saw what spooked Tree Shaker. Engrossed in my microphone logistics, all I heard was a clatter of hooves, then Sally whirled, heading right for the biggest pillar in the tunnel. Tree Shaker was skittering rapidly toward us, 1,200 pounds of scared, high-speed equine muscle heading our way.

Instinctively, I curled my legs even higher than the stirrups allowed, hoping to avoid the concrete post. At the last minute, Sally ducked back in the opposite direction, sparing my legs and shoulders from pillar damage, but knocking my ear mike off.

As suddenly as it had begun, the episode was over. Tree Shaker regained his composure and Sally caught her balance. Riva and I exchanged glances, then shrugged, an "Oh well" hanging in the air between us.

The sound guy came back, checking our microphones one last time. The previous act's paint horses exited from the opposite gate, their black-and-white legs moving in unison. I hurriedly slapped at my drooping earpiece, its clips pinching my lobe. The microphone floated in front of my mouth, ready to amplify my voice as soon as our act began.

The gate swung open — we were on! Riva and I rode together into the arena.

The crowd was on the left side, their seat rows rising above the white arena walls. Riva and I tracked to the right, riding side by side. Our routine had been hastily planned the night before, during an impromptu conversation in the exhibit area.

I had suggested, "So how about if we split off — I'll go in front of the crowd with Sally and talk about racehorses not being psychotic. I want to show off the lightweight racing tack, maybe point out how it affects racehorse behavior. And then you could do dressage moves with Shaker behind us."

Riva had grinned. "Hopefully Shaker won't buck! We haven't been able to practice much."

"I'll talk for five minutes, then introduce you and Shaker."

"Better make your talk a little longer. We'll need the warm-up time. Especially if Shaker's feeling extra good." Riva had sounded delighted at the prospect of a playfully bucking demonstration horse.

I had nodded, but privately vowed to turn the spotlight over to Riva as soon as possible. Any audience would prefer her performance to mine, especially one full of equestrians.

Now, as Riva and I rode past the announcer, the arena looked strangely familiar. The thick walls, the color of the seats, even the crackle of the loudspeakers created a déjà vu sensation. With a start, I recognized the layout. It was the same ring that had housed Ray Hunt's large exhibition two years ago — the clinic that had included the tearful blonde and her rein-yanking paint horse. I did my best to ignore this unhelpful memory, my breathing already rapid.

Music bellowed over the speakers and the announcer introduced us, "And now, the Thoroughbreds..."

Sally was nervous, trying to peek at the crowd over her blinkers. She trotted daintily but kept an ear cocked toward me, listening for my cues. The music thumped intensely, a rhythmic, ominous beat. Sally's head began bobbing, then jerking, just as we rounded the corner and headed toward the crowd.

The music sped up. Then suddenly I heard a BOOMPF with each of Sally's steps. As we rode in front of the crowd, the sound got louder and faster — BOOMPF BOOMPF BOOMPF. Sally started whipping her head back and forth, trying desperately to see what was chasing her. She was terrified, starting to spin — just as I was supposed to begin speaking about how racehorses have that unfair reputation for being crazy.

I could feel the crowd become confused, then embarrassed for us. Sally grew frantic as the mysterious sound continued — it was my breathing, somehow getting distorted in the microphone. "Shshsh," I murmured to Sally, hoping to soothe her. My whisper became a whooshing Niagara Falls, amplified into a disaster movie sound effect.

I sat there a moment, my equestrian life flashing before my eyes. I heard Tory in my mind: "Ride or die," she commanded. Ray's voice was silent, no doubt in disgust. My internal cinema played endless loops of Rusty bucking me off, again and again, in front of his owners. "Are you one of those rescue ladies?" asked Doug, his eyes amused. I saw myriad horse pros from my past rolling their eyes at my ambition to be a horse trainer, telling me to toughen up and ride it out of her. "Don't let that horse win to you, use your whip."

Embarrassed chaos flooded my mind, along with my ever-present debate — was I amateur or expert? Trainer or student? Man or mouse?

More urgently, I could feel Sally. She needed help — and fast.

A whisper. "Think."

I swung my feet out of the stirrups and dismounted, right there in front of the crowd, the film crew, and Riva. Silence in the audience. I took a deep breath. Now what was I going to say to them again? About the non-crazy racehorses?

My face on fire, I led Sally in front of the crowd. She was upset, trotting

rapidly around me. The audience narrowed to the people in my immediate field of vision, sitting in the first few rows. Looking at their faces, I saw
concern, even sympathy — but no contempt. Turning back to Sally, I
watched her pirouette madly within the four-foot loop of reins.

I pulled my microphone into what I hoped was a better position. Keeping my voice low, I began talking to the faces, asking them what they
thought was happening. "What could be bothering this mare?"

A middle-aged woman in a rhinestone vest answered promptly. "All
the people."

"No, it's the microphone and the loud music," said a teenage boy, leaning forward to catch my eye, a belated "Ma'am" following his reply.

Encouraged, I nodded. "Why would those things make her so
excited?"

Three people shouted out, "She thinks it's racing time. She's back at
the track again."

As we diagnosed Sally together, a change settled over the crowd, Sally,
and me. "I need your help retraining this mare," I said. "Let's figure out
what she's thinking, so we can calm her down, maybe convince her it's not
racing night."

As I launched into a description of the race tack's design and how racehorses are taught to run, my words began flowing more easily. Sally's frenzied orbit around me slowed, her eyes shifting from frightened to curious.

By the end of my impromptu talk, Sally was standing peacefully beside
me, gently touching her nose to my shoulder. The crowd was enthused,
peppering me with questions about racehorse retraining, applauding Sally
warmly.

The emcee sidled into the ring, cueing me to wrap it up, our fifteen
minutes almost finished. Hastily, I turned the remaining thirty seconds
over to Riva. As she and Tree Shaker showed off their elegant teamwork,
I walked Sally in front of the stands. Hands stretched out to pet her, admiring her sleek coat. Sally arched her neck; the Prom Queen was back on
the job.

Exiting the arena, we headed back to the stalls. A knot of spectators spilled over to our booth, engaged and full of curiosity, crowding our exhibit for the rest of the afternoon.

One Quarter Horse trainer touched the small racing saddle, marveling at its tiny size, and drawled, "I've been working with horses all my life. Never knew why racehorses acted so nuts. Now I see they weren't crazy, just trained different. It all makes sense!" Another lady asked me if Sally was trained to act up on cue. "It looked like you all planned that whole thing," she declared.

A stocky woman approached, tripod in hand. I recognized her from Aaron's booth — she was the head of a video company, the one that had produced his colt-starting DVD. "I have it all on film," she said. "Your presentation was really unusual."

I nodded ruefully.

She continued, "Listen, we do horsemanship videos for a trainer audience. I think there are a lot of professional horse trainers who'd want to see your demonstration. If you ever want a DVD produced, please let me know. We'd be very interested in working with you. It's hard to find experts." A slick business card slid into my hand, her cell phone number circled on it.

Startled, I stammered, "No, I'm an amateur. A student, I guess you could say."

But she'd already turned away, heading off to network with a cluster of cowboys. I started after her, eager to set the record straight, then stopped, my head buzzing with sudden perspective.

My novice status was my biggest strength — it gave me an open mind and a healthy lack of cynicism. I could focus on what Sally needed instead of how I would look to the crowd. Without it, I would never have been able to convert Sally's fear into a dynamic teaching opportunity.

I was an adult beginner — and I wouldn't have it any other way. As I led Sally into her stall, I heard a soft sound in my mind, a gentle thud, the sound of a past reconciling, an arc ending and a new lesson beginning.

EPILOGUE

Many adventures have continued to unfold for the horses and me. As of this writing, a total of 145 horses have come to the LOPE ranch, while our website listing service has helped nearly 600 other ex-racehorses find new homes as well. When I started this work, I never would have predicted that so many people and horses would find each other through our program. It's been the most rewarding, humbling, and non-numeric career I could ever imagine.

Lightening Ball, the gangster horse, resisted all adoption attempts, spurning every prospective owner by spooking randomly, showing his famous sneer, or refusing to move faster than a plodding trot. Finally getting the hint, I adopted him myself — and have been delighted by our mutual trust under saddle. However, he still shies at strangers in the pasture (just to be on the safe side).

I also adopted Sally, the Prom Queen mare. After our experiences together at the Ray Hunt clinic and the Equine Expo, I couldn't part with her. She is now my steadiest ride, calm and unflappable at the farm and on trail rides. Her diva side still emerges occasionally, such as when new geldings arrive here or when we ride in an arena with microphones. But her antics now remain limited to flirtatious head tossing and other playful ploys for attention. She seems to know she's the star of this book's last chapter.

Tulsa remains my favorite horse, his intelligence and talent for mischief a constant source of entertainment. He and Zuper are inseparable, two ex-jocks enjoying a mellow retirement together. Zuper continues in his role as our assistant ranch manager — and every day edges closer to taking my job over completely.

Our porch looks out over the horse pastures, the view bordered by century-old trees, the long, winding driveway, and numerous birds in motion. Nearly every day I sit there, contemplating such varied topics as the latest hay prices, the horse riding schedule, and the next veterinary visit. I watch the horses as they meander gracefully before me, tails swishing, their herd dynamics a constant flow of equine social life. Our wildlife population completes the scene, with squirrels, deer, geckos, and an elusive turkey wandering across the fields.

Before getting up and launching myself into the day's work, I often pause on the porch and marvel at the life that is mine now. The subtitle of this book is "What I've Learned from Saving Racehorses." But the reality is that the horses saved me — from a dull, ordinary life lacking purpose, adventure, and growth.

I will always be grateful to them.

ACKNOWLEDGMENTS

WRITING A BOOK IS A SWEATY, arduous task. This one would have never been completed without the support of many, many people (even more than can be listed below):

Elise Proulx, for being a patient and brilliant agent to a first-time author. Without your early encouragement, this book might not have been written at all.

Bonnie Nadell, for shepherding this project from manuscript to publication.

Jason Gardner, for being a wonderful editor as well as a horse admirer — an unusual and much-appreciated combination.

Kelly Leonard and Denise Adams, for their proofreading, editing, and all-around cheerleading skills.

Dr. Damon O'Gan and Dr. Matt Evans of Austin Equine Associates, for making the largest, most critical difference to LOPE and all the horses here. Without you, horses like Storm and Babu would have never made it to the pages of this book.

Ray and Carolyn Hunt, for teaching me (and so many others) that the horse is always right — even when we'd rather that he wasn't.

Allie Conrad of CANTER Mid-Atlantic, for being the best racehorse adoption mentor in the world.

All the racetrack folks who helped LOPE from the start — there are literally dozens of you. Special shout-out to Laura Ardis, Glen Rottweiler, Rachelle Russell, Lane Hutchins, Deirdre Panas, Keith Clark, Robin Powers, Tommy Azopardi, Eric Johnston, and Ann McGovern.

Debbie Mulcahy, for giving us our first individual donation — and then giving us our largest (and most special) horse donation "package" ever.

LOPE's Founders Circle: Robert and Janice McNair, Ruth McNair Smith, John Moritz, Retama Park, Frances and Felix Tapp, Texas Horsemen's Assistance Fund, Joseph DiQuinzio, Jr., Susan Brooks Littlefield, Houston Equine Research Organization, and the Texas Horse Enthusiasts. Thank you for your hugely generous support of the horses!

The Texas Horsemen's Partnership and Sam Houston Race Park for taking a chance on a start-up nonprofit adoption program. Your support from the very beginning is deeply appreciated.

The LOPE sponsors: Texas Thoroughbred Association, Soft-Ride, Equine Express, Hycourt Farm, Equestrian-Network.com, and Eponaire.

Tory, for still being the best trainer I've ever met. Thanks for all the lessons, in horsemanship and life.

Nancy Rorke, for instilling a love of books in me at an early age.

Joe and Marcia Rorke, for helping our ranch dream become a reality (not to mention sponsoring the famous Zuper).

James and Jackie Reardon, for all their support in launching the adoption ranch.

Dano, for being the ultimate Zen master and spiritual leader.

Most of all — my husband, Tom. You listened to hours of chapters being read aloud, put up with my bizarre night owl writing schedule, and edited pages of run-on sentences. Your smooth transition from pet-free bachelor to married ranch owner with a menagerie of horses, cats, dogs, and a disheveled wife will always amaze me. Thank you for bringing the qwan to LOPE, me, and our life together.

Racehorse Adoption and Retirement Organizations

BELOW IS A LIST of some of the larger and more well-established racehorse placement groups in the United States. There are also smaller organizations in nearly every state, all worthy of support. If you would like to help racehorses in your area, please search your local horse rescue resources to find the group closest to you.

Angel Acres Horse Haven Rescue • Pennsylvania
www.angelacreshorsehavenrescue.com

CANTER
(Communication Alliance to Network Thoroughbred Ex-Racehorses)
Chapters in California, Illinois, Ohio, Michigan (national headquarters),
Mid-Atlantic, New England, and Pennsylvania • www.canterusa.org

Exceller Fund • Kentucky • www.excellerfund.org

Finger Lakes Thoroughbred Adoption Program • New York
www.fingerlakestap.org

Friends of Ferdinand • Indiana • www.friendsofferdinand.org

Mid-Atlantic Horse Rescue • Maryland • www.midatlantichorserescue.org

New Vocations • Ohio • www.horseadoption.com

Old Friends • Kentucky • www.oldfriendsequine.org

Rerun • State chapters and satellite farms in Kentucky, New Jersey,
New York, North Carolina, and Pennsylvania • www.rerun.org

TB Friends Horse Rescue • California • www.tbfriends.com

Thoroughbred Retirement Foundation • Farms and facilities in Florida,
Kentucky, Missouri, New York, South Carolina, and Virginia • www.trfinc.org

ENDNOTES

CHAPTER 4: TAWAKONI

Page 69, *We got ready to cut [geld] the other colts:* Richard Chamberlain, "C. W. Cascio and Dash for Cash Were a Team from the Beginning," *American Quarter Horse Racing Journal*, October 2002.

CHAPTER 5: CAPTAIN BOO

Page 84, *An average of 67,000 horses were slaughtered each year:* "US Horse Slaughter Statistics," Society for Animal Protective Legislation, http://www.saplonline.org/horses _stats.htm (accessed October 15, 2008).

CHAPTER 8: SUGARFOOT

Page 138, *When we got her she was pretty small, but we started her:* Paula Hunt, "Off the Track," *San Antonio Express-News*, August 18, 2006, Life section.

CHAPTER 11: BRIDGE PLACE

Page 202, *Although only small in size, he was large in stature:* "Polar Falcon Dies in England," *Thoroughbred Times*, December 7, 2001, http://www.thoroughbredtimes.com /breeding-news/2001/December/07/Polar-Falcon-dies-in-England.aspx.

CHAPTER 13: LIGHTENING BALL, AKA "LB"

Page 234, *So when the race starts, your heart is in the right place:* Mickey Herskowitz, "Horse Owners Catch Lightening in a Ball," *Houston Chronicle*, November 27, 2000, Sports section.

ABOUT THE AUTHOR

L YNN REARDON IS THE FOUNDER and executive director of Lone-Star Outreach to Place Ex-Racers (LOPE), a nonprofit racehorse placement agency near Austin, Texas. Prior to LOPE, she worked in nonprofit finance and administrative management in the Washington DC–area for too many years.

She lives on the LOPE ranch with her husband, Tom — and Zuper, the equine assistant ranch manager. Their current household includes Sophie the dog, multiple cats, and a herd of ex-racehorses up for adoption.

Bowing to inevitable occupational hazard, Lynn has adopted three LOPE horses of her own: Tulsa, Sally, and Lightening Ball.

Visit Lynn at www.lopetx.org.

NEW WORLD LIBRARY is dedicated to publishing books and other media that inspire and challenge us to improve the quality of our lives and the world.

We are a socially and environmentally aware company, and we strive to embody the ideals presented in our publications. We recognize that we have an ethical responsibility to our customers, our staff members, and our planet.

We serve our customers by creating the finest publications possible on personal growth, creativity, spirituality, wellness, and other areas of emerging importance. We serve New World Library employees with generous benefits, significant profit sharing, and constant encouragement to pursue their most expansive dreams.

As a member of the Green Press Initiative, we print an increasing number of books with soy-based ink on 100 percent postconsumer-waste recycled paper. Also, we power our offices with solar energy and contribute to nonprofit organizations working to make the world a better place for us all.

Our products are available
in bookstores everywhere.
For our catalog, please contact:

New World Library
14 Pamaron Way
Novato, California 94949

Phone: 415-884-2100 or 800-972-6657
Catalog requests: Ext. 50
Orders: Ext. 52
Fax: 415-884-2199
Email: escort@newworldlibrary.com

To subscribe to our electronic newsletter, visit
www.newworldlibrary.com

Environmental impact estimates were made using the Environmental Defense Fund Paper Calculator @ www.papercalculator.org.